THE QUESTION OF LITERATURE

MANCHESTER
UNIVERSITY PRESS

ANGELAKIHUMANITIES

editors
Charlie Blake
Pelagia Goulimari
Timothy S. Murphy
Robert Smith

general editor
Gerard Greenway

Angelaki Humanities publishes works which address and probe broad and compelling issues in the theoretical humanities. The series favours path-breaking thought, promotes unjustly neglected figures, and grapples with established concerns. It believes in the possibility of blending, without compromising, the rigorous, the well-crafted, and the inventive. The series seeks to host ambitious writing from around the world.

Angelaki Humanities is the associated book series of
Angelaki – journal of the theoretical humanities

Already published
EVIL SPIRITS: NIHILISM AND THE FATE OF MODERNITY
Gary Banham and Charlie Blake (eds)

ABSOLUTELY POSTCOLONIAL: WRITING BETWEEN THE SINGULAR
AND THE SPECIFIC
Peter Hallward

THE NEW BERGSON
John Mullarkey (ed.)

ANGELAKIHUMANITIES

M
45,
B4

THE QUESTION OF LITERATURE

the place of
the literary in contemporary theory

edited by elizabeth beaumont bissell

POPLOAN

MANCHESTER UNIVERSITY PRESS
MANCHESTER AND NEW YORK

distributed exclusively in the USA by Palgrave

010114403

9/05

Published by Manchester University Press
Oxford Road, Manchester M13 9NR, UK
and Room 400, 175 Fifth Avenue, New York, NY 10010, USA
http://www.manchesteruniversitypress.co.uk

Distributed exclusively in the USA by
Palgrave, 175 Fifth Avenue, New York,
NY 10010, USA

Distributed exclusively in Canada by
UBC Press, University of British Columbia, 2029 West Mall
Vancouver, BC, Canada V6T 1Z2

British Library Cataloguing-in-Publication Data
A catalogue record for this book is available from the British Library

Library of Congress Cataloging-in-Publication Data applied for

ISBN   0 7190 5744 2 *hardback*
       0 7190 5745 0 *paperback*

First published 2002

10 09 08 07 06 05 04 03 02   10 9 8 7 6 5 4 3 2 1

Typeset
by Northern Phototypesetting Co Ltd, Bolton
Printed in Great Britain
by Bell & Bain Ltd, Glasgow

CONTENTS

LIST OF CONTRIBUTORS

Charles Altieri teaches twentieth-century poetry and literary theory in the English Department at UC Berkeley. His most recent books are *Postmodernisms Now* (University Park, 1998) and *Subjective Agency* (Oxford, 1994), and he is now hoping to finish a book *Aestheticizing the Affects*.

Derek Attridge is Leverhulme Research Professor at the University of York. His books include *Peculiar Language: Literature as Difference from the Renaissance to James Joyce* (Ithaca, 1988), *Poetic Rhythm: An Introduction* (Cambridge, 1995), and *Joyce Effects: On Language, Theory, and History* (Cambridge, 2000). He is currently completing books on literary singularity and on the fiction of J. M. Coetzee, and working on a history of poetry as performance.

Elizabeth Beaumont Bissell has researched on modernist literature and literary theory at Exeter and Hertford Colleges, Oxford, and at Princeton University. She has taught in these areas at various Oxford colleges, and has published articles on T. S. Eliot and theory, especially deconstruction. She currently works for Oxford University Press.

David Carroll is Professor of French and Chair of the Department of French and Italian at the University of California, Irvine. His books include *French Literary Fascism: Nationalism, Anti-Semitism, and the Ideology of Culture* (Princeton, 1995); *Paraesthetics: Foucault, Lyotard, Derrida* (New York, 1987); and *The Subject in Question: The Languages of Theory and the Strategies of Fiction* (Chicago, 1982). He has also edited a collection of essays entitled *The States of Theory* (New York, 1990). He is currently working on a book on Albert Camus and Algeria.

Timothy Clark is Reader in English at the University of Durham and author of *Embodying Revolution: The Figure of the Poet in Shelley*

(Oxford, 1989); *Derrida, Heidegger, Blanchot: Sources of Derrida's Notion and Practice of Literature* (Cambridge, 1992); *Charles Tomlinson* (Plymouth, 1999); *Martin Heidegger* (London, 2002). He is co-editor of the *Oxford Literary Review*.

Marianne DeKoven is Professor of English at Rutgers University. She is the author of *A Different Language: Gertrude Stein's Experimental Writing* (Madison, 1983), and *Rich and Strange: Gender, History, Modernism* (Princeton, 1991), and the editor of *Feminist Locations: Global and Local, Theory and Practice* (New Brunswick, 2001), in addition to numerous articles in the fields of feminist criticism and theory, and twentieth-century literary and cultural studies. She is completing a book entitled *Utopia Limited: The Sixties and the Emergence of the Postmodern*.

Thomas Docherty is Professor of English, Director of Research, and Director of the Kent Institute for Advanced Studies in the Humanities in the University of Kent. He previously taught in Oxford, at University College Dublin, and at Trinity College Dublin, where he held the Chair of English (1867). He has published a number of books: *Reading (Absent) Character* (Oxford, 1983); *John Donne, Undone* (London, 1986); *On Modern Authority* (Hemel Hempstead, 1987); *After Theory* (London, 1990; 2nd edn, Edinburgh, 1996); *Postmodernism* (New York, 1993); *Alterities: Criticism, History, Representation* (Oxford, 1996); *Criticism and Modernity: Aesthetics, Literature and Nations in Europe and its Academies* (Oxford, 1999); and numerous articles on literature, criticism and theory. His current work is on hypocrisy, confession, and love in modern European culture.

John Frow is Regius Professor of Rhetoric and English Literature at the University of Edinburgh. Recent publications include *Cultural Studies and Cultural Value* (Oxford, 1995), *Time and Commodity Culture* (Oxford, 1997), and (with Tony Bennett and Michael Emmison) *Accounting for Tastes: Australian Everyday Cultures* (Cambridge, 1999). He is currently writing books on genre and on the moral economies of everyday life.

Peggy Kamuf is Professor of French and Comparative Literature at the University of Southern California. Her most recent book is *The Division of Literature, or the University in Deconstruction* (Chicago, 1997). She has also edited and translated work by Jacques Derrida and Jean-Luc Nancy among others.

Adrian Page has taught Literature and Media Arts, and is currently a Principal Lecturer in Media Arts at the University of Luton. He has published on literary theory and aspects of the adaptation of literature. He is the editor of *The Death of the Playwright?* (London, 1992), and has recently published a book entitled *Cracking Morse Code: Semiotics and Television Drama* (Luton, 2000), which looks at television drama from Samuel Beckett to the present day.

Bruce Robbins is the author of *Feeling Global: Internationalism in Distress* (New York, 1999), *The Servant's Hand: English Fiction from Below* (New York, 1986), and *Secular Vocations: Intellectuals, Professionalism, Culture* (London, 1993). He has edited *Intellectuals: Aesthetics, Politics, Academics* (Minneapolis, 1990) and *The Phantom Public Sphere* (Minneapolis, 1993) and co-edited *Cosmopolitics: Thinking and Feeling Beyond the Nation* (Minneapolis, 1998). He is currently Visiting Professor at Columbia University.

Robert Smith is a former Prize Fellow of All Souls, Oxford. He has published on deconstruction and associated areas. He is an executive editor of *Angelaki: journal of the theoretical humanities*. Currently he is finishing a book on psychoanalytic and philosophical concepts of death. He lives in London and works as a management consultant.

ACKNOWLEDGEMENTS

I should like to thank the contributors whose essays appear here, the peer reviewer (who has been extraordinarily helpful and generous with her time), Derek Attridge and Paul Hamilton (who have also given good advice), and all at Angelaki Humanities and Manchester University Press, for making this book possible.

elizabeth beaumont bissell

INTRODUCTION

In the first place, the question of literature would seem to be a rhetorical one – a question, that is, of its own rhetoric, duplicitously poised between the question that literature asks (itself synecdochic for any number of other more or less specific and inclusive questions), and the question that literature is. As a result of this undecidability, the question of literature would also seem to be rhetorical in the more customary sense – a question asked for effect rather than for its effects, or not so much asked as performed. And as such a performance it would follow that this question (especially raised as it is here, without having been asked at all) is one that does not expect any answer – not least because we do not necessarily know what the question is.

For even the most circumspect approach to the question of literature has already caused it to recede into its own questioning, into conditionals and qualifications which make it less and less likely ever to be identified, let alone asked or answered. Merely to claim that the question is indeed rhetorical, in all the recursive senses which I have just suggested, involves the foreclosing of other questions not of rhetoric – of context or content, for example, or of definition – in a manner which recalls the closure of the rhetorical question itself, whose answer is always supposedly known, if also withheld, in advance.

It is a mark of the appositeness of the rhetorical question to the question of literature, however (as well as of the need to approach both with the appropriate circumspection) that they resemble one another so closely in their limits and their evasions. For the question of literature is one to which literary theory tends to assume, either that it already knows the answer, or that no answer is necessary or possible. Theory habitually retreats from this elusive, difficult question, which also retreats from theory – not only into the labyrinths of rhetorical self-interrogation, but into a variety of other adjacent questions, or, more simply, into silence.

Given the constitutive withdrawal of what is nominally its central question, many literary theorists (including several of the contributors to this volume) unsurprisingly consider literature itself to be in crisis. For some this is the inevitable and enabling condition of literature and literary questions: 'any discipline of literary study cannot but be in a state of continual crisis', Timothy Clark writes, '... and this has been one reason for its vitality'. Others find the apparent benignity of such a crisis rather too convenient: Bruce Robbins argues that literary criticism (in common with many other academic disciplines) is sustained by the paradoxes that seem to endanger it, creating 'a comfortable professional niche' out of the very ruins of its disciplinary object.

But there is also the possibility of a more destructive and less immanent literary crisis, one related to the turn that Clark and Robbins have already introduced into my discussion here from rhetorical to institutional questions. The question of literature is increasingly addressed by and to academic institutions, whether they be universities, departments of literary study, scholarly publications, or the uniquely equivocal institution that is literary theory itself. And although it is not simply an effect of the institutionalisation and theorisation of literature, the literary crisis in my second sense is inseparable from these things, and in particular from literature's perceived dependence upon institutions and theories which no longer depend upon it.

In his 1991 book *Literary Into Cultural Studies* Anthony Easthope asserted what he called 'the basic fact that the books read for literature degrees are no longer read anywhere else'.[1] If this is indeed a 'basic fact' (and it has been contested in equally basic terms, sometimes almost with regret, by theorists citing, for example, the recent commercial success of bargain reprints of the 'literary classics'), it already constitutes a literary crisis, and it has serious consequences for our object here. In the first place, if literature is only read in universities – if it can be implicitly (and circularly) defined as 'the books read for literature degrees' – then the questions that it can ask are constrained, and its social, cultural, and political significance is predeterminately limited. It becomes no more than an academic question.

Secondly, if literature is thus circumscribed by the academic institution, its integrity is at risk from changes and developments within that institution – which, in turn, becomes more responsible than it might like to be for the very existence of its own object of study, liable to the circularity implicit in Easthope's provocative claim. Once the institution itself experiences a crisis or a paradigm-shift (as literary study, moreover, must if it believes so resolutely in its own solipsism, and even if it does not turn out to be as solipsistic as it believes), literature becomes very vulnerable indeed.

Many critics have accordingly identified a literary crisis in the paradigm-shift advocated by Easthope's title, *Literary Into Cultural Studies* – the replacement of '"pure" literary study' with 'the more comprehensive analysis of … *signifying practices*' known as cultural studies.[2] This paradigm-shift – if it is a shift within an existing discipline rather than a result of the emergence and consolidation of a newer one – is at the centre of a debate between left-wing theorists for whom 'the valorisation of literature', as Marianne DeKoven puts it, 'is seen primarily as a tool of conservative cultural hegemony', and reactionaries who regard the devaluation of literature as opening the way to a decadent cultural anarchy.

Much of the argument between these antagonists is no more constructive or pertinent than their respective definitions of the 'cultural', and this volume is not intended to repeat its commonplaces. However, whether we welcome or deplore the shift away from the study of literature as such, that this shift should be most persistently promoted from within an institution still bearing the name 'literary studies' would suggest that this institution is indeed experiencing some kind of crisis. What other discipline so routinely diminishes and decries its own objects? Where else do academics relate to their research interests in terms of 'attacks', 'demolishing', and even 'revolutionary assault'?[3]

It would seem at this point that rhetorical questions are inextricable after all from the institutional ones whose necessity might have seemed to supersede them. The literary crisis may be experienced within academic institutions, but it remains a crisis in the forms and possibilities of the literary question – in what it is legitimate or possible to say about literature both inside and outside its institutions, in the vocabulary available to literary discourse, and the vocabulary (the rhetoric of violent destruction, for example) that literary discourse actually uses – and this crisis is no more merely rhetorical than the institutional one is merely academic.

In the name of what, after all, does the rhetorical become the merely rhetorical or the academic the merely academic? What necessity dictates that a rhetorical question should dismiss itself from consideration because it is unanswerable or already answered, or that a question asked by scholars is for that reason negligible and irrelevant? Assuming that these questions are neither merely rhetorical nor merely academic themselves, one answer that would in any case impart its own relevance to them, though it would not lessen their equivocation, is: politics.

Politics, and in particular what David Carroll calls here 'the different politics of gender, race, ethnicity, or culture' (although one should not ignore in this context the narrower politics of education policy and funding), is of course almost as often implicated in the literary crisis as the rise of cultural studies is. The former sort of politics is also just as suspect to literary conservatives. But, 'sterile polemics aside', as Carroll affirms, for politically committed theorists as much as for those who reject such commitment, once politics is invoked, it immediately and authoritatively asserts priority over all other considerations. 'And it is for this reason perhaps more than for any other', Carroll concludes, 'that literature and art ... appear to be in crisis, not any longer even secondary concerns "after politics", but so marginal that they risk being of no concern at all'.

Even those who argue that it should be set aside for political reasons, however, acknowledge that literature itself is thoroughly political: 'it has the most intimate relation', Terry Eagleton writes, 'to questions of social power'.[4] For theorists like Eagleton the politics of literature and literary questions is nearly always 'objectionable' – most forms of literary theory, he argues, 'have strengthened rather than challenged the assumptions of the power system'.[5] The existence of literature as a category, indeed, can be seen as a reflection of that system, reproducing social divisions and inequalities in a domain which affects to transcend them, and foisting the tastes and aspirations of the privileged classes upon the rest of society in the form of literary value judgements.

But this is not the only sense in which the question of literature may be considered political, nor is the only possible literary politics conservative. There is also a long and varied tradition, dating back at least to the Romantics and including revolutionaries (both bourgeois and Marxist) and dissidents of every kind, in which literature has been seen as oppositional, subversive, emancipatory. '[H]istorically', as Timothy Reiss writes, 'literature has as often served subversive and revolutionary goals as it has those of established authority'.[6] It cannot therefore be dismissed as reactionary any more than it can be ignored as politically irrelevant. What may be treated more dismissively, perhaps, is the assumption that literature has a single determinable (or determining) political significance, that the question of literature is indeed political before it is (say) rhetorical or institutional, or that it has a decisive political answer. Reiss argues that the opposition between a conservative and a radical literary politics, in all its reductiveness, 'hints that those on both sides of the argument are neglecting a few aspects of the question. A major one is that they know what *literature* is'.[7]

Like so many other theorists, it might be added, Reiss's political partisans have also neglected to ensure that they know what the question is. As I have sought to demonstrate, this is by no means straightforward: there are as many literary questions as there are ways of asking, and to nominate one in particular as the question of literature is daunting and doubtless mistaken. But this is not to say that theory should renounce such difficult questions altogether. If literature and literary studies are indeed in crisis, and if we consider it presumptuous to assume that this is inevitable, necessary, or good, then these questions need to be asked. Otherwise there is a danger that literary theorists (if not readers) may find themselves renouncing literature itself along with its questions without so much as recognising what they are giving up.

In the first place, it is worth asking whether the question 'what?' is in question here at all. 'The first problem to confront us is, obviously, the subject matter of literary scholarship. What is literature?', Wellek and Warren's *Theory of Literature* confidently asserted, and this 'problem' is often taken to be identical with the question of literature itself.[8] Attractive both in its brevity and its inclusiveness, 'what is literature?' minimises its own extension yet maximises its scope giving a satisfying impression of concision, comprehensiveness, and control. Nevertheless, to assume that literary theory's first problem is necessarily literature's decisive question remains no more than a prejudice, if a tempting and influential one. Despite its apparent succinctness in getting to the point – 'we have to hit the nail on the head', as Jean-Paul Sartre insisted – this question turns out to be no more than a transition between points, a fugitive detour between other questions.[9]

For Sartre, the question quickly splinters into three more ('What is writing? Why does one write? For whom?'), and these are succeeded by a multiplicity which sense and grammar themselves seem unable to contain: 'perhaps we may at this time attempt to answer the only question which is urgent for us: what is the situation of the writer in 1947; what is his public; what are his myths; what does he want to write about; what can he and what ought he write about?'[10] Wellek and Warren likewise end their discussion of 'what is literature?' by turning aside from it to other questions. 'A modern analysis of the [literary] work of art', they acknowledge, 'has to begin with more complex questions: its mode of existence, its system of strata'.[11]

The fugitivity of the question 'what is literature?', however, should not be taken as indicating that it is not complex itself – Wellek's and Warren's very inconclusiveness suggests quite the reverse. Neither the authors of *Theory of Literature* nor the many writers who have come after them have been able to exhaust the possibilities of this first, most minimal, and most general, instance of the question of literature: 'disagreement is widespread', as Paul Hernadi testifies, 'even concerning the *kind* of answer demanded or admitted by that deceptively simple question'.[12] It is for this reason, rather than because of any privilege accorded to its brevity, scope, or ontological directness, that 'what is literature?' remains, if not identical with the question of literature, at least necessary to it. The kinds of answer, the admissions and the new demands to which it has so productively given rise make it a useful guide to literary theory's past presumptions, present crisis, and future possibilities.

In some cases what theory presumed in the past about this crucial question has become unrecognisable, almost incomprehensible to us in the critical present. In 1960, Laurence Lerner wrote: '[a]ll answers to the question What is literature? can, I suggest, be reduced to three: that it is knowledge; that it is the expression of emotion; and that it is the arousing of emotion in the reader'.[13] Lerner's very terms – knowledge, emotion, expression – seem dated now, almost quaint, but the premisses that underlie them are more so. His concern to defend a notion of intuitive literary knowledge against the austere authority of scientific truth belongs to the debates surrounding I. A. Richards thirty years before him, and is quite alien, forty years later, to the contemporaries of Alan Sokal. And the importance that Lerner ascribes to emotion in literature – whether the arousal of a reader's emotion or the expression of the author's – depends upon narrow social expectations ('believing that people are like one another') that more recent theory has put aside as harmfully exclusive.[14]

Although Lerner asserts that his book begins with knowledge, emotion, and expression, moreover, his first sentence suggests another equally dated, if rather different, approach to the problem of what literature is. 'There are several ways of answering the question What is Literature?', *The Truest Poetry* opens by declaring: '[t]he simplest is to draw up a list of books'.[15] This may be less immediately foreign to the twenty-first-century reader than Lerner's later conclusions: literary theorists still draw up lists, though even Harold Bloom did not claim for his Western canon anything so audacious as simplicity. Like the question 'what is literature?' itself, the literary canon has proved as complex and variable as its principle would appear durable and straightforward, and it too has changed beyond recall.

For many, indeed, the canon has not so much changed as disintegrated – along with literature itself, it is widely perceived to be in a state of crisis. '[T]he binary which excludes popular culture as an outside while conserving as an inside a canon of specially literary texts simply cannot be sustained as a serious intellectual argument', Anthony Easthope wrote in 1991.[16] And this sense of unsustainability is as apparent in the tone of the canon's defenders as it is from sceptics such as Easthope: 'the means to destroy canons', Bloom lugubriously observed in *The Western Canon*, 'are very much at hand, and the process is quite advanced'.[17]

As if to reaffirm that no argument about the literary canon (serious or not) can be sustained simply, however, while Bloom's curriculum of great books would seem to be in decline, canons of other kinds are now more often created than destroyed. Using the basic taxonomic principle in order to differentiate rather than discriminate between works and genres, critics have rearranged the literary past into new canons which describe plurality instead of conferring privilege, and which certainly do not exclude popular culture. As Howard Weinbrot writes of the eighteenth century, for example: '[o]ther canons included those of religious controversy; practical or philosophical political theorizing; cookery books; travel books ... any number of poetic subspecies ... periodical essays; the ever popular drama; and of course numerous kinds of fictions, some designed for women, some for children, some for sexual voyeurs, and some for conventional human beings seeking the pleasure of a good read'.[18]

Although, as Weinbrot shows, there would seem to be more literary canons now than ever before, it is also true that no one writing today is likely to answer the question 'what is literature?' with a list. The very number of these new canons has prevented any one of them from identifying itself with literature as such, and the shift from a prescriptive to a descriptive principle has taken from them a powerful means of doing so.

For Laurence Lerner the answer to 'what is literature?' began with 'a long list which would be accepted by almost everyone who has thought seriously about the subject', and from which 'we could then move on to ... ask what these works have in common, and so construct a definition. This definition in turn could be used to settle the claims of doubtful items on the list'.[19] But according to today's theorists definitions such as Lerner's do not settle doubts so much as create them – not only about individual items, but about the validity of the list itself. As Peter Widdowson writes:

> [W]e can argue that the works which are in the Canon – rather than being there because they are, in some anterior sense, self-evidently 'great' – have their 'greatness' conferred on them, or at least continually reconfirmed, precisely by being in it: they *become* 'canonic texts', and therefore remain reference-points for other literary production. However, they do so no longer as benchmarks of 'artistic merit', but as symptomatic instances at once of formal and ideological productions of past cultural conjunctures, and of the values descried in, and inscribed on, them in their reproduction in subsequent cultural history.[20]

The disparity between Lerner's and Widdowson's views of the same selection process could scarcely be more extreme. The latter rejects the authority of literary canon-formation for precisely the same reasons that led the former to assert it. Lerner sees the establishment of a canon as an external check upon the prejudices of the individual critic, whereas for Widdowson it is no more than the institutionalisation of such prejudices in ideology.

The explanation for these sharply differing perspectives, as for the abandonment of dated literary determinants like knowledge, emotion, and expression, is once again to be found in the changing nature of literary theory's underlying premisses – in what, and how much, it is assuming in the anterior sense. And the most obvious change (explicitly acknowledged by Widdowson, indeed) is the one which has taken place in attitudes to literary value. Most theorists and critics today have abandoned the belief in self-evident 'greatness' or 'artistic merit', without which Laurence Lerner's canon (like its diverse but powerful ancestors in the work of T. S. Eliot and F. R. Leavis) may be exposed as the merely circular ideological reaffirmation that Widdowson attacks. Without a shared assumption as to the existence of literary value, attempts to establish its presence, let alone its nature, can only appear arbitrary and culturally arrogant.

The importance (whether liberating or destructive) of this transformation for literary studies and its questions – and for literature itself – has been very great. It is one of the strongest reasons, not only for the decline of the prescriptive canon, but for the more general literary crisis that has already been discussed. The tendency of literary theory to disparage its own objects is persuasively explained if it refuses on principle to place a value upon them, as is its need to look elsewhere (towards history, politics, or philosophy) for legitimation. If it is now inconceivable that, in Laurence Lerner's words, 'almost everyone who has thought seriously about the subject' might be expected to accept the same list of major literary works, this is not only because such an acceptance would be naive and insular in an age when there are so many canons and so many literatures. There is also a doubt as to whether anyone should still be thinking seriously about this particular subject at all.

The present situation, however, contains at least two ironies. The first is that as theory has become less interested in value judgements, it has also become more preoccupied with them. For Lerner, 'the concept of literature is partly descriptive … and partly normative', but 'this mingling of the two is not a hindrance to clear thought, nor in any way to be regretted; it is something which follows from the nature of literature'.[21] Far from insisting upon the primacy of the normative principle in his definition of literature, Lerner is content to accept a hybridity which more recent commentators could only find deeply troubling. For despite their pluralism, literary theorists today are more dogmatic in rejecting value judgement than their predecessors ever were in practising it. Accordingly a composite definition such as Lerner's is likely to be suspected of exploiting its harmlessly descriptive element to hide the sinister influence of the normative. '"Literature"', as Widdowson has written, 'is … being recognised as the construct of a criticism which, while assuming and proclaiming its "descriptiveness", its "disinterestedness", its ideological innocence, has so constituted Literature as to reproduce and naturalise bourgeois ideology as "literary value"'.[22]

In comparison with Widdowson's own ideological proclamations Laurence Lerner's relaxed attitude to literary definition might start to seem, if not innocent, then at least refreshingly pragmatic. Even today it is impossible to use the term 'literature' without implying some relation to value judgement, and its meaning in everyday usage is openly honorific. To deny this fact merely produces an effect of assumed innocence, different from, but no more plausible than, the ideological equivocations of the bourgeois canon itself. If combining normative and descriptive elements in a single definition only disguises and 'naturalise[s]' ideology, excluding the normative altogether will produce a definition which is just as ideological but somewhat more contrived.

Simply to appeal to 'the nature of literature' as Lerner does, however, is no way out of his own predicament or Widdowson's. As a preliminary to asking what literature is, such an appeal merely ensures that the question will turn out, like so many other literary questions, to be rhetorical. It is both unanswerable and already answered, because it assumes in advance the very thing that it is setting out to define. Nothing is learnt in this process about the legitimacy of literary value judgement, or about the constructedness of literary definitions. All that takes place is a familiar interrogative detour by which the question 'what is literature?' is deferred in favour of 'what is the nature of literature?'

The futility of a definition of literature thus dependent upon the presumed nature of its own object does at least confirm that the nature of definition itself is also worthy of distrust. And in particular, it casts doubt upon the initially attractive idea that literature should necessarily be defined compatibly with everyday usage. For like 'the nature of literature', usage takes for granted exactly what a definition should be seeking to determine. Moreover, its assumptions may indeed reflect the 'naturalise[d] bourgeois ideology' which is attacked by Widdowson and others. In 1978, E. D. Hirsch wrote: 'if [definitions of literature] deviate in the least from the usage of educated men, it is the definition that is wrong, and not common usage'.[23] No doubt changes in usage itself have made this claim sound more like a declaration of prejudice against men from some social backgrounds, and against all women, than it once did. Nevertheless, like some of Laurence Lerner's statements, it relies unduly upon the expectation that readers of literature will be socially and culturally homogeneous, and that their usage will indeed be common to all.

Alongside the abandonment of explicit value judgement, the shift from an account of literature based upon homogeneity – that is upon what texts and readers share – to one based upon difference, has been amongst the most significant changes to theory's underlying premises in the second half of the twentieth century. It is reflected not only in the diversification and divergence of literary canons, but in the principles upon which these canons – and definitions of literature more generally – are formed. For if the assumption that 'people are like one another' has been rejected by literary theorists in recent years, so too has the corresponding assumption about texts. Definitions of the kind advocated by Lerner, which move from a canon of works agreed 'by almost everyone who has thought seriously about the subject' to a prescriptive definition derived from 'what these works have in common', have been displaced in favour of an increased emphasis upon 'the unique specificity', in Peter Widdowson's words, 'of all literary works *by definition*' as the very criterion of their literary status.[24]

This refusal of all shared literary assumptions is no less profound in its implications than the more specific rejection of assumptions about literary value. It too contributes to the sense that literature and the canon are in crisis, since without some minimal agreement about subject-matter, even referring to literature becomes difficult, let alone evaluating or defining it. And the lack of such an agreement also helps to explain theory's abandonment of another once urgent but now dated preoccupation – the attempt to define literature on the basis of its formal properties. For Wellek and Warren, 'distinguishing the particular use made of language in literature' was (at least provisionally) 'the simplest way of solving the question' as to what literature is.[25] More recent writers, however, have had no difficulty in dismissing this solution – and along with it the large and influential critical traditions of formalism and structuralism – as unsuccessful, unconvincing, and 'no answer at all'.[26] Like normative ones, formal definitions of literature need to assume their own object in order to determine the traits which may then be used to define it, and if the object is placed in doubt, the definition likewise becomes arbitrary and unreliable.

This apparent loss of literary theory's sustaining certainties brings us to the second irony implicit in its present crisis, which is that the refusal of shared assumptions about the aesthetic value or formal characteristics of literature is itself an assumption which literary theorists share. The consensus necessary to asking and answering questions such as 'what is literature?' has not in fact disappeared but changed, and in many ways it has changed for the better. Theory's preconceptions have become more sophisticated as they have become more limited and tentative, and certain obvious prejudices have positively been overcome.

The persistence and the transformation of literary theoretical assumptions, moreover, importantly demonstrate that those assumptions are more than prejudices themselves. If theory cannot rely upon its own premises, it cannot do without them altogether. As Barbara Herrnstein Smith has influentially observed: '[w]e do not ... move about in a raw universe', and all discourses upon any subject whatsoever must take account of the 'pre-interpret[ation]', 'pre-classification', and 'pre-evaluation' that this implies.[27] Though it may be a mistake to assume the nature of literature in advance, or to conform uncritically to 'common usage' in defining it, this does not mean that making assumptions about literature – or asking questions about it – is therefore futile.

And if the theorists of the past had their characteristic orthodoxies, so too do those of today. The ascription to literature of 'unique specificity' is now a common theoretical given, as is the belief that literature can (only) adequately be understood as a historically contingent social construct. Even the apparent crisis and collapse of literature, its questions, and its assumptions, are no more than a particularly paradoxical example of literary-theoretical orthodoxy. None of these assumptions is fatally prejudiced by the mere fact of its being orthodox, and what prevents them from turning into prejudices is a continual and necessary reinterrogation and reformulation, to which the present volume is intended to contribute, and which, by a final irony, is one of the few traits to have remained constant throughout literary theory's troubled development.

For as I argued at the beginning of this introduction, literary questions – including, but not limited to, the question 'what is literature?' – are always in principle rhetorical. This may mean that they tempt theory to believe that it cannot or does not need to answer them, and that they are negligible, even frivolous, for the same reason that they are ostentatious. But at the same time, the rhetorical status of such questions gives them an effectiveness as well as an affectation. Implicitly interrogating themselves and their own rhetoric, they issue more readily in further questions than they do in answers, and they constantly and self-consciously refine themselves to the demands of their equally mutable and fugitive object.

Each of the essays collected in this volume accordingly responds to the question of literature by transforming it, but they are united in their sensitivity to the precise nature of that question and its consequences. Charles Altieri's opening piece, for example, offers 'five axioms upon which I hope agreement can be reached ... because they provide cogent procedural grounds for exploring the problems that underlie the quest for definition on this topic'. Altieri's restraint in resisting definition itself to concentrate upon the questions that precede it enables his argument to be exceptionally attentive to the historical, cultural, and especially ethical, complexity involved in describing a text as literary. He focuses upon literature's value claims beyond the limits of the merely aesthetic, and its place in the larger philosophical concerns of the human subject. Through an encounter with the 'limitations of ethical criticism' in the work of Wayne C. Booth and Martha Nussbaum, Altieri proposes 'an ethos-based version of the literary' which is able to understand literary texts as 'manifestations of qualities and powers that establish what is possible within certain ways of engaging with the world'.

Derek Attridge, too, starts from an acute sense of the literary question's inherited mysteries: '[i]t is as if the linguistic and intellectual resources of our culture do not permit direct access to a property or a process or a principle whose effects and importance they nevertheless register, and to which the term "literature" and its cognates serve as indirect witnesses', he says. His scrutiny of this elusive 'property or process' results in a theory of 'literary invention' as an event which happens to, and a performance of and by, both the readers and the writers of literary texts. Attridge works through the pivotal terms of his theory, notably 'singularity' ('the quality whereby a cultural object … differs from all others, not as a particular manifestation of general rules but as a uniqueness perceived as resisting or exceeding all general determinations') and 'inventiveness' ('the capacity of a cultural product to bring about a refashioning of the norms and habits on which we regularly rely in our understanding of such products') in a powerful recasting of the question of literature which 'does full justice to its singularity' – as he contends, indeed, that all responses to literature must.

For David Carroll, as I have already suggested, the imperative to do justice to literature takes in the first instance the more straightforward form of a refusal to abandon it entirely in favour of politics. Whilst distancing himself from any reactionary '"defence of literature" against its politicisation', Carroll confronts 'the tendency to downplay or simply to ignore the question(s) of literature' in current theory, arguing that 'such questioning [should] not be seen as a rear-guard assault on progressive, multi-cultural, gender-conscious theory and politics, but rather on the contrary made a component of them'. He turns to the debates between Sartre and Camus during the 1940s and 1950s – and in particular to their differing views of the connections between literature, freedom, and democracy – to demonstrate that literature itself is politically significant, and to 'show why to forget (or ignore) the question(s) of literature is at the same time to trivialise the question(s) of politics'.

Timothy Clark shares with David Carroll the pressing awareness of a literary and literary-theoretical crisis. Clark, however, considers this crisis in relation to literature as an institution and within academic institutions, tracing its particular relation to the development and legitimation of the university. He identifies 'two ways in which conceptions of the university as a whole have determined the object "literature"' – through specialisa-

tion and 'the ideal of the autonomy of the discipline', and through generalisation as the 'centre of a process of liberal education'. These determinations are now in crisis as the university itself mutates into 'the modern
"University of Excellence" – an institution that seems geared to no higher
ideal than its own maximised self-perpetuation according to input/output
ratios'. But even without external ideological intervention, Clark suggests
that literature is necessarily inimical to institutional determination. For
like Attridge, he attributes to literature the power to refashion norms –
including those which institutionalise it. Accordingly 'any discipline of literary study cannot but be in a state of continual crisis as to its relations
with other disciplines, to the university as a whole, and to the question of
criticism's relation to the university's outside' – but this crisis becomes a
measure of its 'vitality' rather than a symptom of its decline.

In 'The literary as activity in postmodernity', Marianne DeKoven also
sees literature as engaging in an agon with its own institutionality, and
experiencing a crisis as modernist determinations of the institution give
way to postmodern ones. Though she agrees with John Guillory that 'the
object of literary study' needs to be 'reconceptualized', she affirms its continued cultural relevance despite a susceptibility to 'dehistoricisation and
conservative appropriations'. Drawing upon Ian Hunter's theorisation of
aesthetic 'practices of the self', as well as on Derrida, Barthes, and Cixous,
DeKoven shows how 'writers from non-hegemonic groups', who are
ostensibly marginalised by the literary institution, can engage in a different and subversive appropriation of that institution's powers, 'seizing the
tools' in Donna Haraway's words, 'to mark the world that marked them as
other'. DeKoven traces the ambiguities and possibilities of such appropriation through an extended analysis of William Burroughs, a writer whose
work is situated at the very border between modernist and postmodernist
literary paradigms, and who can be shown to adapt the techniques and
practices of the one to the changing imperatives of the other.

Thomas Docherty's incisive essay on 'The question concerning literature' is a self-confessedly polemical demystification of some of literary theory's most familiar convictions. Docherty attacks the view articulated by
Terry Eagleton that because literature cannot be satisfactorily defined, it
does not therefore exist as a category. Eagleton, he argues, takes advantage
of 'the difficulty of proposing some stable definition for something that
develops historically and culturally' in order to 'be able to divert attention
from the question'. '[A]ll that is implied in accepting that there *is* a category
called "literature"', Docherty explains by contrast, 'is that I agree to participate in meaningful discussion of the topic'. In his own subsequent discussion, Docherty explores the political consequences of accepting and
defending the category of literature within academic and educational insti-

tutions. In particular, he concludes, 'we must reconsider the claims for the supposed intrinsic link between literature and democracy'. Docherty comes to reject the 'ethically and politically attractive' contention that the opening of the literary canon 'has served a positive political purpose'. 'Those versions of contemporary theory that dispose of the exclusivist category of "literature"', he writes, 'manage to circumvent the complexity of the relations between literature and politics. In particular, they depend upon a simplistic version of "identity-politics" in which the task is to legitimise an authentic identity for the reader. Yet ... such "authenticity" is itself that which exerts a *limitation* on the possibilities of democracy'. Citing Wittgenstein's 'private language' argument, Docherty asserts that 'if I speak "authentically", that is, always in the pure presence of my own proper voice, then, quite simply, I do not speak (or think) at all'. He maintains that in order to be empowered 'to participate adequately in meaningful dialogue', and therefore in democracy, 'one must be literate ... able to speak in different voices, in different registers, in order to assert one's autonomy'.

According to John Frow, '[t]he difficulty is not that the question "What is Literature?" cannot be answered, but that many perfectly valid answers are possible'. Frow examines the particular tension between 'the emergence of the literary' understood as 'an event which occurs in (or *as*) an act of reading', and literature as 'a structure of historical value which is variably consolidated in an institutional form'. He adapts Mircea Marghescou's concept of the regime – originally the 'semantic code regulating the informational potential of [a] linguistic code' – to designate a flexible and heterogeneous set of relations capable of mediating between these two apparently incompatible formulations. For on the one hand, 'the concept of regime shifts attention from an isolated and autonomous "reader" and "text" to the institutional frameworks which govern what counts as the literary', but on the other, 'the literary regime has no reality beyond the shape it gives to acts of reading'. Frow uses his theorisation of 'literature as regime' to 'redefine and redirect what goes on in a good practice of reading', and to advocate a novel 'rapprochement' between literary and cultural studies which would result, not in some conventional expansion of the literary canon to include underprivileged works, but, rather in ending literature's own 'exclusion' from the broader project of cultural criticism. In this process 'literary studies would learn to attend in a more routine manner to the social relations of signification, and cultural studies would in turn be reminded of the constitution of its major explanatory categories in practices of reading'.

Peggy Kamuf locates the essence of literature, the thing which 'if anything, should be saved from the ruins' of the literary crisis, in 'a certain notion of *fiction* or the fictional operation'. 'Essentially', she writes, 'literary theory takes *fiction* seriously' – something which philosophy, equally essentially, refuses to do. '[O]ne of the most consistently recurring gestures of philosophical discourse makes out literary fiction in particular ... to be essentially dependent or parasitical on, therefore secondary to, the whole presumed realm of "non-fiction"'. Kamuf traces this symptomatic dismissal and exclusion of fiction through the work of J. L. Austin and its critique by Derrida, and she appropriates Austin's term 'voiding' to propose a definition of fiction as that which *'marks and lets be remarked* the voiding of the referent'. 'Fiction', she continues, ' ... suspends the sign as sign of a referent which otherwise, without the mark, would be presupposed'. For Kamuf, indeed, fiction suspends or voids the presupposition of existence in general, including the existence of the reading and the writing subjects. She pursues the implications of this claim, this time through Blanchot's reading of Kafka, substituting Blanchot's term 'neutralisation' (which 'is said to be the effect of the literary or the fictional on philosophy') for 'fiction'. Ultimately, Kamuf displaces 'fiction' once again, to conclude by adopting another of Blanchot's terms, the *'récit'*, to express the importance that she attaches to literary and fictional discourses. The *récit*, she concludes 'criticises ... all that language presumes to name; that is, it both sets and lifts the limit of language, keeping thus *at stake*, in possibility, the opening to the other'.

The question of literature's material as well as its institutional future is raised by Adrian Page's exploration of the literary effects of new computer technology. Does hypertext offer qualitatively new possibilities for literary expression, and create new relationships between the producers and readers of texts, or is it no more than a cumbersome elaboration of techniques that are already available in more traditional media? Page is shrewd in his assessment of some of the more ambitious claims made by theorists such as George Landow, who treats hypertext as 'the embodiment of Derrida's theories of language'. On the contrary, as Page shows, hypertext has the effect of constraining the forms and linguistic possibilities of texts, exerting control over the ways in which they may be read, and over the nature and extent of the reader's participation in them. 'The use of hypertext', he writes, 'is not to permit a glimpse of unrestricted textuality, but to compel the reader to follow certain ideas and to pursue certain processes'. Page compares hypertext to 'the deictic use of the camera in an adaptation of literature for the cinema', and he draws on Brecht's ideas about film to suggest ways in which it might be used to open up texts by 'the simultaneous presentation of internal and external perspectives on character and action'. He concludes with a detailed and revealing examination of the potential for hypertext adaptation of two novels, Thomas Pynchon's *The Crying of Lot 49* and Anne Michaels's *Fugitive Pieces*.

Bruce Robbins provides a richly sceptical account of literature's institutional definition as an evasive and paradoxical object of inquiry 'defined by a perpetual rebellion against the necessary one-sidedness of professional perspective and the chastened orderliness of disciplinarity'. Rebellion, he argues, functions as 'a badge of professional membership' for literary theory, 'a paradox of [its] own', but then confounds itself by its embarrassing success, overflowing disciplinary boundaries and 'surrender[ing] its claim to a unique power of subversiveness'. 'All disciplinary objects', as Robbins writes, 'seem obliged to stake out and defend a large degree of inscrutability', and sustain their respective disciplines 'only by perpetually threatening to escape from their possession and undermine their work'. He identifies this generalisation of literature's defining instability with what Ian Hacking calls 'social constructionism', a predisposition in the humanities 'which remains literary in the precise sense that its project of de-naturalising involves showing to be products of human imagination, creativity, and discourse, in other words showing to be like literature, concepts in many fields that had been taken to be "natural givens" and therefore inalterable'. Robbins investigates the consequences of this literary imperialism for the non-literary disciplines that it has overrun, and in particular the consequence of the creative freedom – the freedom to 'pretend what you like' – implicit in the literary model. In this connection he contrasts Martha Nussbaum's objection to Judith Butler's excessive literariness with the internal – and literary – conditions of Butler's own 'perform[ance of] the normativity she denies'. Butler's practice of writing, he suggests, 'offers a stylistically creative response' to the tensions of constructionism, and therefore 'does valuable work of self-legitimation for her fellow academics even as she apparently refuses the legitimacy of the collective project, and perhaps collectivity and legitimacy as such'.

Finally, in 'Literature: repeat nothing', the only essay in this collection to start from psychoanalytical premises, Robert Smith 'transpose[s] to the creativity involved in literary works' a notion of 'libidinal energy' whose 'sustainment and repetition over time' may paradoxically be seen 'equally as deathly and reductive and as creative and life-affirming'. Working through successive theorisations of creativity in relation to obsession, the repetition compulsion, and the death drive, from Freud and Klein to Leo Bersani and Derrida, he shows how the conventional Freudian assumption that creative works 'mark the devious and formal or "aesthetic" accommodations of repressed and refracted wish' inexorably leads to 'a break in the continuum from psyche to literary artefact' which abolishes the universal psychoanalytic subjection of artistic creation to unconscious impulses. This happens at first through the ambiguity by which the repressed itself 'lodg[es] "within" the psyche like a kind of outside or unbroachable recess',

and then through the more radical disjunction imposed by 'formal accommodations' of the repressed themselves. For 'even the most esoteric form
becomes, qua form, a repeatable event and, in this regard, potentially public', and therefore when repression is sublimated formally, the result once
again divides itself from the psyche and 'develop[s] separate status'. Its
'separateness', moreover, is not that of 'a discrete, bordered, framed unity',
since the very formalism which enables it to escape the psyche 'will have
had to jeopardise its singularity': 'in the becoming-formal lies the element
of the literary's power', Smith concludes, 'but the formalisation does not
rectify; it, like an ideological apparatus, institutes an aberration'.

In addressing the question of literature it will be apparent that none of
the contributors to this collection are referring to exactly the same question (although 'what is literature?' does remain an important point of
departure). Nor do they agree as to the question's premises, or as to
where, how, and why it should be asked. We are no nearer to deciding
what the question of literature is, let alone answering it, at the end of the
book than we were at the beginning. I would argue, however, that this is
as it should be, and I have purposely arranged the contributions in alpha-
betical order by author, so as to avoid imposing upon them any prejudicial
organisation or set of conclusions.

For the enduring strength of literary theory in all its crises and trans-
formations has been the ability to keep its questions open, and to see the
limitations and the compromises of its own answers. The essays collected
here re-examine many of theory's current orthodoxies: Peggy Kamuf, for
example, refines the paradoxically familiar idea of literature's absolute
alterity through her reading of Blanchot as a possibility 'not of sameness,
nor finally of strangeness, but of the neutral that withdraws from even this
difference'. And John Frow is able to reconcile the social construction of
literature with its integrity as a 'mode of being' so that 'the "text" is at once
a closed aesthetic space, with lines of force radiating inwards from the
framing conditions that establish its closure, and a space of opening which
begins to merge with its edges, its borders with the non-textual or the hetero-textual'.

A number of the contributors also return to older theoretical preoccu-
pations such as the formal properties of literature, and even the nature and
existence of literary value itself. As well as offering a provocative re-exam-
ination of psychoanalytic ideas about creativity, Robert Smith's 'Literature
– repeat nothing' reinstates form and style as central to our understanding
of literature's 'power' and 'authority', while Charles Altieri uses literary
value as a way to resist the impoverishment of 'a world in which "right"
and "wrong" constitute the only relevant value judgements that we make'.
And throughout the collection, the use of words like 'power' (Smith,

Altieri, Attridge), 'force' (Clark, Smith again), and 'rich[ness]' (Altieri, Frow) marks the need for literary and cultural theorists to value literature, whether or not they evaluate it.

The purpose of *The Question of Literature*, after all, has been to affirm as well as investigate the degree to which literature matters to present-day culture, and the place of literature within and beyond its changing institutions. This book testifies to the persistence, importance, and diversity of the theoretical debate in which it takes part, and names a question that the debate cannot finally resolve but must go on asking.

Notes

1 A. Easthope, *Literary Into Cultural Studies* (London, 1991), p. 172.
2 *Ibid.*, p. 5.
3 *Ibid.*, p. 42. P. Widdowson, *Literature* (London, 1999), pp. 90, 60.
4 T. Eagleton, *Literary Theory: An Introduction* (Oxford, 1983), p. 22.
5 *Ibid.*, p. 195.
6 T. Reiss, *The Meaning of Literature* (Ithaca, 1992), p. 1.
7 *Ibid.*
8 R. Wellek and A. Warren, *Theory of Literature* (1949; repr. Harmondsworth, 1993), p. 20.
9 J-P. Sartre, *What is Literature?*, trans. B. Frechtman (London, 1950), p. vii.
10 *Ibid.*, pp. vii, 119.
11 Wellek and Warren, *Theory of Literature*, p. 28.
12 P. Hernardi, 'Introduction', in Hernardi (ed.), *What is Literature?* (Bloomington, 1978), p. xi.
13 L. Lerner, *The Truest Poetry: An Essay on the Question What is Literature?* (London, 1960), p. 2.
14 *Ibid.*, p. 76.
15 *Ibid.*, p. 1.
16 Easthope, *Literary into Cultural Studies*, pp. 5–6.
17 H. Bloom, *The Western Canon: The Books and School of the Ages* (New York, 1994), p. 4.
18 H. Weinbrot, 'Notes towards a fertility theory of the eighteenth-century canon', *Eighteenth-Century Life* 21:3 (November 1997), 87–8.
19 Lerner, *The Truest Poetry*, p. 1.
20 Widdowson, *Literature*, p. 23.
21 Lerner, *The Truest Poetry*, p. 3.
22 P. Widdowson, 'The crisis in English studies', in Widdowson (ed.), *Re-Reading English* (London, 1982), p. 3.
23 E. D. Hirsch, 'What isn't literature', in Hernardi (ed.), *What is Literature?*, p. 27.
24 Widdowson, *Literature*, p. 104.
25 Wellek and Warren, *Theory of Literature*, p. 22.
26 See A. Easthope, 'Paradigm lost and paradigm regained', in R. Bradford (ed.), *The State of Theory* (London, 1993), p. 95, Easthope, *Literary Into Cultural Studies*, p. 66, and Widdowson, 'The crisis in English studies', p. 2.
27 B. Herrnstein Smith, *Contingencies of Value: Alternative Perspectives for Critical Theory* (Cambridge, Mass., 1988), p. 43.

2

charles altieri

THE LITERARY AND THE ETHICAL: DIFFERENCE AS DEFINITION

One major benefit of anti-foundational thinking is its freeing us from obsession with definitions. We recognise that there are many phenomena in cultural life without strictly definable boundaries, so there is no possibility of delineating necessary and sufficient conditions for many of our basic concepts. Conversely, one major liability of anti-foundational thinking is its making it extremely difficult to characterise error (as opposed to simple difference). For then it cannot sustain any kind of dialectical movement. Without powerful terms for specifying error there seem no imposing demands on us to reach beyond specific inherited modes of life to make theoretical corrections in our assumptions or, more important, to understand processes of self-correction as fundamental to how we appreciate our own historical being. And if we cannot establish general conditions for making errors, we have considerable difficulty in determining how large social groups can hold together: we have no principles for establishing values that might satisfy a range of cultural perspectives, and we find it very difficult to ground any values at all by processes of argument or even by invocations of historical memory.[1]

Definition offers one basic means of allowing those with different perspectives to agree on conditions that bind all their descriptions and hence that make comparison possible among their perspectives. Our culture has to find anti-foundational ways of imposing analogous pressures on our thinking. So here I will address questions of defining literature by beginning with a set of five axioms on which I hope agreement can be reached – not because they somehow capture the real, but because they provide cogent procedural grounds for exploring the problems that underlie the quest for definition on this topic. Ideally these axioms will establish a framework allowing us phenomenological experiments testing what we share when we carry out the kind of reading that may lead us to worry about how we might define literature.

(1) *What needs defining is not literature per se but whatever allows claims that there is a 'Literature' to make certain demands on us.* Clearly 'literature' is indefinable because the term tends to be used so loosely that it covers an almost infinite range of writings. There can be little hope of establishing significant boundaries separating literature from some other domain because simply determining that something is literature tells us nothing about the demands it thereby makes on readers or on the values that the readers might hope to realise if they are responsive to those demands. With 'Literature' on the other hand, there are at least substantial historical efforts to establish just such boundaries. As heirs of those discourses, we find the use of capital letters bringing to bear on texts frameworks of expectation and value questions that we also employ when we deal with the range of fine arts. It is that connection that sustains intricate and ambitious value claims based not simply on what texts claim but on how they go about engaging readers in their concerns. Theorists may ultimately decide that it is counter-productive to grant texts the arrogance to claim that 'all the rest is literature', but even the fantasy of such power seems necessary to postulate if we are to appreciate how the field of high art Literature was constituted and may continue to be significant for contemporary culture.

(2) *We cannot adequately characterise the qualities sanctioning a distinctive category of the 'literary' if we remain bound to a purely aesthetic vocabulary.* Theorising about pleasure and about form simply will not provide a sufficient basis for the range or scope of values that have commonly been attributed to this class of works (if only by those who make a living by elaborating such values). As Alan Singer points out, when criticism relies on an aesthetic vocabulary it tends to preserve the specialness of art by atrophying its connection to life.[2] There is much more that has to be done if we are even to make sense of claims like Shelley's that poets are legislators of the earth or Sidney's that 'poesy is full of virtue-breeding delightfulness'. And it has been these claims that have shaped those practices most influential in determining twentieth-century assertions about literariness. So if we are not simply to dismiss those assertions, we have to understand why such value claims seem deeply woven into our understanding of literariness. Such understanding of course is not incompatible with ultimately dismissing them as evasive efforts to secure cultural capital, but it does make possible a rational discussion of the issues involved.

(3) *Defining literariness is not a matter of locating necessary and sufficient conditions, but rather of identifying what seems shareable and generative in how this concept plays a central role in basic (Western) practices of*

interpreting texts and of making value claims about literary experience.
Rejecting strict standards for definition is not simply a matter of asserting
fealty to anti-foundational practices. There are also several difficulties with
regard to definition that are basic to concepts developed within the
humanities. For example there seems to be no specific physical attribute
or even cultural expectation that provides a single overt marker of literariness; nor are there specifiable correspondences that regularly link particular textual features to the more general value claims that literariness is
expected to mediate. Several different traits can sustain the same value
claims, since one can locate what matters for the literary in an emphasis on
particular aspects of articulation, on qualities of concreteness, or on the
overall effects of structural relationships. Similarly the concept of literariness can take quite different forms in different practices, and it can have
different degrees of centrality for those practices. Finally, it is by no means
clear that providing abstract discursive formulations gives us the best
means of identifying literariness or of clarifying what comes to depend on
those identifications. We may learn this concept largely by interrelated
examples and by a range of experiences within which various cues or contexts indicate that readers are to pursue certain ways of approaching texts
and of drawing out consequences from the reading. Yet because the modes
of reading do have a great deal in common, we need some single concept
to indicate that commonness and to invite our then specifying relevant differences in particular cases.

Given this need and these intricacies, this axiom suggests that literary
theory alter its focus: rather than base its sense of literariness on traits or
qualities shared by a set of objects, it has to turn to what seems shared and
shareable in the various frameworks that readers bring to bear when they
treat literariness as an important value. This means we have to locate literariness as a concern within a variety of literary practices. In many
respects this shift compounds difficulties because there are no clear
boundaries among practices. Moreover, there are severe problems about
what practices have to be honoured when we are talking about a phenomenon like literariness that derives a good deal of its shape and most of its
authority not from present production but from the histories that our definitions enable us to write.

Circularity abounds. Yet we can find a manageable way of determining
which practices (and which level of the practices involved) have to be
addressed and honoured in relation to this topic if we are willing to accept
two sets of criteria – one historical, the other conceptual. If we are concerned with literariness, we have to be able to make provisional identifications with those practices that over time have been most influential in
establishing the relevant values: we have to understand from the inside

why certain canons are honoured and how they effect what we expect from our reading of the works they foreground. And our responsiveness to the historical shaping of our understanding is most effective when it can also show how the modes of memory established within these practices help to clarify the pressures on and the accomplishments of serious contemporary work. For the conceptual modelling of the relevant practices, I think we have to concentrate upon how we might find within a range of approaches to literariness the richest discourses attempting to link how we read to how we might attribute cultural values to those readings. In what follows I shall try not to align myself with any one specific practice but to rely on a version of literary history and of theoretical speculation abstract enough to be responsive to a range of perspectives. Risking banality seems a small price to pay for eliciting agreement because we then have terms on which to build.

(4) *Rather than define literariness in specific positive terms, it is more prudent to work by negatives, establishing what matters in terms of shared dissatisfactions with other ways of construing literary texts.* This axiom provides the abstractness that I need to escape fealty to any specific theory of reading, and it enables us to address the many limitations that theory has to face when it turns to positive formulations. For when we rely on cultural practices rather than definitions, it is extremely difficult to defend any assertion about values – the values reside not in discrete properties or arguments but as aspects of modes of life which are often not specifiable from the outside. Even the simple determination of literariness is not something we arrive at by reasoning from descriptions to conclusions. Rather we enter certain contexts, and because of various possible signs we adapt our attitudes towards materials that give us access to various paths: we might continue to follow our preferred practices or we might see the need for adjustment and experiment. Imagine then how much more tacit and incompletely formulated are the projections about possible satisfactions we experience when we approach texts as 'Literature'. In those cases we assume that if we pay attention to certain particulars and ask some of a range of possible questions we will be rewarded by relatively intense particular experiences and by at least a vague feeling that we are in touch with certain more general values that theory attempts to clarify and stabilise conceptually. Too much articulateness about how we read or what we seek comes to seem a disturbing straitjacket imposing structure where we want the feeling of discovering how to proceed by the kinds of attunements that specific texts invite.

Therefore I think the best way to appreciate the positive force within practices devoted to concerns about literariness is to proceed negatively. If we can develop situations in which the felt boundaries of the relevant practices are clearly violated, we can begin to examine just what seems to be negated and why that negation blocks access to important values that are possible within other attitudes towards reading. In the body of this essay I will adapt this weak version of dialectics to the limitations of ethical criticism, since its confidence about values creates substantial shadows where we can observe the active presence of quite different forces. But to illustrate this dialectic here I would like to dwell for a moment on how theorists of literariness might use the sociological challenges posed to such theorising by thinkers like Pierre Bourdieu. Here there arises a strong temptation to make counter-assertions, but that ought be accompanied by a sharp awareness of the dangers that occur if we succumb.[3]

Sociological criticism's account of literariness depends on a strict methodological understanding of what can count as a plausible positive assertion. From a sociological perspective, self-consciousness is the most untrustworthy mode for interpreting values because its workings are so obviously yet so indecipherably influenced by the agent's needs, desires, and fantasies. To have any knowledge about values we have to get beyond what people say to what they do, since their activities make clear what their interests actually are in such thinking and in such saying. Attending to what people say about themselves is to pretend that symptoms are part of the answer to the theorist's questions, so it is prudent to seek measures of real interests less subject to the need for self-congratulation that seems to pervade theory in the humanities. But perhaps this need for self-congratulation is not something to be dismissed as an illusion but a dynamic feature of our investments in literariness and so a phenomenon to be explored in its own right. Perhaps what seems self-indulgent involves working out terms by which we can represent ourselves to ourselves in ways that satisfy deep conative needs.

If these hesitations produce any reason to maintain one's distance from sociological accounts of value in the humanities, two consequences follow. First we begin to see that the very assertion of independence based on an ability to dismiss the testimony of self-consciousness and focus on behaviour may itself bring with it severe limitations. There may be some areas of experience where it is impossible to understand values unless one can provisionally take seriously how people describe their investments and their satisfactions. In these areas the sociologist's stance involves a willed blindness that has no justified privilege by which to translate one kind of experience into another. Then the second consequence emerges. Where imposed theoretical distance from the subject fails, we have good reason to turn instead on phenomenological self-awareness. However we have to be careful how we handle this contrast. If we proceed directly to the making of positive arguments, we may be acting as though we were in the same basic discursive structures as the sociologist, where evidence can be mustered and conclusions tested, even if the kind of evidence we invoke is quite different. Yet it is by no means clear whether the relevant phenomenological analyses will produce what might count as evidence, or that argument is a feasible basis for establishing the values that matter to those committed to some version of literariness. For the workings of the psyche in relation to such values remain fluid and mysterious: the psyche simply may not be the kind of object that allows the same kinds of understanding that the sociologist pursues.

If, then, we try to talk as if we could make the relevant observations in the form of objective descriptions, we are likely to become vague, abstract, and pious. And that in turn transforms us into exactly the characters that the sociologists insisted we were all along, so we sanction the suspiciousness driving the sociological inquiry in the first place. Therefore we might be both more convincing and less vulnerable if we were not so eager to fill the void that our criticism of the sociologist seems capable of producing. Perhaps we should be content to establish most of our positive account by keeping pressure on the sociologist's perspective – in part by indicating what it cannot cogently subsume, and in part by showing how at times that perspective is likely to extend itself beyond its own parameters by invoking value terms that depend on the modes of consciousness that it rejects.[4]

(5) *Offering a rough phenomenology of lyricism may provide the best concrete index of the basic values that attach to literariness in many of our reading practices.* For there is no better contrast to ethical criticism, since that criticism tends to concentrate on narrative. Lyricism on the other hand need not be a property exclusively present in lyric poems. I use the term to refer to various ways that texts delight in their use of their medium and stress the expressive registers that this excess beyond denotation can not only produce but also compose into complex modes of reflection. By attending to these registers we can develop value complexes very different from those stressed by ethics, yet capable of playing equally important roles within cultural life. And we have a firm basis for insisting that there are aspects of literariness that cannot be reduced to formalism because they are tightly woven into questions about expressivity and self-reflexiveness, even in narrative. Where a contrast with sociological criticism clarifies what is and is not possible within radically different perspectives, contrasts with ethical criticism promise a more finely grained set of differences: both attribute values to how specific texts unfold, and both celebrate distinctive powers of reading, but the specific claims of ethical criticism simply cannot be fully responsive to the modes of agency basic to fully lyrical states. And that calls attention not only to values within the lit-

erary that extend beyond the aesthetic, but also to the possibility that philosophy may not be able to cast itself as the arbiter of how we talk about these values.

Now my argument must grow indirect. I will try to clarify what I mean by ethical criticism so that we can recognise the basic points of tension that arise when we try to adopt that stance as our preferred way of engaging texts. Then, as we come to see the various claims of ethical criticism grow increasingly problematic, we should be able to recognise just what aspects of literary experience seem to require alternative values – not simply because these values are better attuned to the aesthetic dimension of works, but because they better fit the capacity of the aesthetic to address existential concerns. Ethical criticism occurs in at least three activities – in how individuals evaluate motives and actions in texts, in readers imagining or actually entering moral conversations about their assessments, and in the effort to link what readers and critics do to the discourses about morality carried out by professional philosophers. All three activities stage reading as a culturally vital practice because they require us to test what our moral vocabularies can encompass, make careful distinctions in our judgements, and even assess public policies. But all three activities also involve substantial risks of subordinating what might be distinctive within literary experience to those frameworks and mental economies that are attuned to modes of judgement shaped by other non-textual, and (usually) less directly imaginary worldly demands. Therefore it may be necessary now to push against claims about the ethical in the name of a richer model for approaching questions about ethos. This path enables us to develop models that in the long run allow literary experience to affect what we take ethical judgement to involve.[5]

For example literary modes like lyric often ask us to participate in states that are either too elemental or too transcendental or too absolute or too satisfyingly self-absorbed to allow ethical criticism a foothold. Yet these states can have enormous impact on how and why we are concerned with values of all kinds, including those that we pursue by ethical reasoning. Minimally they bring to bear examples of positive intensities that any ethics might have to take into account. And at their richest these works explore the limitations of all judgmental stances by requiring complex blends of sympathy and distance, thus eliciting fascination with extreme states of mind while complicating any possible grasp of how one might put such states into the categories of commensurability on which ethical judgement may ultimately depend. We become attentive to the selves that are possible when we manage to deploy distinctive powers of mind and sensibility. And we find ourselves often less concerned with questions about the world per se than we are with the dispositions of our readerly psyches, especially with the strange interaction between quite particular senses of alienation and the corresponding awareness of what goes into what we call the will. Attending to literariness provides one important means by which we learn to demand of ourselves something more grand and perhaps more threatening than that we be justified in our actions, or that we be able to appreciate how others might be justified or not justified. For we find the will engaged not simply in terms of languages of justification but also in terms of principles of satisfaction. It does not suffice to have made the best decision among available options. Rather for the moment one seems to see what it takes to make the world of a happy person different from that of an unhappy person. And then one understands how there is a dimension of ethics that cannot be put into words but must be approached by thinking about how we might understand Wittgenstein's dictum that ethics and aesthetics are one.[6]

Finally, developing contrasts with ethical appropriations of literariness will require us to alter the conceptual models we have for the emotions fundamental to the reading enterprise. Rather than dwelling within the parameters of approval and disapproval generated by empathy and sympathy we realise the need to explore how attributing literariness invites us to participate in passions that range from fear and desperation and confusion about identification to the fullest models of imaginative satisfaction our culture provides. These models range from visions of surrendering the self to values it engages to what Yeats called the 'self-delighting, self-appeasing, self-affrighting' soul realising that 'its own sweet will is heaven's will'. As Yeats knew, it is precisely the relation between such states of soul and possible dispositions of will that makes the lyrical fundamental to the ethos within ethics: without it we may find ourselves comfortable judging others, but we will have impoverished terms for putting into our moral calculi both what satisfactions are most important to pursue for ourselves and what, within ourselves, might imperil those satisfactions.

In a longer version of my argument about ethical criticism I try to show what is problematic in four basic critical orientations.[7] The first two are mirror images of one another. Each stresses the ethical importance of attending to dense concrete presentations of particular actions because such attention provides a powerful supplement to more abstract and categorical modes of ethical inquiry. At one pole we have an emphasis on how involvement in concrete situations enriches our capacities for making discriminations and keeps our judgements in close relation to the emotions of sympathy and empathy; at the other we have a deconstructive concern for an ethics of letting be that is acutely aware of the imperialising work usually done by professions of empathy and of sympathy, since it is the responder who gets to specify what those emotions involve. And the latter two shift the focus from properties of texts to ethical powers developed in readers by the specific kinds of experience that literature provides for them. Here I will concentrate only on the last two, since these discussions most emphatically dramatise the contrasts leading us to have a rich, if not especially articulate, grasp of the values that our practices for dealing with literariness make available. The first of these provides a version of perfectionism, the second an effort to align literary experience directly with public moral thinking.

There is no better brief summary of how literary experience participates in perfectionist values than Wayne Booth's emphasis upon reading as the exploration of desires that we may come to desire: '[w]hat sort of character, what sort of habits, am I likely to take on or reinforce' as 'I decipher this immensely compact bundle of actions, thought, and allusions?', '[w]hat "better desires" does it lead me to desire?'[8] Formulations like these enable Booth to provide a powerful answer to how texts mediate ethical values, without his having either to subsume texts under general principles or to insist upon their close fit with moral philosophy. The values that matter emerge through comparisons we make among the qualities of experience in texts 'that are both like and unlike' each other.[9] For we appraise works by examining whether an experience can be seen as '*comparatively* desirable, admirable, lovable or, on the other hand, comparatively repugnant, contemptible or hateful'.[10]

Such appraisal is not merely a matter of intuitions or the expression of sensibilities. Booth shows there are clear standards that enter our judgements. For ultimately ethical criticism asks how texts contribute to virtue. To address this concern we have to begin with the issue of intentionality, for we cannot have virtue without agency. We must postulate implied authors, then engage these authors in terms of the roles they might play in conversations about ethical values. Then the 'key question in the ethics of narration … becomes: Is the pattern of life that this would-be friend offers one that friends might well pursue together?'[11] Now we have both an object of ethical reflection – the friendship relation – and we have an obvious locus for making assessments of texts. We are invited to ask whether the basic qualities of the text contribute to forging such imaginary friendships or if it presents hindrances to friendship such as hidden designs or lack of respect for the audience or shoddy reflection on the activity presented. In either case Booth shows that by thinking about texts in terms of questions about the company we keep, we do not need abstract principles as grounds of their worth because we have clear personal measures based on how the modes of desire for desire that they delineate stand up in relation to works to which they can be compared. We do not determine who our friends are because of the conditions they satisfy; rather the relevant choice is how we determine who we are in terms of the quite concrete company we choose, and the company we reject. Responsibility remains a matter of individual self-definition, yet it brings with it appropriate contexts in which choices can be characterised and judged.

In my view Booth's is a powerful theoretical position precisely because it appeals so directly to matters of ethos. Nonetheless I find it difficult to accept this figure of friendship as an adequate principle either for the qualities distinguishing individual valuations by readers or for the frameworks that give such choices public significance. And it is this difficulty that I think establishes the contrastive base we need to tease out what might be distinctive literary ways of engaging in questions about ethos. First, it seems obvious that the figure of the friend simply forecloses the full range of values explored by literary texts while also suppressing the intensity of contradiction that we encounter as we explore that range. Booth's concern for the company one keeps does support a limited pluralism (no single principle is likely to determine our range of friendships). But it leads us also to recognise that some of the literary texts we most value prove interesting enemies rather than admirable friends – not only because of the challenges they pose to our convictions but also because they fascinate us by their refusing to contour themselves to the models of dialogue that are allowed by a virtue-based model of friendship. More important, the idea of virtue as a primary criterion for the friends who contribute to happiness comes to seem a somewhat pious and inaccurate one, at least if we use literary experience as our measure of existential possibilities. Invoking 'virtue' allows the appearance of combining plural possibilities with a generalisability based simply on examples and cultural traditions. Yet attention to imaginative intensities reminds us that *'virtu'* is an irreducibly equivocal concept, because in one register it is simply a measure of power or conative strength, with no distinguishing 'ethical' qualities, while in another it brings an aura of satisfying certain deep moral values in a society. Consequently Booth's effort to keep the moral force of 'virtue' can be said to confer on texts an awkward intimacy that is too public for most forms of affection and fascination, while at the same time he fails to develop an adequate public model of what might count as virtue or satisfy specifically ethical conditions of judgement.

Given this ambiguity around virtue when it is definable only in terms of affective relations, it is not surprising that most philosophers seek different grounds for ethical criticism. Here I will concentrate on Martha Nussbaum's *Poetic Justice* because that book offers the best case that I know for bringing narrative literature into close proximity with the concerns and the language of traditional moral philosophy. Making clear how this work matters and what we can learn from its limitations will take me somewhat more time than I have spent on Booth, but spending that time will also allow us eventually to return to Booth from a perspective enabling us to capitalise on the Nietzschean possibilities within his argument.

Nussbaum's previous writings on literature and ethics had stressed the importance of concrete moral discrimination, but always with a keen sense of interpreting that concreteness as a contribution to concerns basic 'even to Kantians or Utilitarians'.[12] *Poetic Justice* is distinctive for its efforts to extend the 'fit' between narrative fiction and moral philosophy beyond the judgement of individual actions to questions of public policy. There are then no better grounds upon which to test the degree to which one can make literary concreteness into a medium for more overtly generalised moral discourses. Nussbaum argues that reading narrative fiction actually provides 'insights that should play a role (though not as uncriticized foundations) in the construction of an adequate moral and political theory', while at the same time the particular interpretative processes that the narratives invite help to develop specific 'moral capacities without which citizens will not succeed in making reality out of the normative conclusions of any moral or political theory, however excellent'.[13] If it is to pursue these ends ethical criticism has two basic tasks. It must establish a context for the literary text to operate in moral terms by bringing to bear the relevant issues formulated from within philosophy; then it must show how the text 'exemplifies and cultivates abilities of imagination that are essential to the intelligent making' of the relevant 'assessments, in public as well as private life'.[14] For if literature really has philosophical force, then it ought to exercise that force in the same public domain that philosophical concepts try to influence. Where Booth talks of texts as friends, Nussbaum wants to create a context in which we can see deep links between the roles of reader and of judge.

But are readers primarily judges? The closer Nussbaum brings literature into the sphere of public policy the more one begins to feel resistance because so much of what is basic to literary experience seems to be pushed towards the margins. Consider for example the fact that to make the arguments of *Poetic Justice* work she has to turn away from James and from Proust, the major figures of her earlier work on ethical criticism, to the Charles Dickens of *Hard Times*. While Dickens is clearly a major writer, there are few literary theorists who would want to use *Hard Times* as their exemplary text, for exactly the reasons that do tempt Nussbaum to make the effort. For whereas developing ethical claims from James and Proust requires one to stress the play of a very complex intelligence perhaps working at the limits of dominant notions of morality, developing claims from the Dickens of *Hard Times* entails stressing, not so much the processes of judgement in particular dense situations as the need to develop public moral stances towards large social issues. This Dickens is less interested in assessing how characters engage with intricate situations than he is in displaying how agents can respond adequately to the demands of general social conditions. Consequently, he subordinates the density of textual relations to the quite different kind of weight afforded by intense sentimental investments.

Much can be accomplished by this subordination. *Hard Times* gains its moral scope from its extraordinary ability to manipulate pathos and hence to position a responsive audience in a situation where it both registers suffering and understands plausible public causes of that suffering. Nussbaum then is quite right to argue that this novel shares with some contemporary philosophers the project of defending 'an approach to quality of life measurement based on a notion of human functioning and human capability, rather than on either opulence or utility'.[15] Dickens's pathos allows his fiction an immediate and compelling 'measure of how people are doing' because he can bring emotional resonance to questions of 'how well their form of life has enabled them to function in a variety of distinct areas, including but not limited to, mobility, health, education, political participation, and social relations'.[16] From this the leap to contemporary philosophy is not a large one:

> Since we read a novel like *Hard Times* with the thought that we ourselves might be in a character's position – since our emotion is based in part on this sort of empathic identification – we will naturally be most concerned with the lot of those whose position is worst, and we will begin to think of ways in which that position might have been other than it is, might be made better than it is ...
>
> If one could not imagine what it was like to be Stephen Blackpool, then it would be all too easy to neglect this situation as Bounderby does, portraying workers as grasping insensitive beings. Similarly, to take a case that will figure in my next section, if one cannot imagine what women suffer from sexual harassment on the job, one won't have a vivid sense of that offense as a serious social infringement that the law should remedy.[17]

This stress on pathos allows the empathic imagination to leap directly to large value frameworks and it produces an inherently socialising dimension for literary texts because it seeks imaginative agreement about ways of redressing suffering. Yet I think that it is important to ask whether these advantages outweigh the disadvantages of allowing our literary ethics to be so dependent upon that one emotional attitude. James for example is careful to make characters tempted by the appeal of pathos, like Hyacinth Robinson, have to learn to make judgements critical of the temptations to self-righteousness that occur when one lets one's awareness of public issues outweigh the need for concrete self-understanding. And one could argue that this emphasis on pathos allows precious little room for a corresponding emphasis on the various modes of ethos that many of our received practices stress as basic to literary imaginations. In fact one could use this contrast between ethos and pathos as a basic way of challenging assumptions fundamental to Nussbaum's ethical criticism and perhaps to any criticism that is content to ally itself with moral philosophy. This contrast is especially important for clarifying the various roles that accounts of the emotions might play in our perspectives upon literary values. For once pathos is the central link between the literary and the ethical, then Nussbaum's cognitive theory of emotions clearly provides the dynamic energies securing the interactions between the two domains. In my view, however, the cost exacted by this method of linking the domains makes it crucial that we turn from pathos to ethos, and see what conceptions of emotion then best articulate the values provided by a distinctively literary version of experience.

Nussbaum identifies three specific means by which the emotions elicited within literary narrative can support and extend the work of moral philosophy. The first is mentioned only in a passing remark, yet I think that it has to play a major role in a full statement of her theory. I refer to the need to make moral sense of the simple but elemental fact that literature seeks to confer pleasure. What kind of pleasure instructs, especially when pathos is the vehicle of instruction? Nietzsche would suggest that we be suspicious of the kinds of pleasure we take in identifying with other people's suffering, since nothing secures bourgeois self-satisfaction so well as sympathy with those who lack the same possessions. Nussbaum is more generous and in some respects more subtle. She sees that pleasure affords a means of making identification attractive, and hence of allowing us to orient cognitive interests towards suffering, while resisting the need to locate the pleasure in our own melodramatic consciousness of ourselves as pity-producers. For to the extent that we take pleasure in particular characters from underprivileged situations, we are likely to find their company attractive so that we are drawn further into their world and into sympathy with their interests.[18] We do not have to let the pleasure be absorbed within our own sense of self-importance.

However any effort to link literary pleasure to moral philosophy produces a problem that haunts ethical criticism in many of its activities. It cannot suffice to praise concreteness in perception or in our pleasures unless one can say which pleasures contribute to moral values and which do not. Otherwise Plato's fear of the dangers in such ungoverned concreteness must remain a constant threat. Nussbaum addresses that issue by linking her remarks on pleasure to a more general cognitive theory of emotions. If emotions can provide a kind of knowledge in their own right, then we can secure their role in moral thinking without prescribing in advance what emotions we will allow. And indeed there are many respects in which emotions produce knowledge and complement what on other grounds we establish as truths. Emotions clearly establish salience by stressing what might matter in particular perceptual fields, and they bring to bear belief contexts that we have to go on to assess if we are to understand how and why particular options for action might matter to us. The emotions organised by a sense of pathos provide excellent examples. For pathos attunes us to the facts contributing to someone's suffering, and it brings beliefs to bear that orient us toward specific actions if they prove true (just as pleasure facilitates identifications). As Nussbaum puts it, 'the person deprived of the evaluations contained in pity seems to be deprived of ethical information without which such situations cannot be adequately, rationally appraised'.[19] Yet because the emotions are bound to belief, they do not lock us into attitudes but can be modified by relevant information (such as the information that the one bidding for our sympathy is faking it).

The greater the cognitive claims for emotions, however, the more pressing is the dilemma of concreteness that I have just mentioned. Doubtless there are emotions that provide sustenance for reason. But how do we decide which emotions do and do not have the power to modify reason, especially when we are dealing with imaginary constructs? It seems as if these emotions have to be tested by reason in order to be worthy of having such an influence. But then what is to influence rationality must be influenced by rationality, and again we face a vicious circle. Nussbaum is not daunted. She turns to a version of Booth's position where specific human exemplars afford the mediating principles defining how emotions can affect what we take reason to be. But rather than invoke the figure of the friend, she relies on Adam Smith's model of the 'judicious spectator' because this enables her to tie emotions to dispositions of character. Her focus then is not on how we come to desire to desire but on how we attach ourselves to the particular forms of idealisable desire that constitute ethical lives.

Smith develops his model in order to address the fact that many emotions obviously do not prove good guides for our actions. So to ensure that the emotion is appropriate, we have to determine that it is a 'true view of what is going on'.[20] And then we have to be sure that the viewer will not overdetermine that truth because of problematic private interests. Theory can make the appropriate distinctions if it can find a way of assuring that the emotion is that 'of a spectator, not a participant'.[21] In a single stroke literary experience moves from being marginal to philosophy to having claims for centrality, since there is no better ideal for the psychic economies Smith calls for than the self-discipline fundamental to attentive reading. Reading reduces its object to banality if it simply imposes an individual's needs and desires. Conversely, the promise held out for readers requires that they assume spectatorial roles through which they manage both to feel the relevant emotions and to appreciate them for the energies and values that they organise. Reading shows how we can treat anger or grief or love as if we could identify with their intensities while at the same time maintaining the distance necessary to make judgements about and through our involvement in the particulars.

Suggestive as this account of reading is, Nussbaum is less interested in the specific analysis than she is in the social implications that she can draw from it. For the figure of the 'judicious spectator' allows her to insist upon a distinctive care demanded by literary practice, then to extend that power into the dynamics of making social judgements. Hence the dramatic climax of her book consists in an elaborate effort to place reading as a judicious spectator at the heart of how judges make decisions. Judges have to know principles and procedures. But they also have to know the limitations of the abstractness built into principles and procedures, and they have to find ways to make the imaginative projections necessary for producing justice in particular situations.[22] So if one can make literary experience an exemplar for the working of an impartial yet sympathetic judgement, one can then treat the 'poetic imagination' as 'a crucial agent of democratic equality'.[23] This imagination not only tries to sympathise with all of the relevant points of view, it also builds on its own impartiality to seek from that sympathy those actions which comprise the greater social good. And this imagination requires the casting of that understanding in plural and qualitative terms based on those ideals of human flourishing which repeated acts of sympathy enable us to keep in the forefront of our vision.

I dwell on Nussbaum at such length in part because I want to dramatise the ambivalent feelings that she produces, and then use those feelings to articulate what I take to be the basic problem confronting anyone who wants to insist on aspects of literariness that do not allow smooth transitions to the ethical and hence that cannot be so directly connected to reformist and egalitarian desires. On the one hand, I am made uneasy by the self-confident and imperialist philosophising that reduces the great imaginative range of literary experience to the intellectually undemanding yet practically important moral and political truths that are promulgated by a philosophy devoted to spreading the values of human flourishing. On the other hand, I am not happy with myself for being so easily seduced into the equally distressing arrogance of the literary critic appalled at our marvellous complexity being oversimplified merely because someone who has devoted her life to the project wants to use literature for making the world a better place to live for large segments of its population. I am forced to confront the fact that my view of the experiences offered by the practices that for me establish literariness can promise only moderate modifications in how some individuals view the world. My view cannot even approximate the kind of social impact that Nussbaum projects for these texts, and that writers like Dickens are in fact capable of producing. Yet I still want to argue that the very grandeur of her enterprise leads our attention away from those concrete processes by which literature does affect individual lives in ways that noble sentiments about public welfare simply cannot produce. While this alternative perspective may not be able to demonstrate how literary experience makes better moral agents of us, it can show how attending to qualities fundamental to the literariness of works does offer society substantial values which are very difficult to get elsewhere.

In Nussbaum's story literature can be replaced by any other means of training discernment and eliciting thoughtful pity. We do not even need literary examples to develop the theoretical importance of concentrating upon plural qualitative measures of values. And while literature proves useful in resisting the utilitarian and rationalist models of assessment that Nussbaum attacks, its relevance in this regard stems less from the passions it mediates than from the inadequacies of those philosophical stances in the first place. Therefore rather than heed Nussbaum, we may do better to concentrate on what we lose when we ask reading and criticism to pursue clearly defined, public ethical ends. It should be immediately evident that we risk losing sight of what are usually the most compelling and most persuasive experiential qualities that the relevant texts produce, yet we gain little more than ideological reinforcement for what has its driving energies and relevant conditions of judgement elsewhere.

Nussbaum is especially useful as a contrastive figure because opposing her requires a good deal more than returning to some kind of aestheticism or adapting discourses about singularity and difference and empowerment. The literary values that I want to foreground have much more substance, and hence require as background the strenuous over-moralising of a Nussbaum. In this context we begin to see the working of imaginative powers that might be capable of resisting the claims of ethical criticism while engaging essentially the same concerns about the quality of lives embodied within the text. There emerge forces capable of establishing what I think is a necessary tension between the principle-based orientation required for ethics and the projective modes of self-exploration that are fundamental to elaborating what might count as forms of ethos worth honouring for individuals and for society. Therefore I will close by being as clear as I can on what I take to be three insuperable problems in contemporary ethical criticism, in the hope that we can deepen our appreciation of those aspects of literariness that are capable of challenging philosophical stances seeking to make imaginative work submit to their conditions for praise.

We have already addressed the first problem, which lies in the logical structure of ethical criticism. This criticism insists on there being something distinctive in how concrete texts engage our moral attention and yet it has to interpret the value of that engagement in terms of the very philosophical methods and generalisations from which the concrete reading deviates. As Derrida might put it, ethical theory wants the concrete both to establish values and to supplement value schemes, yet the very role of supplement undercuts the concreteness by making it dependent upon abstractions, and it undercuts the abstractions by making them dependent for their realisation on something that philosophy apparently cannot provide on its own. Because I have nothing more to say about the abstract form of this problem I will shift to a quite specific and I think telling manifestation of the issues that is brought into focus by Nussbaum and, indirectly, by Booth. When we realise how philosophy has to strain for the fit that melds it with literary experience, we also understand the pressure to let pathos take over from ethos, or to become the sole relevant ethos, and we understand why it is so tempting to vacillate between different meanings of 'virtue'. That realisation in turn leads us to what I am claiming are the shadows or margins of ethical discourse, where we might value literary experiments in ethos precisely because they do not depend upon the same kind of underlying distinctively moral sentiments as do examples drenched in pathos. More important, these experiments allow us to appreciate imaginative states as directly affecting our experience of values without our having to postulate those underlying reasons. Examples of ethos make their appeal to us in terms of the dynamic capacities they afford our quite particular states of self-awareness as we explore the energies they make available, with no sanction beyond the textual qualities eliciting intellectual, emotional, and intersubjective intensities.

There is no better contrast to the ethics of literary pathos than W. B. Yeats's poem 'He and She':

> As the moon sidles up
> Must she sidle up,
> As trips the scared moon
> Away must she trip:
> 'His light had struck me blind
> Dared I stop'.
>
> She sings as the moon sings:
> 'I am I, am I;
> The greater grows my light

The further that I fly'.
All creation shivers
With that sweet cry.[24]

The first stanza tries to render something like the essence of pathos. For here the character cannot speak for herself but must be represented by another, except for the one moment when she gets to utter her dilemma. Every move seems driven by forces to which the character is unwillingly bound. By the second stanza the very intensity of the pain seems to open a possible fascination with the opposite pole, with more assertive egocentric states that poetry might not only represent, but also help to focus. At first this stanza also depends upon a narrator in order to situate the speaker. But after one line the content of the singing takes over from its visual representation, and the mode of consciousness within that singing then entirely dominates the scene. The absoluteness of the singing in turn suffices to produce an assertion of an 'I' identical to itself: there simply seems to be no gap between the subject singing and the objective state that is the song made physical.

Technically speaking, such assertions cannot have any philosophical force, since only God can experience the complete coincidence of subjectivity and objectivity. But the poem is less interested in the truth of its assertion than in the energies and desires that it can make visible by the effort to purify song of everything but the 'I' who as its singer, or better as its singing, manages to glimpse what it means to experience the coincidence of subject and object states. While there is no empirical test of the truth of this assertion, there are important formal features of the poem that at least give a kind of substance to the desire itself. The utter simplicity of the situation, for example, shaped only by a contrast with the dependency of the first stanza, gives us a world in which there might be nothing but the singing, with all impurities driven away by the need to separate oneself from the kind of psyche that can be dominated by the moon. Here lyric seems to approach its own inner possibilities – presenting not any one role, one version of ethos, but the essence of what any role becomes when it can be entirely the matter of song. And, as song, the poem's physical qualities deepen the all-absorbing nature of the 'I am I'. Long *I* sounds literally take the poem over, spreading the light produced by and as the 'I' of the singing. That intensity in turn becomes so great that self-absorption cannot rest in narcissistic states. Just as the 'she' of the first stanza is bound to the ways of the moon, the 'I' of the second must return to its setting. Only now the self-absorption comes to constitute a fantasy lover bringing into creation its deepest sexual pleasure because finally creation has an opposite active enough to make its own presence felt. Resistance to the force of the moon enables the second lyric to treat creation itself as once again something to be loved and not merely feared or respected or moralised.

Had I the time I would go on to poems that explore the same level of intensity attached to quite different emotional orientations. Yeats's 'Lullaby' for example completely absorbs the ego within that traditional folk form, using literary self-consciousness as its vehicle for giving to care itself a mode of absorption that extends far beyond what would suffice for moral judgement. But my one example is strong enough to allow my going directly to the generalisation that what matters most in these literary states is not how they might be justified morally but how they justify themselves by their invitation to imaginative participation within what the text elicits from its ways of bringing the world and the psyche into language. Excess lies down with extreme, precise care; no wonder creation shivers.

And perhaps ethics can learn from this display. For it seems to me arguable that here we have a telling illustration of how the lyrical dimension of experience influences what Booth calls the desire for desires – not simply because specific states appeal to us, but also because we encounter specific qualities of those desires that become exemplars for what a range of emotions might provide were we attuned to appreciate their intensities. Both ways of encountering emotional fields then have the power to affect how we adapt or modify ethical stances. Lyrical emotions can make certain states attractive because of the modes of self-identification that they allow – here the best example may be the qualities of moral responsiveness that we find in the great epic poets. Or these emotions can affect ethics by giving us standards for the levels of emotional life in which we might feel able to take pride as we explore possible dispositions only some of which are thematisably moral. By this logic we might even claim that concerns about ethos prove central to how we let ourselves be affected by pathos.

The second of the three basic problems that I see facing ethical criticism will help us to appreciate aspects of our emotional intensities and their consequences for us which are largely ignored or displaced when literature is asked to carry ethical weight. For in its eagerness to establish moral seriousness ethical criticism is rarely sufficiently attentive to the qualities and values that writers work hardest to produce (at least those writers who accept practices in which literariness remains a crucial concern). We then have to use contrasts with how this criticism stages emotions in order to clarify what is most dynamic about the affective lives created by those authorial concerns. Within ethical criticism discourse about the emotions faces the same problems that we have been tracing in relation to its concreteness claims. For ethical criticism has to assert that it gives moral philosophy access to emotions mediating kinds of knowledge and investment not available within the conceptual modes of judgement usually called upon by ethical theory. Yet while the emotions have to be different they also have to be contained, overtly or covertly, by the very rationality that they are seen as supplementing – hence Nussbaum's reliance upon the cognitive theory of emotions.

Nussbaum provides one example that will make clear the stakes in how we represent literary emotions. The case in point is her effort to develop Richard Wright's *Native Son* as a moral exemplum even though this labour tends to repress much of the work's emotional force. Nussbaum claims that readers of this text clearly find their emotional responses also serving as cognitive instruments – both in generating sympathy for Bigger Thomas and in pushing whites to examine their assumptions towards such young black males. And, Nussbaum shows, Wright is careful to complicate and qualify that sympathy so that it meets real world conditions. Rather than make the easy appeal to figures of universal brotherhood, the novel demands we acknowledge the degree to which social factors have also made literal brotherhood very hard to envision, at least for bourgeois whites. The result of that demand is a deeper sympathy leading the judicious spectator to feel and to think that '[t]his is a human being, with the basic equipment to lead a productive life; [for we] see how not only the external circumstances of action, but also anger, fear, and desire have been deformed by racial hatred and its institutional expression. The unlikeness that repels identification becomes the chief object of our concern'.[25]

But Nussbaum's rich analysis of the difficulties that whites feel in relating to Bigger makes that unlikeness more problematic than her theory allows her to grant. It is clear that Wright's text deepens our capacity to understand Bigger in his unlikeness. Yet the more deeply that whites come to appreciate how wounded Bigger is by his upbringing in a racist society, the more difficult it is for them to link that knowledge with an unequivocal sympathy. He raises a complex set of emotions in whites, and perhaps not only in whites, involving fear and self-preservation and the resulting need to evade self-contempt. And once those emotions enter it is not possible simply to translate the sympathy that Bigger elicits from the judicious spectator into a moral orientation towards specific actions.

Nussbaum is confident that 'the reader, while judging Bigger culpable (the degree of his culpability is certainly debatable), is likely to be, other things equal, inclined to mercy in the imposition of punishment, seeing how much of his character was the product of circumstances created by others'.[26] Yet I am not sure that the emotions he raises produce that judgement, nor that Wright even wanted that judgement.[27] The sympathy Wright calls for engages us with a seriously wounded psyche that for many readers will not elicit mercy, at least in relation to what they expect of the legal system. It is perfectly possible to respect Bigger's independence so much that one wants him kept away from the white world at all costs. Once sympathy aligns us with his character, and not just with his actions, we have very good reason to think that nothing so merely institutional as a relatively short jail sentence is likely to produce any change in Bigger. Instrumental reason then may well find itself using this sympathy to seek ways of eliminating the threat rather than improving the condition of the one found threatening.

Almost anyone reading this essay is likely to share a desire that mercy temper punishment in cases like Bigger's. But I suspect that we cannot arrive at this judgement because of anything our emotions for him tell us. In fact the motivating force here has very little to do with our emotional relation to Bigger's specific condition. Rather what moves us to mercy is our affective investment in certain images of ourselves based on our overall political commitments. These investments do seem to me crucial to politics and are certainly affected by literary experience – but not quite by the experience of sympathy, or any other pathos-orientated attitude, and certainly not by what Nussbaum celebrates as the emotions of a judicious spectator who manages to control the impulses of the empirical self. For what in part leads us to go against what we know from our sympathy with Bigger is an intensely personal commitment to aligning ourselves with the politics of hope rather than the politics of despair, and with a willingness to take political risks rather than to insist on safe order. These impulses are strengthened not by sympathy per se but by developing investments in positive identifications, if not with specific role models then with imaginary worlds that literary texts help us to envision and to populate with possible judges whom we want to please by acting as nobly as we can. Nussbaum's cognitive model of emotions can neither handle the dangers attendant on what we do come to know in passionate ways nor address the role of non-cognitive fantasised identifications as fundamental to morality and to the impact that literary experience can have in affecting morality by influencing identifications.[28]

If I am right, the limitations of Nussbaum's cognitive theory of emotions provide a superb contrastive stage on which to put our spotlight back on Yeats's poem. It seems clear that her position cannot adequately address either of the fundamental lyrical states in the poem – the dependency by which the speaker understands what power is, and the assertiveness by which she explores her own access to it. Both are extreme states that require the spectator to suspend impersonal judiciousness. What matters is not what we come to know about the world but what our participation in the poem makes available as concrete, elemental abstraction. So from Yeats's point of view it is reason that must learn to accommodate states like those that the poem can make so intensely real and so appealing, as if we were encountering representations of what the desire for desire might look like in its pure form. Yeats's poem sets ethos against pathos, insisting that while rationality may require Nussbaum's view of cognitive emotions, there are strong features of literary experience that sharply oppose it, features like Richard Wright's desire to leave his audience in despairing awe at Bigger's life. Where cognition might have been, there Yeats wants fascination to reign, since fascination opens the reader to what we might call pure lyrical power and its capacities to produce modes of satisfying self-reflection. And where Yeats is, there too we might find writers as diverse as James and Shakespeare and perhaps even Dante in his effort to characterise a loving intellect whose reason is far beyond any representations that we might produce for it.

My praise of these states does not mean that we as agents can survive without heeding the claims of reason. It does mean that we as agents are not likely to thrive until we recognise how much that is in our possible interest is in conflict with what we are likely to understand as the imperatives of reason, or at least with how philosophers like Nussbaum understand its imperatives. Reason has its claims because we have to act in a world where accurate information is crucial, where laws of all kinds need to be honoured, and where society needs shareable principles for assessing actions and agendas. But these claims take precedence for us only when we actually need to justify actions (and non-actions) or when we have to make analogous judgements about actions or agendas. Then we need disciplinary ethics, and disciplinary ethics always needs the background provided by discussions in moral philosophy. But our lives also engage us in quite different modalities where justifications can be assumed or where they are clearly after the fact and hence not fundamental. In these domains the worry about what is right is less pressing than the need to discover what is possible for us to feel and to project and even to speculate upon.[29] And in these domains the social impact of our actions proves less central than the possible impact on our private lives produced by specific imaginative states and related energy fields.

And so I come to the last positive point that I think is sharpened by dwelling on what is problematic within ethical criticism. I want to show how an emphasis on ethos helps to clarify both the kinds of willing that are fundamental to literary experience and the terms on which it might make sense to use so tricky a concept as the 'will'. In order to do this we once again have to recognise that while cognition is fundamental to moral judgement, there is a specific element of decision or affirmation in such judgements which cannot be explained in purely cognitive terms. Nussbaum's cognitive theory of emotions seems to rest in part on an assumption that the fit between philosophical reasoning and discriminating, sympathetic literary experience is matched by a direct fit between what we come to think is right and how we go on to act. Therefore if one can specify the fit between what one recognises and how one feels, one has the appropriate terms for handling those psychological dimensions enabling ethical reading to carry over into influencing ethical practice. Booth, on the other hand, introduces what seems a crucial third term for this psychology. In his scheme one has to move beyond the complex of recognitions and emotions to attribute some distinctive motivating force. What we feel must connect with some model of self-regard or force of desire before it will have a decisive impact on how we act.[30] Indeed that is why 'the company we keep' is so central a figure for Booth. When we read we do not simply interpret texts; we also position ourselves in relation to them by the company in which we put them. Then by entering such company texts even take on the power to judge us because they provide contexts for assessing the desires that we desire. Hence they reflect back to us whether we are aligning our desires with our ideals, and they maintain the power to display to us whether we are living up to the conditions of membership in an imagined community.

Booth, however, sets unnecessary constraints on how these communities are constituted. So we have to use his claims contrastively, locating in our dissatisfactions with them a more comprehensive range of motives and interests by which literary experiences influence both the decisions we make and the self-representations or modes of awareness that shape our understanding of those decisions. The image of texts as friends simply does not capture the many different kinds of intimate relations that texts enter in our lives, nor does it quite address the variety of productive energies brought into play by those intimate relations. Our affective lives can be strongly touched by pleasures, fascinations, and challenges that have their power because they refuse the domesticating ideal of friendship for other less stable and less comforting modes of presence. Moreover these pleasures, fascinations, and challenges are not as easy as to subsume under criteria compatible with moral discourse as are appeals to friendship.

When we go beyond the confines of friendship relations, our ideas about how the will functions in our reading have to be substantially modified. Even when we do find texts affecting our decisions about actions or about values, we need not base that determination upon any specific categories or idealising languages under which they fit. Texts appeal as particulars with their own distinctive promise of a relation that allows us to feel ourselves endowed with specific powers because we seem capable of maintaining certain images of ourselves – by identification or by active struggle against domination. Indeed the more identity issues seem directly at stake, the more we find it impossible to interpret specific affirmations as relying on concepts or on specifiable criteria. In such cases we often exert our will simply as an extension of where we find our energies satisfyingly disposed. Consider again how identification is invited by Yeats's poem – not because the poem somehow provides us an idea affording a specific image for the self, but because we find ourselves taking on the poem's own work of gathering an intensity of productive self-consciousness as its response to the utter loss of personal power represented in the initial situation. For in our experiences of the lyrical at least, the will often emerges less through an interpretation of what is true or good about the text than as an attachment to what is powerful within it. And the good then becomes less a matter of how actions can be assessed than of how fully we find ourselves able to take part within the worlds they afford our imaginations.

This claim about the will is not incompatible with the capacity of literary texts to state the truth or to represent the good. For the willing elicited by imaginative power occupies a different plane: it can accompany a range of judgements or perceptions because it simply determines the degree to which a person places stakes upon a particular state. So even when we do stress the truth value of an intense literary experience, our affirmation of it as an experience may depend less on the truth it offers than on our finding ourselves intensely identified with how its specific efforts at articulation provide a sense of discovery or sharpen what we thought we knew. We may affirm a text for the way in which it represents moral situations, or we may affirm ourselves in relation to that text for the way we find ourselves becoming moved in its presence. And, analogously, when we are moved to pity, we may respond directly to the object of pity or to the states of subjective intensity that the text offers us as agents capable of developing this specific intensity and scope of pity in relation to the world evoked.

Here then we enter another possibility for appreciating why Wittgenstein thought ethics and aesthetics were one. There is a deep connection between how we affirm our own relation to the states or actions we inhabit and how we ultimately come to affirm the sense of completeness and of intense participation afforded us by works of art. From the point of view of ethics the comparison to aesthetics foregrounds how closely our awareness of various exemplary states becomes fundamental to our own senses of identity. This is how ethos takes on cultural force. We are what we will most intensely, whether that be our investment in reason or our investments in what provides material for reason to work upon. In both cases one important measure of who we are as persons consists in the range of passions that we can occupy self-reflexively so that we take responsibility for the roles they play in our lives and in our representations of our lives. Therefore rather than attributing literariness to some condition of form, I think that in our basic practices of reading 'Literature' we respond to an invitation to explore the degree to which texts can offer states of mind so powerful and distinctive that we understand what it would mean to identify fully with them (even if the identification is with the undermining of identity), and hence to make them part of what we desire about desire.

Approached from this perspective, literariness seems ultimately less a quality created by specific features of the work than a marker that we are expected to assume a willingness to take on in imagination the force that the work may be able to muster as a whole, as a specification of modes of agency and of consciousness capable of making demands on how we forge identifications. Literariness challenges us to examine who we become by virtue of the modes of participation within which we find ourselves engaged.[31] When we make affirmative judgements in response to such challenges, it seems as if we cannot but want this text to be part of our world and we cannot but want ourselves to make this text part of how we see possibilities for affirming our own capacities within that world. On some occasions we could give ethical reasons for such judgements, but we also often find emotions themselves capable of modifying the quality or degree of investments once relegated only to moral categories.

One sign that I am right about literariness is the fact that the company we keep in our reading readily expands to include the kinds of texts that challenge moral values and, more generally, the primacy of morality as a measure of human worth. But such texts need not be treated as friends. It suffices that they afford imaginative presences capable not only of defining the most powerful and fascinating states of consciousness we know, but also of holding out the promise that by identifying provisionally with them we are likely to encounter ourselves at our most vital and most capacious. Where ethical criticism is forced, often against its best instincts, to treat texts ultimately as examples of something that philosophy can clarify and help assess, the ethos-based version of the literary that I am proposing deals directly with the examples as manifestations of qualities and powers that establish what is possible within certain ways of engaging the world. When we reflect on these examples, we may decide that we have to reject any long-term claims they make upon our loyalties, because what they offer us in moments of intensity simply will not fit with the economies that we work out as ways of directing our lives. But if we have experienced them fully, we are hard-pressed to dismiss them as simply behaviour that we can judge or mistaken identifications we can easily dispel. Think of the continuing impact that Shelley and Milton have had on poets who think they should know better. So these presences remain with us as challenges and as measures of the levels of intensity and commitment that we can continue to offer those texts with which we continue to identify.

Now I need no longer be indirect. The more carefully we attend to ethical criticism, the more clearly we see by contrast not only what might be embedded in our practices for postulating literariness but also why it matters to continue to explore what those practices offer us. It seems as if ethical criticism is willing to accept a painful compromise: if we are to feel we have moral control over ourselves and if we are to see reading as the fostering of social values, we may have to limit our imaginative worlds to prevent their displacing what reason tells us constitutes our best selves. But yielding to this compromise seems to me to involve surrendering to a false sense of urgency and to ignore the at least equally important psychological states that emerge as we simply explore what versions of ethos might ultimately have the force to modify those imperatives shaping our sense of right and wrong. Or perhaps it is better to say that ignoring the many ways that literariness invites us to reflect on how texts elaborate emotional economies and stage intensities reduces us to a world in which 'right' and 'wrong' constitute the only relevant value judgements that we make. In that kind of world, moral consciousness easily becomes self-satisfied and hence runs the risk of providing little more than wardrobes we adapt for social purposes. Where literariness is central, on the other hand, our values have to present themselves with a certain flash in their eyes and tilt to their carriage. The imagination offers us at least that opportunity for correlating life and art.

Notes

1 These remarks are strongly influenced by Alan Singer's analysis of discourse about 'error' as providing an alternative to the brute negatives invoked for art by Adorno, and by those desperately seeking in art some kind of uncategorisable resistance to dominant cultural mores.

2 A. Singer, 'Beautiful errors: aesthetics and the art of contextualization', *boundary 2*, 25 (Spring 1998), 7–34, p. 8.

3 I do not base my case on contrasts with sociological criticism because the arguments on both sides are by now quite predictable, and the differences in value perspective are almost impossible to negotiate.

4 I take this last point from a very interesting critique of Bourdieu by Alan Dunn. Let me also use this note to present the passage from Wittgenstein's *Remarks on Colour* on which I base my language of blindness and sight: '[c]an one explain to a blind person what it is like to see? – Certainly; the blind do learn a great deal about the difference between themselves and the sighted. And yet we want to answer no to this question. – But isn't it posed in a misleading way? We can describe both to someone who does not play soccer and to someone who does "what it is like to play soccer",

perhaps to the latter so that he can check the correctness of the description. Can we then describe to the sighted person what it is like to see? But we can certainly explain to him what blindness is! I.e. we can describe to him the characteristic behavior of a blind person and we can blindfold him. On the other hand, we cannot make a blind person see for a while; we can, however, describe to him how the sighted behave'. (L. Wittgenstein, *Remarks on Colour* (Berkeley, 1978), p. 53). I think sociological criticism can do no more than describe how the sighted behave.

5 Philosophers have long been aware of the need for some such distinction between ethics as concerned specifically with processes of justification, and more general questions about values and ends. Perhaps the most useful contemporary formulation can be found in Martha Nussbaum's *Love's Knowledge*, where she distinguishes between ethical theory as 'the theoretical study of substantive ethical positions' and 'moral philosophy' as a 'general and inclusive rubric covering ... many different types of ethical investigations'. This is certainly preferable to the popular distinction between 'ethics' as somehow the domain of high principle and 'morals' as the mere social coding of those principles in different circumstances because it gets at the distinctive roles played by theorising within professional philosophical discourse and more general speculations on 'how human beings should live' (M. Nussbaum, *Love's Knowledge: Essays on Philosophy and Literature* (New York, 1990), pp. 169, 15). Yet the very generality that Nussbaum wins for the rubric 'moral philosophy' runs the risk of bringing literature's general concern with how values are pursued within a discourse that turns out to look very much like 'ethics', because assessing those values turns out to require the specific terms of moral philosophy and hence also to seek 'reasons' for the kinds of action that are beggared by assuming that we arrive at them by moral calculuses. Moreover these philosophical assumptions are probably not sufficiently attuned to the deep conflicts in how even to talk about values that emerge among different cultural practices.

6 L. Wittgenstein, *Tractatus Logico-Philosophicus*, trans. D. F. Pears and B. F. McGuinness (London, 1961), 6.421–6.43. Conversely, the richer our alternative to standard ethical criticism, the better the case we can make that ethical analyses be limited to situations where we are concerned with the justification of specific actions or with the characterisation of how we might go about making these assessments. Rather than treating most questions about value as ethical, we can insist that these concerns be relegated to the general cultural theatre where we have to acknowledge constant struggle not only over which specific aspects of ethos will prevail, but also over which ways of determining among the values make the most practical sense.

7 See C. Altieri, 'Lyrical ethics and literary experience', *Style*, 32 (1998), 272–97. Reprinted in T. Davis and K. Womack, (eds), *Mapping the Ethical Turn* (Charlottesville, 2001), pp. 30–58. The remainder of this essay repeats that argument with some variations.

8 W. C. Booth, *The Company We Keep: An Ethics of Fiction* (Berkeley, 1988), p. 274. Strictly speaking Booth is not a perfectionist, because when he wrote *The Company We Keep* there was no such label available. Stanley Cavell has popularised the concept in relation to literature, but I have already written a good deal on Cavell, and Booth is much cleaner in his formulations. I should add that the best philosophical articulation of perfectionist principles that I know is the treatment of poesis developed by Richard Eldridge in his *Leading a Human Life: Wittgenstein, Intentionality, and Romanticism* (Chicago, 1997). However, Eldridge's actual application of this model to literary texts seems to me hampered by the effort to make his dramatic analyses correlate with statable principles for what constitutes human flourishing.

9 Booth, *The Company We Keep*, p. 70.

10 *Ibid.*, p. 71.

11 *Ibid.*, p. 222.

12 Nussbaum, *Love's Knowledge*, p. 27. Let me support this claim with specific quotations. This is the literary Nussbaum: 'certain truths about human life can only be fittingly and accurately stated in the language and forms characteristic of the narrative artist' (*Love's Knowledge*, p. 5). Repeated acts of complex sympathy and empathy in relation to these narrative situations help forge a 'distinctive ethical conception' (p. 26) in their own right, because they help us to envision what constitutes a good life for human beings, and what values make that life shareable. But then on the very next page she is content to argue that we should '*add* the study of certain novels to the study' of classical works in philosophical ethics, 'on the grounds that without them we will not have a fully adequate statement of a powerful ethical conception' that we 'ought to investigate'. I find the claim that only 'certain novels' should be studied especially difficult to reconcile with any argument that there is a distinctive contribution to be made to ethics by literary experience. At best one can argue that these certain novels support or enrich her enlightened Aristotelianism.

13 M. Nussbaum, *Poetic Justice: The Literary Imagination and Public Life* (Boston, 1995), p. 12.

14 *Ibid.*, p. 52.

15 *Ibid.*, p. 51.

16 *Ibid.*

17 *Ibid.*, p. 91.

18 *Ibid.*, p. 35.

19 *Ibid.*, p. 65.

20 *Ibid.*, p. 74.

21 *Ibid.*

22 *Ibid.*, p. 82.

23 *Ibid.*, p. 119.

24 W. B. Yeats, *The Poems of William Butler Yeats*, ed. Richard Finneran (New York, 1983), pp. 286–7. Reprinted with the permission of Scribner, a Division of Simon & Schuster, Inc., from THE COLLECTED POEMS OF W. B. YEATS: REVISED 2nd EDITION, edited by Richard J. Finneran. Copyright © 1934 by Macmillan Publishing Company, copyright renewed © 1962 by Bertha Georgie Yeats.

25 Nussbaum, *Poetic Justice*, p. 94.

26 *Ibid.*, p. 95.

27 In conversation, Bryan Glaser has pointed out to me that Wright himself uses the courtroom parts of his novel to raise questions about judgement which seem to lead away from any possible institutional response to Bigger: to sympathise is patronising; to execute utterly inhumane. Wright can do this because his larger ambition is to make us see the forces which produce our impasse, and in order to do that we cannot just sympathise, we have to make our sympathy one feature of a complex political judgement which remains suspicious of all dreams that moral identities matter very much at all in relation to what needs to be done.

28 In conversation Richard Wollheim has made clear to me the cost involved in linking emotions only to perceptions as cognitive theory does, and hence in denying all the fantasy dimensions that give the emotions their intensity and their hold on our lives. For a good example of problems that arise when this fantasy dimension is overlooked see Nussbaum, *Poetic Justice*, p. 64.

29 In the book I am writing I argue that the cognitive theory of the emotions makes a perfect fit for ethical criticism's emphasis on narrative fiction because the kinds of emotion stressed are those that can be negotiated by the *phronesis* providing the basic mode of judgement in that domain. But the realm of affect contains much more than the emotions that enter this fit. If one comes to the affects through the experience of lyric states two other affective domains become at least equally important. These are the feelings, which I take to be the range of ways that our affective being spreads out into the world in particular moments, and the passions, which I take to be those emotions in which the identity of the agent is overtly and intensely at stake.

30 One could argue that Nussbaum's judicious spectator creates the same problems of moving between ethical reason and empirical personal situations that haunt both Kant and Rawls. I find Bernard Williams, *Ethics and the Limits of Philosophy*, the most useful treatment of this topic, but I should also mention Michael Sandel's influential critique of Rawls along these lines. In Kant motivation is not an issue because will is inseparable from reason: if one can enter the impersonal domain of reason one will have to will – reason is active and self-defining.

31 This is what Wittgenstein probably was referring to when he said that ethics and aesthetics are one.

derek attridge

SINGULAR EVENTS: LITERATURE, INVENTION, AND PERFORMANCE

Understanding 'literature'

One of the traps that await attempts to provide a clear account of the terms *literature*, the *literary*, and *literariness* is to take them to be names of entities in the world and to ignore the degree to which they are culturally produced concepts with a long history and multiple (and not always consistent) uses. There have been many discussions of that history, and of the closely related (though significantly different) histories of similar concepts named in other Western languages, which serve as valuable reminders of the complicated past and continuing ambiguity of these words. But in order to understand the importance today of this cluster of interrelated terms and concepts to the broader web of ideas and practices that make up Western culture, and thereby perhaps to encourage fresh thinking about the future direction of that culture, it is necessary to embark on something other than lexicographical investigation or cultural history. Among or within the many uses of the terms can be discerned (often at the places where consistency is most put at risk) something more than the simple naming that takes literature to be, for example, a category of writing determined by its fictional status or its institutional function, and something other than the straightforward valorisation that awards the label 'literature' to what are regarded as superior examples of what is sometimes called 'imaginative writing'. This 'something more' or 'something other' remains obscure, however, although many different attempts have been made to describe it.[1] It is as if the linguistic and intellectual resources of our culture do not permit direct access to a property or a process or a principle whose effects and importance they nevertheless register, and to which the term 'literature' and its cognates serve as indirect witnesses. These are not the only terms that perform this function, but the purchase they offer is a distinctive one, shared by no other concepts.

Discursive language is already beginning to break down in my attempt at lucid exposition. I have employed *property, process,* and *principle* to refer to what it is that literature might be said to witness or point to in the full knowledge that all these words are unsatisfactory, as, in this sentence, are the use of the word *it* and the notions of 'witnessing' or 'pointing'. This difficulty is, of course, a direct outcome of the state of affairs we are discussing: were it possible to find unambiguous names, to use pronouns with confidence, to talk in terms of simple acts of reference, there would be no need to ascribe to the non-discursive mode of literature a peculiar potency not possessed by other linguistic practices. There is something fundamentally paradoxical, perhaps even wrong-headed, in an attempt such as the present one to use a non-literary discourse to convey what literature, most importantly, can do. Nevertheless, there might be some profit in pursuing the attempt to the extent that theoretical language will allow it, as a corrective to other – often even more reductive – accounts of the literary, and as a complement to the primary activity of the reading of literary works. Such reading has to be primary, for we are not engaging in a purely linguistic-philosophical exercise here, analysing the use or conceptual underpinning of a set of terms without reference to what it is they name and how it functions socially, psychologically, and somatically. Although I have been stressing that the entities denominated by these terms – the (ill-defined) phenomenon of literature, individual literary works, the practice of reading those works, and the literary as a property of certain texts – are produced by the concepts that designate them, it is also the case that the difficulties that beset any theoretical analysis derive from the resistance of those constituted categories and entities to all fixed conceptual determinations. If the term *literature* does not uncomplicatedly name something in the world, it does not uncomplicatedly bring something into being either. Rather, by putting the processes of denominating and constituting into play, by, in a sense to be developed later, *performing* them, it complicates that very opposition. Our task, then, is both to acknowledge the cultural construction of the literary and to investigate why this construction does not result in stable and clearly delimited categories.

Singular inventions

At the heart of what I have called the peculiar potency of literature – the possibility held out by literary works of an encounter with a non-discursive, non-rational potential in language and signification – is its inseparability from two properties, which we may call, without too much violence to normal usage, *singularity* and *inventiveness*.[2] *Singularity* names the quality whereby a cultural object of a certain kind differs from all others, not as a particular manifestation of general rules but as a uniqueness perceived as resisting or exceeding all general determinations. This uniqueness is generated not by a substantial core of pure materiality or contingency on which the general frameworks we use can gain no hold but by a specific configuration of properties that, in constituting the object, goes beyond the possibilities pre-programmed by the system of norms with which a culture's members are familiar and through which cultural products are understood. (Singularity is therefore dependent upon what we can call *reception*: it does not exist outside the responses of those who encounter it. This point will be developed in due course.) *Inventiveness* is a closely related quality, to which we shall also return; for the moment, we may take it as naming the capacity of a cultural product to bring about a refashioning of the norms and habits on which we regularly rely in our understanding of such products (and of many other entities and practices). Again, inventiveness is not an inherent property of objects, but exists only in their effects.

Singularity and inventiveness are not, of course, peculiar to literature or indeed to the arts; if we confine ourselves for the sake of brevity to verbal productions, we can point to philosophical arguments, historical descriptions, or reports of scientific experiments that, when they appear, cannot be accounted for or understood in terms of existing norms, and bring about permanent changes in those norms. In the following discussion, I shall focus at first on verbal but not necessarily literary inventions, and then attempt to specify what determines the specifically literary invention. I shall not attempt to broaden the argument to non-verbal invention and the non-verbal arts, other than by way of the occasional hint of what might be entailed in an extrapolation of the argument to this wider realm.

Inventiveness and alterity

Inventiveness, as we have noted, is not an inherent property of a text, nor is it a property of the act that produces a text, since it depends on the text's reception.[3] If one wished to designate some feature of the text itself, one might want to refer to its 'potential inventiveness', but this is not a property that could ever be measured, since there is no place outside the varied events of reception where one could stand in order to do the measuring. A text that is received as inventive within a cultural field we term an *invention*, a word whose usefulness lies in part in its equal applicability to the *act* as to the *result* of inventing.

What exactly is it that is invented in an act of invention, in the inventive articulation of a sentence as it occurs in the writing of a text, say, or the development of an inventive philosophical argument? It is extremely difficult to talk about this process, which usually remains mysterious to the inventor, but one way of putting it would be to say that it is a creative handling of language whereby *otherness*, or *alterity*, is brought into, or manifested within, a particular cultural field.[4] Otherness is that which is, at a given historical moment, outside the framework provided by the culture for thinking, imagining, feeling, perceiving. (An alternative might be *newness*, but this term has the disadvantage of suggesting a historical narrative whereby the old is constantly displaced by the new, whereas in fact it is often through the old that the quality of otherness makes itself felt in an invention.) Because that which is other is outside the available framework, it is not something that the inventor could simply take hold of, as an idea, a formal possibility, a mathematical equation, and so on. The creative mind can work only with the materials to which it has access, and it can have no certain knowledge beyond these; it therefore has to work in ignorance of its destination. Accounts of invention, in a number of fields, regularly use terms like *hunch* and *guess*, *trial and error*, *lucky break*. The very term *experiment* paradoxically combines the notions of a controlled, repeatable physical process and the unpredictable trying-out of new procedures.

The event of invention

Because of this peculiar property of the inventive process, to call it an *act*, as I have been doing, is to misrepresent it; it is as much an *event* that happens to the inventor, and to the culture within which the invention takes place, as it is a willed action of a conscious individual. (This is not the place to discuss the possibility that invention is, in part at least, an 'act' of the unconscious: my argument could certainly be recast in psychoanalytic terms, although there is some danger that this might serve only to multiply the obscurities.) It is for this reason (that invention is as much *event* as *act*) that invention has been called not just the invention of otherness but, in a phrase with a double meaning deriving from the ambiguity of the genitive construction, 'the invention of the other'.[5] That is to say, the event that we call invention both *brings alterity into being*, into the realm of the knowable, and at the same time *is produced by alterity*. When I succeed in writing a text that is genuinely original, and does more than simply extend existing norms, I introduce into the cultural matrix in whose terms I think and write a germ, a foreign body, that cannot be accounted for by its norms. I do this not just by fashioning into a new shape the materials at hand – in language these materials are the rules and regularities, codes and conventions, that govern its forms and its operation as well as its sonic, rhythmic, and graphic properties; in philosophy these are concepts and arguments[6] – but, more importantly, by destabilising them, heightening their internal inconsistencies and ambiguities, exaggerating their dangerous proclivities, and exploiting their gaps and tensions, in such a way as to allow otherness to make itself felt. There is always an uncertainty about whether or not otherness will come into being, and the experience of its doing so is always one of being taken by surprise. Inventors are not able to predict the novelty they are about to produce, nor are they in a position to understand its source when it has emerged. The process is both active and passive, therefore, both an act and an event; the 'invention of the other' in both senses of the phrase. However, because I want to stress what we can call the *eventness* of the process, I shall from now on generally prefer the term *event*.

The old meaning of *invent* as 'find' is not irrelevant here: the testimony of countless artists, writers, scientists, and others shows that the experience of invention is an experience of *coming upon* a form, a phrase, a solution that seemed, in retrospect, to have been waiting in advance, or even of being *found by* the form, phrase, or solution in a moment of illumination (that is, of being illuminated as much as illuminating).[7] The event need not be dramatically sudden, however; it is often a gradual process of false starts and wasted efforts, erasures and revisions, slowly inching nearer to an outcome that, it is hoped, will be the desired one, or arriving at it in fits and starts. There is always an element of risk in the event of invention, of trusting to the future, of a certain passivity and helplessness in the face of what may be coming. Failure is frequent, when the otherness that seemed to be on the horizon turns out to be another version of the same; and success can often look like failure at first. In any case what the creator trusts is an invention only becomes one in its reception by the culture at large. Otherness is a strictly relative term – it is always otherness *to* an existing subjectivity or state of affairs – and this is why the inventor has to be exceptionally well attuned to his or her cultural surroundings. Many a work that in the view of the artist or philosopher who created it brings something new into the world turns out, when received widely, to be the familiar in superficially different dress.

Innovation in language

The notion of the *event*, which we have already seen to be crucial to invention, is also an important element in the notion of the *sign*, though many discussions of signification ignore this dimension of it. The letter *p*, for example, while it has (*a*) an abstract existence as a collective agreement about a certain configuration of visible material in relation to a set of other configurations, (b) a neuropsychological existence in the brains of those who recognise it, and (c) a physical existence on thousands of pages, computer screens, and other surfaces, functions as a sign in the fullest sense only when an event of recognition, usually coupled with an event of combination and an event of comprehension (in a word or a sentence), takes place.[8] We identify, that is to say, the object before us – the coloured shape on the billboard, for instance – as a 'token' corresponding to a 'type' with which we are already familiar. And this event of identification includes the acknowledgement of purposiveness: what we are seeing is not a random scratch or a piece of driftwood that, as we would say, 'looks like a p' but a shape that some mind (perhaps some way back in a chain of production) *intended* to look like a p – or, more simply, to *be* a p. (The fact that the perceiver can always be mistaken – the p may have been produced by a random scratch, or what looks like driftwood may have been carved – indicates that what is at issue here is not 'historical truth' but the nature of the event we call 'recognition' itself.) Something similar could be said of the phoneme /p/ in the domain of sound, except that its physical existence already depends on a certain kind of event.[9] However, the sound-event does not become a sign-event unless recognition takes place.

Morphemes, words, phrases, sentences, whole texts function in a similar way; they come into existence as events constituted by a hierarchical arrangement of briefer events. And as complex events they are capable of creative manipulation. As we move up the scale from the smallest units of language to larger and larger ones, the opportunities for deviation from existing norms increase while the affront to the interpreting mind produced by deviation decreases: one rarely comes across made-up *letters* or *phonemes*, and they are very difficult to make sense of (the unpronounceable 'sigla' of *Finnegans Wake* are a case in point); the creation of new *words* occasionally occurs, though it is easy to slide from fruitful extension of meaning to loss of meaning (as *Finnegans Wake* also amply demonstrates); creativity in the production of *sentences* is very common, and is much less challenging to the interpreter; and entire *texts* offer limitless opportunities for innovation, and require very marked deviations to produce strong effects. In order to move towards the question of the literary, I propose to make a distinction between two kinds of transgression of existing rules at all of these levels. This will mean slightly sharpening the categorisations enshrined in common usage, but not, I hope, to a degree which will sow confusion. The fact that the distinction I am making is not hard-and-fast does not diminish its usefulness; fuzzy categories can, after all, be as illuminating as clear-cut ones.

Frequently an unusual use of language can be comprehended without difficulty by referring it unproblematically to the norms from which it deviates. One way of putting this would be that new rules which are easily grasped extensions or extrapolations of existing rules are temporarily established. If the key for the letter *t* on my keyboard ceases to function, and I use the ampersand key instead, the reader of my typed text has no difficulty in making the necessary adjustment. No fundamen&al al&eration in &he process of unders&anding is needed. If in my after-dinner speech to the Film Society I bring the name of a famous actor into every sentence, I may (or may not) be applauded for my cleverness, but in itself the trick, though it introduces a new rule not already given in the codes that govern the genre of the humorous speech, is easily assimilated. The event of reading the text with ampersands or listening to the speech with actors' names is on a par with the daily events of textual comprehension we all engage in.

But it is also possible to rewrite the rules of the genre one is using, or to be innovative at the phonemic, lexical, or syntactic level, or to introduce new semantic or affective resonances, in such a way as to create a text that offers a stronger challenge to the reader or hearer. The words I type may have gaps in them that are suggestive but not automatically fillable; the speech I make may leave the hearers uncertain about the degree of self-directed irony I am using. (And *I* may not be certain either, if I have been truly inventive). The effect of such a challenge to the norms may be merely blockage or blankness, a shutting-down of the interpretative mechanism, an experience of baffled perplexity that takes the reader or hearer nowhere. Or it may be a temporary remaking of norms in a manner that does not involve straightforward extension or extrapolation, and that produces not an interpretation but something like an experience of meaning *in process*, the experience of an event, in short. The gaps in my words may heighten the reader's consciousness of the materiality of letters, may flirt perplexingly but engrossingly with signification, may produce fruitful ambiguities; the tonal uncertainties in my after-dinner speech may make my hearers all the more intensely involved in it, aware of the multiple potentialities lurking in a single set of uttered words. The possibilities of this kind of creativity are, of course, limitless, since every rule, every norm, every habit, every expectation involved in the use of language can be stretched, twisted, cited, thwarted, or exaggerated, and in multiply varied combinations with one another. It can manifest itself as a striking challenge to comprehension or as the slightest experience of unfamiliarity haunting the familiar. It can be felt as easily in a work written three centuries ago as in one that is hot off the press, as readily in an old favourite being re-read yet again as in a first-time encounter. This kind of linguistic innovation is what I take to be literary invention.

The institution of literature

Not every linguistic innovation that requires a reformulation of existing norms, therefore, is a literary invention; most, in fact, are not. One could program a computer to produce millions of linguistic items that deviate from the rules of English in this way without a single one being experienceable as a literary work in this sense. It is only when the event of this reformulation is experienced *as an event*, an event which opens new possibilities of meaning and feeling, or, more accurately, the event *of such opening*, that we can speak of the literary. The habits and conventions by means of which most events of comprehension occur are challenged and recast, not merely as automatic extensions but as invitations to alterity, to modes of mental processing, ideas and emotions, conceptual possibilities that had hitherto been impossible. This process of initiation, this movement into the unknown, is experienced as something that *happens to* the reader in the course of a committed and attentive reading.[10]

It will be obvious that my use of *literary* and *literature* here does not accord with some of the commonly accepted meanings of these terms. I employ the terms to designate a body of texts with a certain effectivity, an effectivity that is crucial to the vigour and perhaps the ethical well-being of a culture. (It is not, however, without its dangers – there can be no guarantee that the alterity brought into the world by a literary or other artistic work will be beneficial.)[11] Literature has of course frequently been regarded as having, and perhaps being partly defined by, certain effects on its readers: humanising them, broadening their minds, alerting them to linguistic niceties, enlarging their sympathies, undermining their covert ideological assumptions, and so forth.[12] This is not the kind of effectivity of which I am speaking. It is certainly the case that literary texts may have any of these effects, and a good number of others, but when they do, it is not as a direct result of their being literary. But I would not go so far as to say, as some would, that *all* valorisation of literature is merely ideological, and that we should apply the term 'literature' in a value-free manner to all textual productions of an imaginative or fictional character. There is nothing inherently wrong with such an application: it is one possibility allowed for by our current inconsistent use of the word 'literature'. My only quarrel with the more general use is that accepting it would make it harder to find a word or phrase for the narrower category I am interested in, and which corresponds, at least roughly speaking, to another possibility allowed for in current uses of the term. Phrases like 'genuine literature' or 'real literature' would only exacerbate the problem. Perhaps the best solution, if one wants to maintain the widest sense of the term, would be to distinguish between 'literature in general' and 'inventive literature' (which is not, of course, to be equated with 'serious literature' nor opposed to 'popular literature'), and if the reader wishes to give this gloss to the word in what follows, he or she is welcome to do so.

It will also be evident that the literary in the somewhat specialised sense in which I am using it is not confined to the recognised institution of literature; nor is it the case that everything classified at a particular historical juncture as 'literature' embodies what I am calling the literary.[13] And although it is true to say that within a given culture at a given time a certain body of texts is widely received as literary, the slightest acquaintance with literary history shows that it is a far from stable category.

Performance

If an inventive event in any cultural domain involves the entry of otherness into the existing field of knowledge and habit, the result of the process is that the hitherto unknown has become the known, otherness has become sameness, singularity has become generality. Absolute alterity, as long as it remains absolute, cannot be apprehended at all. And if the hitherto unthinkable becomes the eminently thinkable, it also in the very same moment becomes the imitable, patentable, parodiable. In the case of most types of invention, once it has brought about change to an individual or a culture its work is done: its effects will continue to be felt through those applications, reproductions, and imitations. The artistic invention, however, though it too gives rise to imitations of various kinds, retains its inventiveness as long as it finds a suitably receptive audience. The literary text demands re-reading; its otherness is not something that can be assimilated by the culture whose norms it changes. We have seen that it is only in the event of its reception that language as a mode of signification fully exists. However, that event can function inventively in two different ways: in the non-literary text its *results* are what matter, in the literary text the *eventness* of the event is what matters. The reader experiences, that is, not just the event itself, but its happening *as event*. Another way of putting this is that the literary text exists, as literary text, only in *performance*.

I choose the term *performance* because it points to that element of self-distance that is present in the event of the literary, the event comprehended in its eventness. Most of the sentences we read or hear we do not perform, in this sense; we recognise, apprehend, interpret them, perhaps feel or do something as an immediate consequence, but we treat the words conceptually and instrumentally. Take the referential properties of a text: I may enjoy and learn from my encounter with the concepts, feelings, historical or imagined entities, and so on, to be found in any text, including a literary text (which always functions in ways other than the literary). But when I am reading a text *as literature* (and it may or may not impose this choice upon me) my pleasure and profit come from the experience of an *event* of referring, from a *process* of referentiality, whereby those concepts, feelings, and entities are brought into my consciousness in ways that change it, or to put it another way, whereby my consciousness is altered, at least momentarily, in order to enable this event of referring to take place. (This remains true whether my performance is the reading or reciting, aloud or silent, of a text, or my listening to someone else's reading or reciting of it.) Fiction is not, therefore, identical with literature; a fictional text may simply present fictional characters and events for my apprehension, as in an anecdote or perhaps (this would have to be argued case by case and would always be subject to revision) certain novels that lack inventiveness at any level. Literary fiction involves the *performance* of fictionality, occurring as the experience of an event or series of events whereby the characters and occurrences apparently referred to are in fact brought into being by the language. Similarly, narrative becomes literary when it involves the performance of narrativity,[14] metaphor when it involves the performance of metaphoricity, description when it involves the performance of descriptivity, and so on. In performing the work, therefore, I am taken through *its* performance of language's diverse powers; indeed, I, or the 'I' that is engaged with the work, could be said to be *performed by it*.[15]

Let us take a brief example. Here is a stanza by George Herbert, from the poem 'Easter':

> I got me flowers to straw thy way;
> I got me boughs off many a tree:
> But thou wast up by break of day,
> And brought'st thy sweets along with thee.[16]

To read or hear this as literature is to experience the event of its four lines, to be carried forward by a familiar, rather insistently regular rhythm, to register the easy colloquialism of the phrasing and the simplicity of the syntax, and to counterpoise against these experienced qualities the extra-ordinariness of the occurrence – the rising of a man who was lying dead in a tomb – to which it refers. It is to participate in an ambiguous, perhaps even contradictory, tonal and emotional complex – reverence? whimsicality? awe? disappointment? delight? triumph? – that is singular and unre-produceable. It is to feel, as one reads them, the anticipation built up by the first two lines – the second a variation on the first – and the sudden explosion of meaning in the third on the apparently insignificant word *up*, where a trifling observation about rising from sleep expressed in the most flat and elementary phrasing – 'thou wast up', 'you were up' – refers to an barely imaginable miracle, one that has taken place, as it were, in the moment between the previous line and this one. It is to undergo the transition from this moment of shock to a final line, conveying its finality in metre and rhyme of course, but also in the clinching and calming thought of the sweetness (physical and spiritual) accompanying the risen Christ, outstripping by an unthinkable distance all human efforts at solicitude and celebration. It is also, at the same time, *to be made aware of language's power to do all these things*, to be conscious of their happening as a complex linguistic (but also, and inseparably, a conceptual, emotional, and physical) event.

A reading of the poem that activates such qualities is a performance of it, whether spoken aloud, heard in someone else's reading, read silently on the page, or recited in the mind from memory, and it is in such performances that it comes into being, each time, as a poem. Every performance is different from all others, sometimes in imperceptible ways (an example might be a single reader reading it twice in quick succession) but often in marked ways (as would emerge if, for instance, we could compare a performance in the seventeenth century with one today). Reading the poem as a literary work is different from reading it for, say, the purposes of doctrinal instruction, or as historical evidence; these are not performances but interpretations geared to the extraction of truth. Performing the poem as a literary reader may involve being alert to doctrinal and historical issues – this may be one of the criteria of a good reading of Herbert's work – but it also involves a certain suspension of questions of truth, of morality, of history. One need have no belief in the Resurrection to perform Herbert's poem and to feel the power of its eventness.

My example can be no more than suggestive; as a singular work, whose singularity is renewed in each performance of it, its inventiveness differs from the inventiveness of every other singular work, and no simple extrapolation or generalisation is possible. Imitations are never reduplications. Part of what an inventive work discovers, and makes possible for other writers, is new ways of being inventive. Nor is my example intended to advance a new mode of literary criticism; literary criticism has often commented on literature (especially poetry) in terms that suggest the centrality of inventiveness and singularity, and the way in which these properties are realised in performances. Criticism, it is true, has sometimes failed to distinguish between the performativity of the literary work and other, non-literary aspects of it, such as its referential accuracy, its moral stance, its political usefulness, its formal complexity, and so on. Often it has been the most inventive of writers who have responded most fully to other literary works, and this is hardly surprising: commentary on a text that seeks to do justice to its eventness must find a way of conveying that quality in a second text, and this is most likely when it too has a performative dimension.

Performance as invention

The question of performative criticism leads us to a further dimension of literary practice. Up to now, we have discussed inventiveness in literature as if it were confined to the writing of literary works, and as if the performance of the literary work, although it is different each time it occurs, were the predictable outcome of the particular situation and psychological make-up of the reader in question in conjunction with the given words. This, of course, is largely true of the *linguistic* event; language would not function if its receivers did not operate in predictable ways. But a literary work, one that is inventive and singular in relation to a particular reader or group of readers, demands something more: because it disjoins the cultural matrix to the point of allowing alterity to arise, only a matching inventiveness can fully respond to its achievement. An uninventive response would either fail to apprehend what was singular and inventive in the work, or register it as a blank or a mistake. In the inventive performance of a work (which, remember, is as much a matter of being performed as of performing), the reader's own habitual terms of reference give way to something unforeseen, and this happens as an event which is not separable from what we have been calling the event of the work's invention. Just as inventiveness in production can be described both as an act and as an event, so can inventiveness in reception; and in both cases, the activity involved is a creative handling of existing modes of thought and feeling – a willingness to open up invisible fractures and explore sealed recesses – to make possible the origination of otherness. And although the event of reception is, at its best, a response to the event of the work that does full justice to its singularity, it cannot be a mere repetition of the work; its inventiveness, too, is singular. What is performed, in fact, is the singularity of the work, which, in the case of the literary work, is a verbal singularity. It is also, if I can put it like this, an always-for-the-first-time singularity – that is to say, an inventive singularity as well as a singular invention. Other kinds of invention, including non-literary textual inventions, can possess many kinds of singularity, including conceptual, spatial, sonic, and visual singularity. In the philosophical realm, singularity is experienced as an argument, in the aesthetic realm as an event. The literary event is experienced as the invented singularity of a series of specific words in a specific order.

A performance that does justice to the inventiveness and singularity of a literary work, then, is one that is itself, in a closely related sense, inventive and singular.[17] Although it is based on the normal process of recognition and interpretation of language, it does not confine itself entirely to existing modes of interpretation, or slot the concepts it encounters or emotions it arouses into existing grids; it inventively finds a way of revising those modes and recreating those grids.[18] Reception is therefore itself a mode of production: in performing a work I give it a singular existence as an event. Production, by the same token, can be said to be a mode of reception: the writer creates by inventively reading, or by hearing, what it is that is coming into being in the work of invention in which he or she is engaged.

There is another aspect of the performance of literature that needs to be taken into account. I have referred on several occasions to the assumption held by the reader of a text as to the purposiveness of the sentences he or she is reading. Whether the assumption is true or false (and fresh evidence as to its truthfulness or falsity may alter the reader's reception of a text), it underlies the ascription of meaning to any text. In the case of a literary text, or the literariness of any text, we have a more complicated sense of that purposiveness. Since what we experience, most crucially, is a performative verbal event, not a set of concepts or series of arguments, we do not interpret purposiveness as some determining intention that we are attempting to reconstruct from the evidence of the words. Rather, purposiveness is manifested as what we may call *authoredness*, the presupposition that the words we are reading (both the choice of words and their particular arrangement) have their origin in a mind or minds. If we know (or think we know) that the words have been produced by a computer, we will assume that the computer was programmed in such a way as to generate verbal strings of a certain kind. If we know that they have been produced by a team of writers, or a series of writers each revising the previous writer's work, the sense of authoredness is grounded in a conception of collaborative or serial labour. If they are presented to us as the result of automatic writing, or as a found poem, or as the product of chance operations, we take them to be literary only if the selection and presentation of the words has the character of an authorial act (which is also, of course, if it is inventive, an event). Our current conception of the literary would draw a limit around human authors; I would like to leave open, however, the possibility that this is a limit that future inventiveness will breach. There can be no intrinsic restriction on the form that the other will take; if there were, it would already be compromised, and not wholly other.

The term *work* that we commonly use is particularly appropriate to the literary text, suggesting as it does that the reader responds not just to the finished object but also to the labour that went into its creation, and in this it corresponds well with the double meaning of *invention*. This relationship is not only one of reader's and the (presupposed) writer's minds; it may involve a relationship of bodies, too. The physical response we often have to a literary work (most frequently to a poem) is not, as it would be in the case of other kinds of text, a simple consequence of the materiality of language, but is a response to what we take to be an event of physical creation re-performed in our own performance.

Objections: repetition and familiarity

In his sonnet 'On sitting down to read *King Lear* once again', Keats bids farewell to 'golden-tongued Romance' and turns to a different mode of reading:

> Adieu! for, once again, the fierce dispute
> Betwixt damnation and impassion'd clay
> Must I burn through; once more humbly assay
> The bitter-sweet of this Shaksperean fruit.[19]

The account I have given of the literary event may seem to allow for no explanation of the phenomenon Keats is addressing: that the repetition of a reading experience can be as powerful as, or even more powerful than, the initial reading experience. But in fact it helps us to understand how this can happen. Since every performance of a literary work that does justice to its verbal singularity is itself an irreducibly singular event, it involves a fresh apprehension (which is also a production) of that singularity – which thereby becomes a new singularity. Absolute repetition, which would mean a diminution of the work's effectivity, does not occur, since the reader, and the cultural context in which and by means of which the reading takes place, constantly change. Moreover, the knowledge of what is to come in a text one has read before and the memory of the experience of earlier readings are both aspects of the singular event of re-reading that Keats is evoking. It is, of course, part of the measure of the inventiveness of a literary work that it can be re-read without loss of power; less inventive works quickly lose their singularity as they become personally and culturally assimilated.

Another objection to my argument might be that we also ascribe literary value to works that reassure us, works that are our familiar companions or that, when we read them for the first time, confirm what we already hold dear. In these cases, it would seem to be precisely the absence of alterity that pleases and comforts. The first point to make in response is that the otherness brought into existence by the work, in the singular performance that constitutes the event of its realisation, need not be disturbing or startling; indeed, it must be, at least in some way, pleasurable. If we could apprehend otherness directly, the experience would indeed be traumatic; but direct apprehension is exactly what is ruled out. What we experience are the shifts of mental and emotional gear that make it possible for what *was* other to be apprehended, now no longer as other. (This is why one inventive work makes possible a host of imitations, since it brings into existence a new framework of understanding that others can exploit.) This experience of increased possibilities for thought and feeling is pleasurable, even though the thoughts and feelings themselves may, as in the case of Shakespeare's tragedies, involve discomfort and distress.

Now the mental and emotional expansion demanded by the work may be extensive and hard to sustain, as with *King Lear*, or it may be very slight. The work that reassures by its familiar rehearsal of what we already know, if it functions as literature – if, that is, it is received by means of a performance of its verbal singularity – is likely to demand only a minimal modification of our habitual patterns of thought and feeling, perhaps only the coming-into-consciousness, by means of a performance, of practices and relations that are usually taken for granted. It is important to realise, too, that the experience is not always one of thinking the hitherto unthinkable: it may be one of capturing in language something already known non-verbally – Pope's 'What oft was thought, but ne'er so well expressed'. (Of course, such an experience may be an illusion, an instance of *Nachträglichkeit*, produced retrospectively by the successful invention.) If the text comforts and reassures by simply confirming prejudices according to well-known verbal formulae, however, it cannot be called – in the somewhat circumscribed sense in which I am using the term – literature.

A related objection might be that to stress the importance of otherness and verbal singularity in literary invention is to privilege certain genres and modes, and certain periods, over others – poetry over prose, and the modernist period over earlier periods, in particular. Again, to make this objection is to misunderstand the nature of alterity as it operates in the artistic sphere. Linguistic and formal inventiveness is only one kind of inventiveness, a kind we associate especially with poetry and with modernism (although of course there are many novels and plays, and many works in all periods, that bring about their literary effects through these types of inventiveness). Many other kinds of inventiveness occur: a work that is conventional in its form and language may be extremely powerful in its apprehension of unfamiliar modes of feeling, its elaboration of hitherto unexplored types of human relationship, its crystallisation of new ideas. What makes these works literary works (as distinct from other kinds of text that have been inventively productive in such areas) is that these new understandings or feelings depend on their specific use of language and come into existence *in the event of performance*. Although they may change the ways people think and feel, their particular newness can be experienced only in this event.

It has remained true throughout the history of Western culture that the artists whose work has been received as the most powerful, the most intensely pleasure-giving, have been those who have inventively recreated the cultural fabric, whether by means of formal and linguistic innovation or by the skilful deployment of existing formal and linguistic possibilities – though in fact it is very difficult to find examples of inventive writers who are not inventive to some degree at the formal level. But the literary event occurs with many degrees of intensity in many readings of many texts, however they are classified, and its value lies just as much in its ever-present efficacy as in the conspicuous achievements of its long past.

Notes

This essay is a fragment of a longer work on questions of literary singularity and performativity. Rather than attempt to signal every specific debt (many of which will be quite obvious), I would like to acknowledge the many writers whose work, theoretical or fictional, has nourished my thinking, including – to name only a few – Jacques Derrida, Emmanuel Levinas, Theodor Adorno, J. M. Coetzee, Jean-François Lyotard, and James Joyce.

1 One indication of this recurrent problem in the specification of literary practice is the long history of the idea of an unfathomable, supplementary *je ne sais quoi* that distinguishes literary from non-literary uses of language. I discuss some significant moments in this history in *Peculiar Language: Literature as Difference from the Renaissance to James Joyce* (Ithaca, 1988).

2 I have discussed the relation of singularity and inventiveness to the literary in 'Innovation, literature, ethics: relating to the other', *PMLA*, 114 (1999), 20–31; what follows is a development of some of the thoughts sketched in that essay, though it unavoidably recapitulates parts of the earlier discussion.

3 To refer to the act of producing an artefact which, from the perspective of the *producer*, breaks new ground in a potentially inventive way, I use the term 'creativity'. This is, of course, a somewhat specialised use of the word; see my discussion in 'Innovation, literature, ethics'. (I shall use the terms *reception, receive, receiver* to refer in the most general terms to the various ways of comprehending and responding to a text. The primary modes of reception are of course reading and hearing, and I shall use *reading* to include both of these, except when it is appropriate to make a distinction between them.)

4 I leave the notion of 'cultural field' deliberately vague here; it could denominate something as broad as 'Western culture' or have a more limited range of reference. Any individual's grasp on the world is mediated by an array of interlocking and overlapping cultural systems, and thus the experience of otherness differs from person to person, and of course from time to time.

5 See the essay by Derrida entitled 'Psyche: invention of the other', in D. Attridge (ed.), *Acts of Literature* (New York, 1992), pp. 311–43.

6 This, at least, is philosophy's predominant self-conception. The unavoidability of mediation via language, and the effects of this on the philosophical project, has been the theme of much philosophical and para-philosophical writing, especially in the last three or four decades.

7 Of the countless descriptions of this process, I will quote only a recent one from J.
   M. Coetzee's *Disgrace*: '[A]stonishingly, in dribs and drabs, the music comes. Sometimes the contour of a phrase occurs to him before he has a hint of what the words
   themselves will be; sometimes the words call forth the cadence; sometimes the shade
   of a melody, having hovered for days on the edge of hearing, unfolds and blessedly
   reveals itself' (Coetzee, *Disgrace* (London, 1999), p. 183). The term *inspiration* has
   traditionally been used to capture this experience of passivity; see Timothy Clark,
   *The Theory of Inspiration: Composition as a Crisis of Subjectivity in Romantic and
   Post-Romantic Writing* (Manchester, 1997).

8 Saussure's distinction between *langue* and *parole* is one well-known attempt to characterise the distinction between, on the one hand, my *a*, *b*, and *c*, and, on the other,
   the event of signification. Unlike Chomsky's reinterpretation of the opposition
   between *langue* and *parole* as an opposition between *competence* and *performance*,
   Saussure's terms highlight the different status of the two modes of existence of the
   sign, as object (psychological for Saussure, although at once individual and social)
   and as event. This difference in status – which is less like comparing apples with
   oranges than like comparing apples with the picking of apples – has led to many mis-
   understandings and misapplications of the distinction. For further discussion, see
   Attridge, *Peculiar Language*, chapter 4.

9 Even if it is a recorded phoneme, its physical correlate in the form of grooves or mag-
   netised particles remains dumb until the event of its translation into hearable sound.
   This remains true when the sound in digitised and the physical medium is an elec-
   tromagnetic wave or a stream of photons.

10 It is important to be aware that, whatever the word *experience* might suggest, this is
   not a psychological description of the event of literary reception. The motions
   through which the mind and the emotions go in reading literary works are doubtless
   of an immense variety, and perhaps not systematically classifiable at all. My claim is
   that whatever the psychological process involved, it has a structural dependence
   upon the kind of event I am describing.

11 This uncertainty is something I have discussed in 'Expecting the unexpected in
   Coetzee's *Master of Petersburg* and Derrida's recent writings', in J. Brannigan, R.
   Robbins, and J. Wolfreys (eds), *Applying: To Derrida* (London, 1996), pp. 21–40.

12 Hillis Miller, in *Others* (Princeton, 2001), makes a rather muted version of the claim
   for literature's effectiveness in the world.

13 Nevertheless, literature is the major repository of the literary, and when we call a
   philosophical or historical work 'literary' it is its affiliation to the body of works historically acknowledged as literature to which we are drawing attention. Although literary inventiveness is something that happens only to individuals, it is the culture at
   large that determines whether this or that text is literary. A significant number of a
   text's readers must experience the alterity brought about by inventiveness before it
   can be called 'literary' from a cultural or institutional perspective. There is often disagreement about this question: a given text may be received as literary by some readers, and not by others.

14 See chapter 10, 'Countlessness of livestories: narrativity in *Finnegans Wake*', in my
   Joyce Effects: On Language, Theory, and History (Cambridge, 2000).

15 The protagonist of Coetzee's *Disgrace* has a similar insight: 'He is inventing the
   music (or the music is inventing him) … ' (p. 186).

16 Quoted from J. Tobin (ed.), *The Complete English Poems of George Herbert* (Harmondsworth, 1991), p. 37. As Tobin notes, the two very distinct parts of what he

prints as one poem are often printed as two, 'Easter (1)' and 'Easter (2)', in which case the cited lines form the first stanza of the second poem.

17 If my brief reading of Herbert's stanza can claim to do justice to the singularity of the lines (for me, here, now) it must itself bear the imprint of my singular response, and those who read it or hear it must find in it an invitation to respond performatively themselves.

18 It can also be said to be a *responsible* reading; this introduces an ethical or quasi-ethical dimension into the demands made upon the reader, a dimension which I have discussed in 'Innovation, literature, ethics'.

19 J. Stillinger (ed.), *The Poems of John Keats* (Cambridge, Mass., 1978), p. 225.

david carroll

THE POST-LITERARY CONDITION: SARTRE, CAMUS, AND THE QUESTION(S) OF LITERATURE

There is no guarantee that literature is immortal. Its chance today, its only chance, is the chance of Europe, of socialism, of democracy, and of peace. We must play it. If we writers lose it, too bad for us. But also, too bad for society. (Sartre, *What is Literature?*)[1]

Literature during politicised times

'Tout est politique' ('Everything is political') and 'Politique d'abord' ('Politics first') are slogans that express the belief (or hope) that politics (will) dominate and ultimately determine, or at least that they should dominate and determine, all essential aspects of daily life, thought, experience, and action. They postulate political theorising as the most basic theoretical activity and political activism as the most relevant or even exclusive form of praxis. Both are calls to accept politics as one's primary calling and acknowledge that every aspect of life is related to or determined by politics. Certainly those of us who were students in the 1960s heard these slogans often and perhaps even used them ourselves at various times.

There are obviously times when such slogans seem more appropriate than others. In complacent times, rallying cries of this type might seem necessary to overcome lethargy, indifference, or self-satisfaction. Their purpose would be to focus attention on the effects of politics on daily life and to encourage political activism. Or, at times of social unrest, a consensus might emerge on its own concerning the dominance of politics and the urgent necessity to act collectively against economic or political inequalities, unjust wars, or political oppression, and such slogans would then express this already-formed consensus concerning the primary importance of politics. In both contexts, at least for those who are responsive to the slogans, the assumptions underlying them and their general political implications rarely if ever become explicit issues, either because of a desire to put an end to political lethargy, whatever the costs, or simply because there appears to be no time for critical analysis given the pressing demands of the present.

During both highly politicised times and times considered not to be sufficiently politicised, then, activities that are not overtly and directly political are often considered by those who are politically committed to be at best of secondary importance, if not simply irrelevant. Art and literature certainly fall within this general category of irrelevance, and not just for hardened political militants for whom perhaps this is always the case. It is also true for the broader group of intellectuals, writers, artists, and students who become convinced not only of the pressing necessity of political activism, but also of the general primacy of politics and its determination over all other aspects of their intellectual and literary-aesthetic activities and pursuits. And if everything is 'political', if politics comes and should come 'first', then this means both that literature and art are determined by politics and that they come at best 'second'.

Some might argue that in the academy we are once again in such a political or politicised time, either as a reaction to social complacency and the dearth of serious political discussion both inside and outside the university or, as the most outspoken critics of the most recent forms of the alleged 'politicisation of the humanities' argue, because ageing 1960s radicals simply will not give up their perverse obsession with politics. Having failed to change the world, they now are accused of having resigned themselves to changing (politicising) academia. Such sterile polemics aside, it is nevertheless undeniable that the different politics of gender, race, ethnicity, or culture – whether in the form of the politics of identity or of multiculturalism and hybridity – have for some time played an increasingly important role in the various departments of the humanities and in the publications of university and commercial presses alike. And it is for this reason perhaps more than for any other that literature and art (the former undoubtedly more than the latter, and this is an interesting problem in itself) appear to be in crisis, not any longer even secondary concerns 'after politics,' but so marginal that they risk being of no concern at all. 'Everything is political' has come to mean for some that nothing of interest is literary, aesthetic or even theoretical. 'Politics first' has come to mean literature comes last, or not at all.

At what point the tendency to downplay or simply to ignore the question(s) of literature (and the conflicting answers of criticism and theory to these questions) began in recent times is difficult to determine with any precision, but it seems that it is today accepted more easily than perhaps at any other time in the last fifty years that literature is practically irrelevant, and theory itself, if not already dead, then increasingly in a state of agony. This is said by some with regret; it is affirmed by others with great glee and a smug 'I-told-you-so' attitude. I would argue that it is in fact no coincidence that an increasing lack of interest in literature accompanies the demise of theory, and that if we are now in, or if a significant and outspoken number feel that we should now be in, a post-theoretical era, an era when theory is seen as a thing of the past, then this is in part due to the fact that many have accepted that we are in a post-literary era as well, with literature seen more and more as a remnant from another, allegedly less enlightened, less progressive time. Except for a certain type of traditional critic, who would hope that the demise of theory would indicate a return to 'true literature', the post-theoretical and post-literary conditions may very well in fact be one and the same condition.

The irrelevance of literature is even or especially being proclaimed, it seems, in departments of literature, where reading and interpretation of canonical literary texts have not just been legitimately supplemented by the study of unjustly neglected non-canonical texts but also in many instances simply replaced by thematic presentations and summaries of diaries, logs, memoirs, films, maps, letters – by everything but a direct and sustained confrontation with literary texts themselves. It is as if it were felt that the prolonged, detailed reading, analysis, and critical discussion of literature have themselves become inferior, outdated, or even reactionary practices.

It is also a sign of the times that in spite of the important contributions made by such developing interdisciplinary fields as cultural studies, ethnic studies, and gender studies, all of which owe much to the theoretical developments of the last decades and thus at least indirectly to the study of literary questions and the question of literature, the serious critical investigation and interpretation of speculative philosophical, anthropological, rhetorical, and psychoanalytical texts are also becoming increasingly rare. Theory is now more often than not seen as an impediment to empirical historical-cultural research – this in fact has undoubtedly always been the case for dogmatic empiricists – and thus, if it is referred to at all, this is only in order to be done with it as quickly and superficially as possible.

Whatever the basis of the apparent consensus that we are now increasingly in a post-theoretical era, the coincidence of the post-theoretical and the post-literary raises important theoretical and literary questions. Especially if we consider the 'post' as Jean-François Lyotard did in his essay, 'Answering the question: what is postmodernism?', not as a discrete historical moment following in line dialectically and coming therefore *after* a previous discrete, well-delineated period – the postmodern following in time the modern – but a tension or conflict already within the period it is supposed to follow, and in the present instance a conflict inherent in both literature and theory from the very start and at the moments both of their greatest triumphs and worst defeats.[2]

What then if the post-literary/post-theoretical condition were in fact an original, constitutive moment of the literary-theoretical condition itself? What if in our haste to move beyond theory and literature, we are forgetting what brought us to where we are, and in thinking we are moving beyond and moving forward with the times, we are actually moving backward into the future, naively repeating and perpetuating the assumptions of preliterary/pretheoretical times – which themselves were not really 'pre' at all but also part of all times, even our own post-times? It may very well be time, then, to refuse to move on simply for the sake of moving on. It may be time to raise once again the question(s) of theory, and along with it (them), the question(s) of literature. This is precisely what I propose to do in this essay.

Even if an increasing number in the academy today appear less and less interested in literary questions or have simple abandoned them to pursue other, allegedly more pressing political, cultural, ethnic, and/or sexual questions, it seems to me important not to follow blindly such a trend but rather to begin to question its basic assumptions and potential implications. My intent, however, is not to mount another 'defence of literature' against its politicisation but rather ·- and without denying or minimising the significance of the political issues currently being raised and debated in academic journals and books – to attempt to understand better the general problem of the relations between politics and literature. I propose in this essay, however, not an extended analysis of the present situation in the academy but rather an investigation of a very different and particularly volatile, highly politicised period in which the question of literature was in fact central to political discussions. The purpose of such an evaluation will be to shed light indirectly on our own situation and point to possible consequences of literature's (and theory's) allegedly impending demise.

I will focus in this essay on arguably the two most influential French writers of the post-war period: Jean-Paul Sartre and Albert Camus. My purpose is to show the centrality of their writings on the nature and function of literature and art to their political writings and to demonstrate why literature certainly cannot be considered for either writer to come entirely 'after politics' – even though it would be equally dubious to assert that it comes simply before politics either. My goal is to understand better the dynamic relation between literature and politics in their work and to show why to forget (or ignore) the question(s) of literature is at the same time to trivialise the question(s) of politics.

Sartre and literary 'engagement'

The epigraph I have chosen for this essay is from Jean-Paul Sartre's *What is Literature?*, an essay written in 1947 and published originally that year in serial form in the journal Sartre had recently founded, *Les Temps Modernes*. It consists of the very last words of the essay, and I have chosen it because of the prophecy or threat it contains. In it Sartre claims that if writers do not immediately reinvigorate literature and make it play the liberating, critical role that he feels it should play in society, if they on the contrary let it become (once again) either dogmatic or irrelevant ('propaganda or pure distraction'), then the consequences for society will be disastrous.[3] And the fault will be no one's but the writers' themselves.

In fact, Sartre claims that literature's only chance – chance for what, he never clearly states – is directly linked to nothing less than the chances of Europe, socialism, democracy, and peace. Conversely, Europe's, democracy's, socialism's, and peace's only chances are linked directly then to the fate of literature. The world can certainly do without literature, Sartre also admits, but the cost of such a loss would be enormous: Europe, democracy, socialism, and peace, and he adds, humankind itself.[4]

For Sartre, then, the demise of literature, even after the recent victory over fascism in Europe, would not just be a sign of tyranny but also constitute a key event in the process of surrendering to tyranny. It is as if he felt that everything that had been accomplished during World War II would be lost – not to Nazism and an invading German army, but to irresponsibility and indifference – if writers did not commit themselves to writing a politically-committed form of literature, and if literature were not read primarily if not exclusively in terms of its historical-political involvement in its own society.

Since nothing is eternal, Sartre admits, literature could disappear, and the world would continue on without it, no matter how badly. But to live in a world without literature would be to live in a world without free men and women aware of their situation in the world and responsible for their own destiny. Sartre's challenge to writers (and critics) is thus enormous. The future of 'the free world', which for him at the time meant the free, socialist, democratic world, rests in a sense on their shoulders. And if writers fail to rise to the challenge, then too bad for them! And too bad for the rest of us and the world as well!

Today, it would certainly be difficult to imagine anyone making such a monumental claim for literature, when both the trivialisation and politicisation of literature (and criticism and theory) seem to be more and more accepted, and when literature, which in the not so distant past was still at or near the centre of humanistic inquiry, is being increasingly displaced to the margins of intellectual concerns, not just in society in general but also or especially in the university. The one site where literature had always been taken seriously and, when necessary, defended and protected from both political censorship and trivialisation – both for better and for worse depending on the form these defences took – no longer offers it much (if any) asylum at all.

If one's goal were to counter and reverse such a trend today, then Sartre's warnings could very well take on renewed relevance and urgency. Not for the sake of literature alone but also for the sake of critical thinking and the continuing search for alternatives to the assumptions and unexamined certainties that support the dominant political notions of Europe, democracy, and socialism, as well as other politicised and political ideas having to do with gender, ethnicity, and cultural identity as well. And this would be so even if the links between literature and democracy, not to mention those between literature and the fate of Europe (and the non-European world as well), socialism, and peace, undoubtedly appear to us more problematical than they did for Sartre in 1947. But those differences, as important as they might be, do not constitute sufficient reasons for dismissing Sartre's call to revitalise literature and recognise its crucial place in critical thought. That is, unless we no longer believe in the value of critical thinking itself.

Sartre states in his foreword that his chief purpose in writing *What is Literature?* was to respond to the 'nonsense' written by critics about his own work and to silence them once and for all: 'since critics condemn me in the name of literature without ever saying what they mean by that, the best answer to give them is to examine the art of writing without prejudice. What is writing? Why does one write? For whom? The fact is, it seems that no one has ever asked this before'.[5] It is as if he felt that once he had raised and answered the basic questions of literature, he could then move on to what he seemed to consider were more important areas of concern: namely, philosophy and politics. The question(s) of literature was (were) something that could be and that had to be answered clearly and decisively, and once answered, that could then apparently be left behind.

In fact, literature and its questions never disappear, either from Sartre's later work, or from the work of subsequent French theorists, whether followers of Sartre or, which is more often the case, representatives of if not anti-Sartrean tendencies in French thought, then at least of non-Sartrean alternatives to both Sartrean existentialism and the specific kind of political commitment he demanded of all writers. Questions of literature will continue to haunt French theory for decades. And it is precisely the difficulty of determining the defining questions of literature and thus providing definitive answers to them as well that will mark French theory and might even constitute the principal characteristic that makes it 'French' and distinguishes it from other national theoretical tendencies.

It could even be argued – thanks both to Sartre and to those who took decidedly anti-Sartrean positions – that 'French theory', assuming such a term makes sense, is distinguished from other national theoretical tendencies by its overriding concern with questions of literature and its investigation of the literary dimensions of theoretical discourse in general. These questions have had a dynamic, constructive role in theory for so long (for over fifty years) precisely because the answers given to them, whether Sartre's or others', have turned out in each case to be both provocative and unsettling, decisive and yet still open-ended. For this reason they continue to haunt theory (and anti-theoretical positions as well), even at a time of its trivialisation and politicisation. Even today.

It might even be possible to claim that theory is most alive and critical at those moments when its complex, paradoxical, even contradictory relations with its 'literary other', an other that is at the same time outside and within it, are analysed explicitly and seriously. Sartre's words on literature are clearly then not the last words, as he seemed to hope, nor it would be safe to say are they, as he claimed, the first words on such questions either, since the basic 'what', 'why', and 'for whom', questions he claims must be asked – along with many other basic and not so basic questions – in fact have a long philosophical, political, and literary history. This is a history that continues today, even when the questions of literature are being marginalised, ignored, forgotten, or suppressed for the sake of other, more directly political or politicised questions.

Question 1: What is it to write? Sartre's desire to answer quickly and definitively the fundamental questions of literature is most evident in the distinction he makes between literary writing (prose) and art (which for Sartre includes painting, music, and poetry). The artist, unlike the literary (prose) writer, works on matter – on colours, sounds, the material aspects of language – as an end in itself, not as a means of signifying. Prose writers signify, and they do or should do nothing else. For poets, language is not even really language. Poets are poets because they are 'foreigners' to the language they use and because they decline to use that language as an instrument to convey meaning. Words are not signs for poets but things, just as a house painted by a painter is not the sign of a house but simply a painted house that signifies only itself, that is only what it is.

All crises of language are thus poetic (and all poetry, representative of a repeated and never resolved crisis in and of language), for what is really in crisis in poetry is the signifying dimension of language itself. Language in crisis or poetic language is language taken as an impediment to communication rather than a transparent vehicle of sense. Poets and poetry impede communication as they make language do both more and/or less than communicate, and any generalised crisis of language would be equivalent to a generalisation of the aesthetic, rhetorical, poetic dimensions of language, and a reduction, complication, or even destruction of its signifying potential. All poetic crises of language threaten to leave politics in a mess as well, for they complicate, obscure, and even risk destroying, communicative links among individuals and groups and thus potentially their freedom. For this reason Sartre implies that the generalisation of the poetic always risks opening the way for tyranny.

As a prose writer, philosopher, and politically committed intellectual, Sartre vehemently opposes such crises (and the individuals, movements, and social classes responsible for them) and tries to do what he can to keep the poetic and the poet outside language and history and at a safe aesthetic distance from (prose) writing, which for him is one of the dynamic forces of history. This separation between prose and poetry and literature and art could even be argued to be the founding principle of his 'politics of prose', for his defence of (prose) literature is a primary weapon in the political-philosophical battles he waged on behalf of freedom.[6] Poetry and theory thus cannot for him in any way overlap without the most serious negative consequences – for both literature and politics.

Sartre's 'defence of literature' thus also aims to be a radical rectification of literature, a depoeticisation or deliterarisation of literature that could itself potentially destroy literature in an attempt to save it. Were prose literature in fact ever to be emptied of its literary-poetic functions – if such a thing were even imaginable – and thus do nothing but serve reality, if literature were thus ever to become exclusively 'utilitarian', then it is difficult to see how even Sartre could still have considered it to be literature. The literal realisation of the Sartrean project for (or myth of) prose literature would thus constitute the destruction of the very literature (and politics) he wanted to save (or serve).[7]

Perhaps Sartre never really intended such a generalisation of his theory of literary commitment after all. In any case, his call for transparent, utilitarian prose was always countered if not contradicted in his own writings by what could be called the poetics not just of his prose but of his politics as well. As Sartre acknowledges later in Les Mots (Paris, 1963), for better or for worse he was 'cursed' with what could be called a, or the, literary disease, a fascination and/or obsession with literature and great writers. And in spite of his repeated attempts to do so and assertions that he had finally succeeded, he was in fact never really able either to live comfortably with the disease or cure himself of it. I would add that such a 'failure' to find a definitive cure for the disease and the different literary illusions in which he believed – one of which was to consider all literature as 'engagée' – was not necessarily the worst literary-political condition to be in, especially when these literary illusions served as antidotes to his ever-increasing susceptibility to specific 'political diseases' or as counter-forces to his various and contradictory political illusions.

For Sartre, the prose writer (*the writer*) 'uses words' and thus is obliged to treat them not as things in themselves but exclusively as instruments, as means of communicating with others. This means that the writer is primarily, if not exclusively, 'a *speaker*' rather than a writer: 'he designates, demonstrates, orders, refuses, interpolates, begs, insults, persuades, insinuates'.[8] When he speaks in order to have no effect on anyone and to say nothing, he can do so without becoming a poet, if to say nothing is precisely what he or she intends to say and he or she is willing to accept responsibility for having no effect on his/her readers. The poet, on the contrary, always *says* nothing but does not use language to speak or signify the nothing he says.

Sartre's view of language is in part militaristic, for he presents language often as an armament. For if 'to speak is to act', sometimes violently, and if words at times function as 'loaded pistols', then to write (speak) can also be to shoot.[9] If one is going to shoot, however, it is of course better to aim carefully at one's target and take responsibility for having shot at and hit it, says Sartre, than to shoot like a child at everything that moves or simply into the air without aiming, just for the 'pleasure of hearing the shot' of one's language-gun go off and causing all sorts of damage for which one then refuses to be responsible.[10] Without a theory of literary *engagement*, Sartre clearly feels historical-political irresponsibility would soon be the rule not just of poetry, where it is acceptable, but of prose as well. Above all, Sartre demands that the writer be responsible for how he shoots and where he aims. There should be no stray, gratuitous, random shots for the committed prose writer. Whether Sartre himself ever came close to living up to such an ideal, or ever really tried to live up to it, however, is not at all clear. What is clear is that writing-as-communication for him means above all shooting straight.

For a word or phrase to arrive at its target or destination and accomplish the principal task Sartre assigns to the writer, which is 'to reveal the world and particularly to reveal man to other men', the writer has to aim well and shoot straight at the world and at other men and women (especially at those obscuring the world or making its revelation more difficult).[11] This means that language must go directly where it is supposed to go and do what it is supposed to do as quickly and unobtrusively as possible. Sartre wants writers to have silencers on their guns, to hit their targets but with as little rhetorical-poetic noise as possible. All 'contamination' of prose by poetry is to be avoided, because it has the effect of making too much noise and clouding the minds of readers who end up not seeing what has been aimed at and what has been hit. It inevitably results in the failure of communication and action – and in the targets that are aimed at being missed and the wrong targets hit. For Sartre, this kind of literary gratuity constitutes a dangerous and unacceptable political-philosophical position.

When it comes to describing language and its utilitarian function, Sartre himself, however, does not proceed very directly, efficiently, or quietly. He in fact makes quite a bit of linguistic-poetic noise in his prosaic endeavour to explain what literature is, and at the end of this first section of his essay it is not at all clear whether he in fact has really hit his main target, language, at all. Rather than the presentation of language itself, his analysis is dominated by a remarkable array of metaphors for language that are intended to reveal both the true nature and function of this 'tool' that the writer uses like any other but to which he or she is never supposed to pay attention.

It is in fact impossible not to pay attention to Sartre's own metaphors as he shoots his linguistic pistol at language:

> When someone is in danger or in difficulty, he grabs any tool whatever. Once the danger has passed, he no longer even remembers if it was a hammer or a stick; moreover, he never knew: all that was needed was a prolongation of his body, a means of extending a hand to the highest branch. It was a sixth finger, a third leg, in brief, a pure function that he assimilated into himself. This is the case for language: it is our shell and our antennae; it protects us against others and informs us about them; it is a prolongation of our senses … We are in language as in our body. We *feel* it spontaneously while going beyond it toward other ends, as we feel our hands and feet. We perceive it when others use it, as we perceive the limbs of others.[12]

Language is thus presented as a 'natural', physical phenomenon that takes the form of a supplementary, unnatural series of figurative body parts that have been so incorporated into us and become so natural that we are not – and should not ever be – aware of them. We can perceive them in others and others may perceive them in us – how would it be possible to miss extra fingers, legs, a protective shell, or antennae in other human beings? – but in no case should we allow ourselves to be aware of them in ourselves. We should use the extra possibilities they provide us for our own protection and for a better understanding and richer experience of the world, but we should not notice or be concerned with how language serves the function of a variety of supplementary limbs. Don't look, don't tell.

The trick of the prose writer is thus never to let this unnatural, supplementary body with multiple and contradictory functions, what might be called his/her imaginary 'writing body' (not a 'corps sans organes' but a 'corps avec organes supplémentaires'), ever become so visible that it would be impossible not to be aware of it, not to marvel at what it does or be fascinated by its unnatural 'naturalness'.[13] When it comes to language, the prose writer should censor him/herself and never look at or be aware of the supplementary appendages that he/she constantly needs in order to write.

There is in fact so much poetic 'contamination' in this description of the nature and function of language that it would be impossible to conceive of language outside the vivid figures used to describe it. At the very moment of his argument when the issue of non-poetic clarity is being proposed as the fundamental characteristic of prose, Sartre's own prose is overloaded with figurative language. The way to prosaic clarity thus turns out to be by means of poetic indirection, inventiveness, and communicational complexity, if not obscurity.

The prosaic and poetic uses of language which are meant to be kept separate thus overlap, with no ultimate distinction possible between them. Sartre has proved a point different from the one he intended, but he has also opened the way for further analysis of the overlapping of literature and philosophy and of literary, poetic language and theoretical, communicative language in general. The direct path to pure communication turns out to be a winding, circuitous one, with literature (and the poetic) inextricably implicated in philosophy and literary and political theory.

Question 2: Why write? The answer for Sartre comes easily and immediately: a writer writes not for him/herself but for others. And here again, the differences between art (including poetry) and (prose) literature evoked in the first section seem to have been forgotten and have in fact become almost irrelevant. For the role of others is as fundamental in art in general as it is in writing: '[t]here is no art except for and by others'.[14] Sartre thus argues that others are necessary to complete the creative project of the writer and give an objective existence to the revelations undertaken by the writer by means of language.[15] But what is given existence is not language or its figures but rather the world itself as it is revealed by the writer. Above all, the dialectic between writer and readers is an act of freedom on the part of the writer that demands the free response of readers to be complete.

It could even be argued that the literary act par excellence – the production and reception of prose – is for Sartre the model for free acts in general, since '[t]he book does not serve my freedom; it requires it'.[16] As language is a transparent tool or a means to an end, the book on the contrary, here treated as being equivalent to the work of art, is not a tool or a means but an end in itself, not a Kantian 'finality without end', but a 'finality as end': '[t]he work of art *does not have* an end; there we agree with

Kant. But the reason is that it *is* an end'.[17] For the work to be an end in this sense is not for it to be a discrete, autonomous object removed from history. Rather the work is seen as a fusion of two separate but interrelated acts *in history*, the act of writing and the complementary act of reading.

As important, if not more important than the freedom necessary for the writer to write is thus the freedom of the reader to respond to the call made by the work, a freedom Sartre characterises as 'pure creative power': '[i]f I appeal to my reader so that he/she will carry the enterprise which I have begun to a successful conclusion, it is self-evident that I consider him/her as pure freedom, pure creative power, unconditioned activity'.[18] The relation between writer and reader thus constitutes an ideal, unconditioned, absolute manifestation of pure freedom, the most transparent, complete, and successful *political* act imaginable.

Literature thus requires as its point of departure what society has never been able to realise in or as itself: the experience of pure freedom. The writer must have total confidence in the freedom of others, his/her potential readers, and reciprocally the reader must respond to this confidence in an 'exercise in generosity' with the 'gift of his/her whole person'.[19] Regardless of the content of the work, as a work of art literature is not just an expression of freedom but freedom itself. It is such a pure act, so total a gift, that one would have to wonder where Sartre could have found a more complete model for freedom, as both concept and practice, and whether his notion of political freedom would not have been severely limited and very different in nature if he had not used literature as the model of an ideal form of freedom unavailable in society.

In an essay from this same period, Sartre defended existentialism as a humanism, but he could just as easily have defended it as an aesthetics or poetics of freedom.[20] Not a poetics removed from the world but an activist poetics of the world, a poetics of political action that models itself after the free relations that allegedly exist between writer and reader (and since in this section he makes no distinction between writer and artist, between artist and viewer as well). The unique subject of the writer, 'a free man addressing free men', and thus of all writing, no matter its form, style, content, or themes, is thus freedom.[21] And in terms of politics, this means that the 'art of prose' – prose, he thus explicitly admits, is or can be an art – is inseparable from the only political regime 'where prose has meaning: democracy'.[22] Sartre could just as easily have said, 'where freedom has meaning', for since prose and freedom are so intimately connected, evoking one immediately evokes the other.

Sartre's radical notion of freedom and of the form of social democracy it implies are thus inseparable from a literary ideal of freedom. Sartre was right to feel obliged to reply to his literary critics, even if he claimed that it didn't amuse him to have to do so.[23] Literature is crucial to his entire philosophical-political enterprise. It is not just one question among many others, for its questions are fundamental to the Sartrean theory and practice of freedom. This is why the future of Europe for him is so intimately connected to the future of literature – and vice versa. In *What is Literature?* this future remains relatively undetermined, and perhaps indeterminable, and literature has an important role to play both in the conceptualisation and practice of freedom, and ensuring its indeterminacy.[24]

Question 3: For whom does one write? One does not write for everyone, says Sartre, even though this may be the explicit ideal, the 'abstract dream' of writers. Rather, '[w]hether he wants to or not, and even if he has his eyes on eternal laurels, the writer speaks to his contemporaries, his compatriots, and his racial or class brothers'.[25] Contemporaries, compatriots, and racial or class brothers, are defined as the people of 'the same period and same collectivity, who have lived through the same events, who have asked or eluded the same questions, who have the same taste in their mouth, who have with each other the same complicity and among whom there are the same corpses'.[26] These 'brothers' (or 'sisters') are the people who will best understand a writer's words and for whom in fact very few words are necessary to evoke common experiences – and using as few words as possible should always be the goal of the writer, even if Sartre himself wrote for the most part very long, dense philosophical and literary-critical works that many have found verbose as well as practically unreadable. Once again, Sartre is trying to keep language under the conscious control of the writer, to root literature (prose) in a communicational context and assign it the primary if not exclusive goal of total and immediate exchange of clear, unambiguous messages, of meanings and feelings that are in fact already in some sense understood and experienced by both parties before being exchanged.

It might be necessary, Sartre admits, to explain everything about life in France during the war to those who did not experience it, especially to Americans who seem to Sartre especially dense and removed from the historical reality of Europe. But few words, figures, and images, are necessary to convey the same experiences to the French, for as Sartre puts it, 'we are "entre nous"'.[27] Language ultimately seems to be unnecessary for those who are of the same race or share the same cultural heritage or national or class origin – assuming, of course, that we are ever really 'entre nous', no matter how we define the 'nous' – for nothing is communicated in communication that isn't in some sense already known.

Sartre hates the abstract universal so much that he is willing to accept the historically formed 'native community' as his point of departure: 'each book proposes a concrete liberation out of a particular alienation'.[28] The freedom of literature, like all forms of freedom for Sartre, begins and ends in concrete socio-historical situations. In the specific case of literature this restriction is imposed by the community of potential first (and allegedly best) readers to whom everything does not need to be explained, or in the best (or worst) of cases, to whom nothing needs to be explained. Even if the effects of writing are always to negate, move beyond, and in this sense be liberated from the situation in which one is originally placed, which means to move beyond the community consisting only of 'ourselves' and to experience perhaps other tastes in our mouth than the one *we* all allegedly already share, literature is nonetheless still limited by the pre-determined 'community' in which what it has to say is known (or tasted) even before being written or read.

What is true of production is also true of consumption. Like bananas, which Sartre claims, 'have a better taste when they have just been picked, works of the mind should likewise be consumed on the spot [*sur place*]'.[29] Sartre's view of literature is thus also a theory of immediate production and consumption, of how and when literary and philosophical works are best consumed and have the best taste and thus are most fully *of the present*.

But if reading books were really like eating bananas – and writing them, like growing and picking bananas – there would be no need for theoretical investigations of what it means to write and read to help us understand the complex dynamics of each. Rather, only a theory of exchange and consumption would be needed, perhaps even a theory of good taste in a gastronomic sense – what tastes good – rather than in an aesthetic or social sense. That theory of 'good taste' could then be applied to literature and to any other consumable object, but it would owe more to Brillat-Savarin than to Kant. And yet it is clear that Sartre would not really have been satisfied with such a theory of literature and would have had to admit that he needed something more from literature than its good taste when it is consumed immediately after, or even better, simultaneously with being produced. He most certainly would have had to agree that eating a banana is one thing and writing or reading literature another, and moreover that this difference is crucial for the 'taste' of both.[30]

What Sartre gets from literature is not in fact a good taste but a view of utopia, a utopia in which the 'first' audience ('native community') would be at the same time concrete and universal – all of humanity – and literature would be totally conscious of itself because its context would be a classless society totally present to itself and whose members' freedom would be unlimited.[31] In such a society, 'literature is, in essence, the subjectivity of a society in permanent revolution', one in which all order, literary and social, is reversed as soon as it becomes fixed: 'in a collectivity which constantly corrects, judges, and metamorphoses itself, the written work can be an essential condition of action, that is, the moment of reflexive consciousness'.[32] And although Sartre acknowledges that such a utopian society is not for tomorrow or perhaps for any time, literature still has the obligation to produce or function as this critical, reflexive consciousness, no matter how impartially and imperfectly, and offer critical alternatives to the present. But to do so, it can't be exclusively or perhaps even primarily of the present. It might even have to be as poetic as it is prosaic to induce such reflexivity; it might have to be as metaphorical as it is literal or communicational.

Whatever the limitations of Sartre's very particular defence of literature, it is clear that it makes no sense in his terms to ask 'why literature?' It would be as nonsensical as the question, 'why freedom?' In Sartrean terms, the post-literary and post-theoretical condition(s) would also constitute a condition after freedom, an era of the deadening of the critical faculties and of the politicisation and trivialisation not just of literature but of all aspects of life. Some form of political-cultural tyranny would result.

Camus: beauty and politics

The artist ... knows that nothing is simple and that the other exists.
(Camus, 'Témoin de la liberté', November 1948)

To separate freedom from justice comes back to separating culture from work, which is the social sin par excellence ... The first task of every dictatorial enterprise is thus to subjugate at the same time work and culture.
(Camus, 'Le pain et la liberté', 10 May 1953)

If the immediate post-war period in France is considered by most to have been dominated by Sartre, Albert Camus would still have to be ranked a close second in influence and importance. Camus never wrote an extended essay on the nature and function of literature and art but like Sartre was concerned with the basic question(s) of literature, even if his questions (and answers) were not the same. Their literary differences in fact played a role in the disagreements between them that most have considered to be primarily, if not exclusively, political in nature – bitter, seemingly irresolvable conflicts over Marxism, communism, the future of democracy, and finally over the FLN and the best political strategy for achieving justice in Algeria.

Thus, politics alone did not separate them, for aesthetics, their formulations of and responses to the question(s) of art and literature, also distanced them from each other. If for Sartre literature has a fundamental role in forming the critical, reflexive consciousness essential for freedom, for Camus art and literature represent critical alternatives to history and politics that are also necessary for freedom, necessary in fact for the freedom from history and politics that for him is a force necessary for their transformation. What is at stake in these differences is a not only a different poetics of prose (and poetry) but also a different political idea of freedom.

In his preface to one of his first published works, *L'Envers et l'endroit* (containing essays written in 1935–36), Camus dramatically links the political question of economic inequality and poverty to the question of beauty, or more precisely, to the problem of the unaesthetic, of the absence or even negation of beauty. In describing the deplorable conditions of working-class suburbs of northern French cities he denounces what he considers the ultimate form of injustice, an injustice which is both socio-economic and aesthetic at the same time, a deprivation of both the basic means of survival and of the pleasure of aesthetic appreciation, what he calls 'the double humiliation of destitution and ugliness'.[33] The absence of natural beauty transforms a geographic space of destitution – horrible in itself – into a space of incomparable, absolute injustice, one to which even 'the extreme Arab destitution [of his native Algeria] cannot be compared'.[34] At least in Algeria, no matter how great the destitution of the Arab population, which Camus in no way ignores or mitigates, the beauty of the North African landscape could not be denied. And in the experience of this beauty, there is still the hope for a different, better life. For the unemployed of the desolate sections of the cities of the north, that experience and the hope that accompanies it seem to be missing.

But what has beauty to do with this economic-political question, a sceptic might legitimately ask? Does it really make any difference to those suffering from political injustice and economic deprivation whether the landscape is beautiful or whether the sun shines brightly and the sea is warm? Economic and political justice must come first, this sceptic might claim, before the question of beauty and other literary-aesthetic questions should even be considered. For compared to the destitution of a people or extreme political injustice, how could any experience of beauty be considered significant? Camus's response would have been that even if aesthetic experience doesn't 'measure up' when compared to the scandal of a starving child, it nevertheless always contains within it the possibility, if not the necessity, of social transformation.[35] It thus represents the hope – even if it does not provide the means – of putting an end to the conditions responsible for destitution and a child's scandalous death.

Beauty by itself certainly does not diminish or mitigate these social and political injustices and the suffering of individuals, groups, and classes. But the total absence of the experience of beauty in the cold, dreary working-class suburbs of northern European cities, what Camus calls an 'injustice of climate', raises injustice to another level.[36] The absence of beauty transforms destitution into a kind of negative absolute, a sign of nothing less than the most extreme, hopeless form of injustice: '[w]hen poverty combines with this life without horizon or hope ... then the final, most revolting injustice is accomplished'.[37] All of Camus's most lyrical, romantic, and nostalgic essays that praise the beauty of the North African landscape could be said in this sense to have been written in protest against the most revolting forms of aesthetic-political injustice. As descriptions of aesthetic experiences, they represent the possibility of alternatives to destitution and injustice, even or especially in their most extreme forms.

The experiences of natural beauty, especially, for Camus, of the North African sun illuminating a seemingly infinite landscape, and of destitution, as it is found in the living conditions of the Arab and Berber populations of his native land or the proletariat of the cities of metropolitan France, are recurring, fundamental, even obsessive elements of Camus's lyrical and political essays and his novels. To ignore the aesthetic dimension of his politics or the political dimension of his aesthetics or poetics would also be to ignore the central question of limits in his work – the limits of both politics and art. It would be both to misunderstand his sense of injustice and to ignore or seriously distort what could be called his political-aesthetic activism, which was directed against the unacceptable conditions of extreme poverty and political oppression and the supplementary but fundamental degradation produced by or accompanying the absence or negation of even the possibility of the experience of beauty. Literature and art are thus inextricably linked to freedom for Camus, as they were for Sartre, even if in a different way.

On the one hand, the direct experience of poverty and the witnessing of the destitution of others impose a limit for Camus on all aesthetic experience and on beauty itself and make it impossible to postulate art as a simple alternative to or escape from social reality and history. Such experiences make it impossible to believe that 'everything is good under the sun and in history', no matter how 'good' beauty is and how much pleasure and sense of fulfilment is felt in its contemplation and appreciation.[38] Camus was always suspicious of and vigorously opposed all aestheticisms and historicisms (or politicisms?) that proposed or implied the contrary: that everything was, or that everything could be either good or beautiful. He was much more of a sceptic than many have acknowledged, not just about history and politics, as his critics have claimed, but about art and literature as well.

On the other hand, the feeling of well-being under the sun and the experience of beauty in general represent experiences different from historical-political experience and thus point to the fact that 'history is not [and should not be considered as being] everything'.[39] In his earliest essays before World War II, therefore, and well before the outbreak of either the Cold War or the Algerian War, Camus cautions against taking history (or politics) as an absolute, even if it is only because an important human experience, for him, one of the most radical and transgressive of human experiences, will be ignored, negated, or simply trivialised if history is conceived as totally determining. For Camus, not just justice but also beauty cannot and should not wait to be realised or experienced at some future time. They both need to be of the present, of each present, not as simple reflections of the present but as alternatives to it.

Camus argues that the ideal of aesthetic experience is at the same time just as problematic as that of historical experience, because as a radical alternative to misery it inevitably encourages a flight from social reality and political injustice. Beauty is thus not everything because it cannot in itself negate and overcome injustice and destitution; just as history is not everything because it cannot negate and overcome the existence of and need for beauty as an alternative for and resistance to total historical-political determination.

Camus does not consider art (including literature) to be a refuge from the world but rather a particular opening to the world. Art thus should not be removed from historical-political reality or considered transcendent with respect to history but must rather be treated as another type of experience in the world and of the world. It represents above all the possibility of other worlds and other types of experience of the world, no matter how destitute one's condition. Aesthetic experience complicates historical experience and constitutes the sign that there is always something other than history within history, something other than politics at stake within politics.

In November 1948, Camus gave a speech before an international meeting of writers in which he defended the rights of the artist against what he called the oppression of politics. 'Le témoin de la liberté' is perhaps his first clear response to Sartre's increasingly militant Marxist politics and what Camus considered his politicisation of literature; it is Camus's most direct refutation of the Sartrean notion of *engagement*. If Sartre defended literature primarily as a form of communication and stressed its role in revealing (and changing) the world and the writer's situation in the world, Camus defended literature as a form of art and a way of resisting and offering alternatives to the historical-political determination of the world. In a world in which Camus claimed polemics had replaced dialogue and intimidation had replaced persuasion, in which death had become an abstraction, a statistic, an administrative responsibility of the state, where murderers and torturers had become government ministers, and totalitarian ideologies, in the name of the salvation of the world, strove for the sterility, silence, or death of all adversaries, in such a world art not politics best resisted oppression and injustice and the ideologies that legitimate them: '[f]or everything that constitutes the dignity of art is opposed to such a world and challenges it. The work of art, by the fact alone that it exists, negates the conquests of ideology'.[40]

This is a bold statement, and one easily misunderstood, especially if it is taken as a sign of Camus's retreat from politics and of a flight from history into art. It could even be taken to foreshadow his eventual retreat into silence during the Algerian War and his rejection of all proposed political solutions for ending the war. But all 'retreats from the political' are not of the same kind or have the same effects; some retreats may in fact be strategies for engaging politics and being committed to politics, but in an extra- or para-political way.

It all comes down for Camus to the difference between two desires that seem quite close but are in fact opposed: the aesthetic desire for unity and the political desire for totality:

> Political action and creation are the two sides of the same revolt against the disorder of the world. In both cases, one wants to give unity to the world … What the [political] conqueror of the right or the left wants is not unity, which is the harmony of opposites; it is rather totality, which is the obliteration of differences. The artist … knows that nothing is simple and that the other exists. The conqueror wants the other not to exist; his world is a world of masters and slaves, the world in which we live.[41]

The (aesthetic) recognition of the existence of the other complicates, differentiates, pluralises, and relativises all unities and makes totalisation or the elimination or levelling of differences impossible. The existence of the other, of an alterity inscribed at the very foundation of art, means that art for Camus is always incomplete, experimental, always undoing the unity that has been achieved in search of other, more complex, more differentiated unities. Art thus offers a model not of unity per se but of a process rooted in the fundamental but disruptive place of the other in all experience. It is this search for unity without the destruction of the other that best explains what Camus means when he said that 'by his/her function itself, the artist is witness to freedom' and that artists are 'by nature the enemies of the abstract idols that are today triumphant, whether they be national or partisan'.[42] National and ideological idols reduce or even destroy alterity for the sake of totality, while the artist for Camus bears witness to the alterity and freedom that resist totalisation.

Freedom for Camus is never exclusively or even primarily individual in the sense that it would be an inherent, inalienable right or attribute of each individual subject. It is not exclusively or primarily collective either. Rather freedom is associated with the other in general, inseparable from and in fact rooted in the recognition of the indestructible otherness of the other, an otherness with no single content or face but, as Camus says, 'with thousands of faces'.[43] The artist bears witness to freedom and to the thousand faces of otherness by resisting totalisation and intervening in politics, but not in the terms dictated by the political. Art (literature) is necessary so that the other and his and her multiple faces will not be eliminated or synthesised into a collective face, whether it be that of a people, class, gender, ethnicity, or race. Freedom is the name of the struggle to create links among the parts of an irreducible plurality without destroying the specificity of the parts.

Artists (writers), through their recognition of otherness, are also witnesses to history, not just to history as it is defined by historians, philosophers, political theorists, or politicians, but witness to what in history is more than or other than history, 'witnesses of the flesh, not of the law' of history.[44] Artists are or should be witnesses to the suffering of the victims of history, to the sorrow of 'the losers' of history for their losses. They are or should be witnesses to the multiple others whose history is not told as history, rather than to the victors and conquerors in history whose stories history has always told. Art in Camus's sense can never be triumphant, for victory is the story of the individual or collective self not the other; it has one, rather than thousands of faces. Literature, as art, is the unfinished story of the multiple.

Literature and the Sartre–Camus political conflict

Sartre is not an enemy; I have had no literary quarrel with him. He was only my adversary on a point that I consider capital for all of us. I also feel, it is true, that he was not a loyal adversary, but that concerns only me. (Camus, 'Réponse à Domenach', *Témoins*, Summer 1955)

In 1947, Camus and Sartre were nominally at least still friends and linked in common literary-political struggles. The emerging Cold War and the question of communism, however, had already begun to create serious frictions between them. It is certainly no secret that in the late 1940s and 1950s they had conflicting views of politics; but what has not been sufficiently discussed is how their political differences were related to and even rooted in very different views of art and literature. If Sartre was first and foremost a philosopher and political theorist who also wrote plays and novels, Camus was primarily a journalist, playwright, and novelist who also wrote essays on literature, philosophy, art, and politics. The different priority given in each case in itself indicates an important source of conflict between them that became increasingly pronounced when it took on an explicitly political form. Even though they disagreed as to what the role of literature was or should be – in spite of what Camus claimed, he did in fact have an extended literary quarrel with Sartre – their concern with literary questions in relation to politics remained one of the most important points of intersection between them, as well as one of the principal points of conflict.

It could certainly be argued that Sartre believed more in politics than Camus, just as Camus believed more in literature than Sartre, but in each case the difference is relative rather than absolute. For Camus understood that what politics had been unable to do, what the ideologies of the nineteenth and twentieth century had been unable to do, what the grand metanarratives of modernity had been unable to do, art certainly could not do either. But as opposed to metanarratives of history and politics, he argued that art never claimed to be able to bring about total peace and harmony among peoples or justice and equality in society. Art and literature's ambitions and claims were and had to be much more modest. Art and literature had to re-emerge, Camus asserted, in spite of or rather because of their modesty, as a central component of human existence. This is why he felt it necessary in a highly-charged political environment 'to recall the place of art on the most humble level of reality and to give it, against its enemies, justifications that would not be privileges'.[45]

Against what he called the haughty arrogance of Europe and its failed humanism, against both its liberal and Marxist metanarratives, Camus humbly proposed art (and literature) as an alternative counterforce, not 'Art' in the grand tradition – which would also depend on and be justified by the same metanarratives legitimating history that he rejected – but 'little' works of art of all kinds, creative products not of the artist-genius but of the artist-worker or artisan. In 'L'artiste et son temps' (1958), Camus addressed once again the problem of the political implications of art and responded to questions having to do with both his political principles and his role as a writer in relation to politics. He denounced the Marxist project to save mankind by linking it and the political ends it proposed to the colonialist project of the redemption of 'the savage'. 'In reality, the end of history can have no definable sense within the limits of our condition. It can only be the object of faith and a new mystification. A mystification which today is no less than the one which previously founded colonialist oppression on the necessity of saving the souls of infidels'.[46] Camus was the enemy of all forms of redemption, whether historical, political, religious, or aesthetic in nature.

Redemption always had for him an oppressive, inquisitorial basis, condemning to eternal damnation all infidels – defined as such in terms of their 'inferior' race, ethnicity, religion, political allegiance, or social class – and projecting a salvation for the faithful at their expense and in the name of a myth of a future which legitimated oppression and even murder in the present. Messianic forms of Marxism were thus for him associated with repression, not liberation, having the same effects as colonialism and the inquisition. They lack both literary-aesthetic and political modesty.

Sartre of course clearly did not agree with such criticisms, at least not in the form Camus made them. He preferred a more immodest form of literature and was clearly tempted by different even more immodest forms of redemptive politics. But it has not been my purpose in this essay to decide who was right or who was wrong in the literary and political polemics that eventually separated and opposed Sartre and Camus. It has rather been to understand better the conflicts themselves and the assumptions inherent in each position. In spite of the many differences separating them, both agreed at least that literature had a fundamental role to play in (and simultaneously 'against') history, and therefore had a necessary internal relation to politics. In spite of an apparent consensus to the contrary, I would argue that it should be one of the tasks of literary studies today, although not the only or necessarily even the primary one, to continue to develop critical strategies that could account for such relations, all the while respecting the differences between and relative specificity of both the literary and the political. And all the while understanding the necessity for modesty in both realms.

The end of literature and the end of the kind of critical theory that is concerned with and attempts to respond to the question(s) of literature would certainly have represented for both Sartre and Camus a serious limitation, if not the destruction, of freedom. Times have certainly changed since their time, but it seems to me still crucial for us, situated as some would have it in a 'post-literary condition', to continue to or to begin once again both to question literature and to pursue seriously the question(s) of literature. This is true even if the questions of literature and the modes of questioning today are necessarily different from those of Sartre and Camus. It is crucial that such questions and such questioning find again an important place in the academy. It is also crucial that such questioning not be seen as a rearguard assault on progressive, multi-cultural, gender-conscious theory and politics, but rather on the contrary made a component of them. Something is still at stake in literature that should not be lost – for both literary-aesthetic and political reasons. And if we are unable or if we simply refuse to acknowledge this, then the words of Sartre would perhaps once again be appropriate: '[t]oo bad for us'.

Notes

1 J-P. Sartre, *What is Literature?*, trans. B. Frechtman (Gloucester, Mass.: 1978), pp. 290–1.

2 J-F. Lyotard, 'Answering the question: what is postmodernism', trans. R. Durand, in *The Postmodern Condition* (Minneapolis, 1984). Lyotard's claim is the following: '[the postmodern] is undoubtedly a part of the modern ... Postmodernism thus understood is not modernism at its end but in the nascent state, and this state is constant' (p. 79).

3 Sartre, *What is Literature?*, p. 291.

4 *Ibid.*

5 *Ibid.*, p. xviii (translation modified).

6 See Denis Hollier's amusing, insightful, but at the same time limited, reading of Sartre's politics entitled *Politique de la Prose: Jean-Paul Sartre et l'an quarante* (Paris, 1982). Jean-François Lyotard, at the beginning of his short essay on Hollier's book, which serves as the foreword to its English translation, summarises the many serious political and poetic differences he (and others on the left) had with Sartre. He calls these differences his own 'prejudices', but in admitting them he actually highlights Sartre's own aesthetic-political dogmatism and 'prejudices'. In this way his foreword highlights a number of important political and poetic questions that Hollier ignores or passes over very quickly in his book, while still presenting it in the best light possible: 'Hollier plainly did not have to overcome such prejudices to approach Sartre. He does not debate "in depth" ... He does not seem to believe in depth ... He is gay, alert, without disdain, without demagogy, at times amused to the point of disrespect, always guided by a meticulous consideration of the surfaces of the text and the life, with a touch of the rake in his delicacy ... I write these notes solely in order to understand how or why, aside from his talent, Hollier succeeded in having his curiosity shared by the worst reader of Sartre [i.e. Lyotard himself] that Sartre could conceivably dream of' (J-F. Lyotard, 'Foreword: a success of Sartre's', in D. Hollier, *The Politics of Prose: Essays on Sartre*, trans. J. Mehlman (Minneapolis, 1986), pp. xv–xvi). Without disagreeing with Lyotard's comments, I am sure I am not the only reader of Hollier who would have preferred at times a more sustained, 'in depth', and less 'rakish' reading of the most important contradictions within Sartre's poetics and politics, some of which are evoked in an amusing but cursory way by Hollier in his study.

7 Suzanne Guerlac, in *Literary Polemics: Bataille, Sartre, Valéry, Breton* (Stanford, 1997) considers Sartre's theory of engagement to be 'a new myth of literature – the myth of prose – which serves as the ideological core of an existentialist humanism and of a democratic socialism. Prose is the myth of language restored to an originary innocence – a pure signifying force – through the healing powers of a literary practice ... In Sartre's analysis of prose, a myth of semiological transparency serves a myth of instrumental force: speech as action' (pp. 58–9).

8 Sartre, *What is Literature?*, pp. 13–14.

9 *Ibid.*, pp. 16, 18.

10 *Ibid.*, p. 18.

11 *Ibid.*

12 *Ibid.*, p. 27.

13 See of course G. Deleuze and F. Guattari, *L'Anti-Oedipe* (Paris, 1972).

14 Sartre, *What is Literature?*, p. 37.

15 *Ibid.*, p. 40.

16 *Ibid.*, p. 41.

17 *Ibid.*, p. 42.

18 *Ibid.*, p. 43 (translation modified).

19 *Ibid.*, p. 45.

20 See J-P. Sartre, *L'Existentialisme est un humanisme* (Paris, 1946). Guerlac argues that Sartre's characterisation of 'the essence of literature as mutual recognition of freedom' constitutes an 'esthetic moment [that] lies at the heart of engagement' (Guerlac, *Literary Polemics*, p. 66). Her point is well taken, even if I think she forces things just a bit when she links the 'esthetic moment' in Sartre to eroticism and 'an economy of excess' in order to diminish the differences between Sartre and Bataille.

21 Sartre, *What is Literature?*, p. 58.

22 *Ibid.*, p. 59.

23 *Ibid.*, p. xvii.

24 In her effort to counter the one-sided political interpretations of Sartrean *engagement* and link Sartre closely to writers to whom he is usually opposed and to whom he appears to have opposed himself – Bataille and Valéry – Guerlac, I feel, overstates the case for Sartre-poet just a bit and is herself overly decisive and one-sided in her own conclusions: 'Sartre's thinking of engagement is not utilitarian. It does not subordinate literature to utilitarian ends or impose values to be upheld or represented in art. Indeed, it has more in common with the pure poet Valéry than with any ideology of social realism' (Guerlac, *Literary Polemics*, p. 91). As her own reading shows, the subordination of literature to utilitarian ends is an important component, although not necessarily the determining one, of the Sartrean theory of engagement. After reading Guerlac, it is certainly necessary to acknowledge that the poetic has a fundamental, non-subordinate role to play in his work as well.

25 Sartre, *What is Literature?*, p. 62 (translation modified).

26 *Ibid.* (translation modified).

27 *Ibid.*

28 *Ibid.*, p. 64.

29 *Ibid.*, p. 68.

30 Hollier has some amusing things to say about Sartre and bananas, especially given Sartre's own apparent taste for canned goods over fresh produce (*The Poetics of Prose*, pp. 147–9). Michel Contat and Michel Rybalka in *Les Écrits de Sartre* (Paris, 1970) indicate that Sartre also begins a short article on jazz entitled 'Nick's Bar, New York City', which was published the same year as *What is Literature?* (1947), with the same comparison: '[j]azz music is like bananas; it is [best] consumed on the spot [*sur place*]' (p. 166).

31 Sartre, *What is Literature?*, p. 149.

32 *Ibid.*, p. 153.

33 A. Camus, *Essais* (Paris, 1965), p. 7. All translations from this collection of essays are my own.

34 *Ibid.*

35 I am of course referring to the comments Sartre made in an interview after the publication of *Les Mots* in which he talks about how he had changed since writing his first novel, *La Nausée*: '[w]hat I lacked [at the time of writing *La Nausée*] was the sense of reality. I have changed since then. I have had a long apprenticeship of the real. I have seen children die of hunger. Compared to a dying child, *La Nausée* doesn't measure up [*ne fait pas le poids*]' (*Le Monde*, 18 April 1964).

36 Camus, *Essais*, p. 6.

37 *Ibid.*, p. 7.

38 *Ibid.*, p. 6.
39 *Ibid.*
40 *Ibid.*, pp. 401, 404.
41 *Ibid.*, p. 404.
42 *Ibid.*, p. 405.
43 *Ibid.*
44 *Ibid.*, p. 406.
45 *Ibid.*, p. 714. Camus defended democracy in two newspaper articles in almost exactly the same terms as an 'exercise in modesty', as not 'the best', but rather the 'least bad of all political regimes'. See 'Démocratie et modestie' *Combat* (February 1947), and 'La démocratie: exercise de la modestie', *Caliban* (November 1948), in Camus, *Essais*, pp. 319, 1582–83.
46 *Ibid.*, p. 801.

timothy clark

LITERARY FORCE, INSTITUTIONAL VALUES

The authentic answer is always the question's vitality. (Blanchot, *The Space of Literature*)

Introduction

Let us imagine that while one was preparing a lecture or seminar, the ghost of, say, James Joyce or of William Blake appeared in the room, asking 'what are you doing with *Ulysses/The Four Zoas*?' The answer comes back: 'I'm teaching it as literature …'. I leave it to you to imagine their response. My point is this: why does this answer, so obviously truthful, seem so inadequate and reductive, almost as if the main effect of studying, or teaching, something 'as literature' were to contain or to curtail it in some way? What is the relation between literary force and institutional value?

This essay follows a path broken by Robert J. C. Young and Bill Readings in arguing that a major if neglected site in debates about literature, 'the crisis in criticism' and so on, is the university institution, its 'idea' and its public status.[1] I contend that many of the debates going on within the walls of English departments about the canon, the authority of tradition, the nature of interpretation, etc. can never be solved. This is because they are not ultimately academic problems at all in the sense of questions that can be formulated and addressed within defined disciplinary boundaries (the way, for instance, that the nature of element 114 is clearly a topic for the physicists). Many major questions in literary studies cannot be solved *in* literary studies, but immediately involve other fields, such as history or sociology, and the cultural mission of the humanities, and an 'idea of the university'. In the second section of this paper I will argue that one way of defending literary study in the contemporary corporate university is to focus on literature's resistance to institutionalised lines of demarcation, and the creative disruptions this entails. In the terms of my title, there is a tension – one which needs to be maintained – between institutional values and literary force.

First, however, I want to offer a schematic account of the various institutional values that have dominated literary study.

Ideas of a university

One of the distinctive features of literary criticism is that its status in the university has always been controversial, if not precarious. Throughout its history it has tried to answer accusations of being little more than a professionalised hobby, a dilettante subject, the poor man's Classics, or an amateurish cultivation of taste and connoisseurship. If one reads the various histories of English that are now available, such as the work of Franklin E. Court, or Brian Doyle's *English and Englishness*, one is struck by the way in which changes in conceptions of the subject and of ways of teaching it are invariably driven by internal, university pressures, especially the need to conform to models of disciplinary knowledge regarded as established in other areas.[2] We see a succession of different methodologies as various as philology, *belle-lettrist* cultivation of taste, and ethnology – to confine oneself to the nineteenth century alone. There is no history of English with the same inherent rationale as the history of physics or sociology, working out various theories and conflicting claims around a common object. Instead, we have a series of usually short-lived quasi-disciplines whose rationale dictates the appropriation of texts in certain ways and the definition of certain texts as literary. These endure for a generation or so before being displaced, with an essentially different academic practice taking their place under the same administrative titles. Even what some people call 'traditional criticism' – the kind of loose untheorised amalgam of historical context and close textual evaluation practised in group-work at most universities – has only been around since the late 1950s and early 1960s.

Is it possible to offer some kind of schematisation of the institutional pressures delimiting literary study in the university? Peggy Kamuf writes that literary study has always been both determined and riven by the double demands of its institutionalisation: (1) the need to dissociate itself from merely amateur literary culture, to claim the status of a knowledge worthy of full inclusion in the modern university, with warrantable procedures of research and the methodology of genuinely disciplinary and pedagogical procedures, not mere impressionism, subjectivism, etc.; (2) the converse need to be differentiated from other parts of the university – i.e. the need to define and delimit a conception of literature and literary value that will not collapse into cross-disciplinary areas under the least intellectual pressure.[3] These are the institutional pressures delimiting literary force.

How might Kamuf's schema apply to the various practices which have taken place under the title of English in the university? In answering this question, I'm going to follow Bill Readings in schematising three major ideas of the university since the modern research university emerged in early nineteenth-century Germany. The first two are what Readings nicknames the 'University of Reason' and the 'University of Culture'. The third I'll come to later.

(1) The 'University of Reason' refers to the idea of the university at work in Kant's *The Conflict of the Faculties* of 1798 (another recent bicentennial).[4] The following question governs the foundation of the modern university: can a life of reason be institutionalised without becoming other to itself, as it manifestly had in republican France? Kant's *The Conflict of the Faculties* presents a model of the university as the institution in which reason gives itself its own law (this is still the crucial component of the idea of academic freedom). Although the university must be allowed to legislate in all matters of knowledge, it is subordinate in power to the state. At the same time, however, the state has a duty to protect the university from any abuse of power that would interfere with the autonomy of reason. Reason is instituted primarily in the so-called lower faculty of 'philosophy' (a term that would now cover the humanities and natural sciences). The three higher faculties of law, medicine and theology are devoted mainly to the training of a professional class in service to the state – lawyers, doctors, and clergy. Yet they are also expected to submit to the legislation of philosophy, of reason, in their own affairs. As a consequence, reason grounds the university as whole, while its influence on professional training enables a peaceful diffusion of enlightenment throughout the state.

One of the practical consequences of trying to institutionalise ideals of the self-determination of reason has been a recognition of the need for a division of labour, to compartmentalise the pursuit of knowledge into discrete departments and fields, each with its recognised objects and procedures. The double demand outlined by Kamuf can be discerned from the very earliest attempts to institutionalise literary study at the University of London up till the present day. The demarcation of 'fields' of expertise is one of the founding gestures of the division of labour within the professional university: '[l]imits and limitation were indispensable for the demarcation of the professional field, but once the latter had been established, the attention to borders (founding principles) became increasingly the exception rather than the rule. Attention was focused on the problems and questions emerging *within* the field, the coherence and even history of which was increasingly taken for granted'.[5] Areas of training and research increasingly ignored issues of their own constitution and history: '[i]ndeed, the very notion of academic "seriousness" came increasingly to exclude reflection upon the relation of one "field" to another'.[6] Academic freedom too is not just a case of free speech: it is a particular and specific freedom linked to the public recognition of expertise in a field. It is inseparable from the division between disciplines: it is accepted that those academics appointed by a department to work within it have a level of expertise in their teaching and research that, ultimately, only peers can recognise or underwrite. What counts as good work in a history department is a matter for historians to decide, what counts as good sociology should not be decided by biologists, etc. Academic freedom is thus an institutional affair, not solely a matter of individual free speech. It depends on the recognised autonomy of departments of learning. Clearly, then, in so far as my account sees literary studies as transgressive of clear disciplinary boundaries, and in fact downright suspicious of some of ways they operate, it may cause problems for this particular notion of academic freedom.

The professionalisation of academic life has had then profound effects upon the changing understanding of literature. This is not a trivial point because the drive for the professional autonomy of literary studies as a discipline in the university affects the very minutiae of thought, especially in the form of the drive or project to discern or isolate some object able to underwrite or guarantee a self-contained disciplinary space. Hence the repeated call to study 'literature as literature' or to isolate some definable or measurable criterion of intrinsic literariness. The ethos of professionalism has been inseparable from a tendency towards formalism, which emerges, in effect, as partly a strategy of disciplinary containment. Such purism is, as we now realise, in tension with the nature of its object, as may be the concept of objectivity itself where literature is concerned. Clearly, even the debate about the merits of close reading, argued by some to be the key practice upon which any independent discipline of criticism might be founded, is largely determined by a certain idea of what a university discipline should be.

Claims that literature should be attended to for itself, without supposedly extrinsic motivation, are a recurrent feature of professionalised criticism. Such a claim is a mirror image of the idea of pursuing knowledge 'for its own sake'. This platitude is a very distant echo of the original German ideal of a rational enquiry that would be 'unconditioned'. Both claims to transcend squabbles about value are, inevitably, value-laden themselves: they affirm a notion of autonomy as the realisation of an essence – i.e. as in the claim that only study of literature as literature will let us see it as it really is, and not distorted by some sort of instrumentalising programme. There is a complicity between aesthetic purism and notions of scientific objectivity. Both can be understood as consequences of the ideal of autonomy inherent in a Kantian idea of the university, as this is reinforced by the culture of professionalisation. Their institutional basis lies in the pressures of such a university towards disciplinarity. The discipline is held to be maintained as an untrammelled disinterested enquiry in which reason gives itself its own law, undictated by the state or distorted by personal motives. Yet such ideals also subserve professional specialisation and tend, at worst, to the kind of irresponsible formalism of which Russian formalism and New Criticism are now often accused.

(2) The second historically decisive idea of the university, distinct in idea if not in practice from the Kantian model, is that which Readings nicknames the 'University of Culture'. The reference here is to Wilhelm von Humboldt's University of Berlin, established in 1810, and to the documents by Schiller, von Humboldt, Schleiermacher, Fichte, and Schelling, that fed into the project.[7] In 1789 Schiller had affirmed an ideal of the university as providing a midpoint [*Mittelpunkt*] from which the unity of all the disciplines can be grasped.[8] The program for the University of Berlin is remembered now, if at all, for making teaching and research inseparable (though, at this time this was in part a cost-cutting measure – why pay two different sets of people to do these two things?). More philosophically, knowledge is held to be not a static body of information but an organic process. The organic, process-like nature of learning demands that the teacher be engaged in research, and the student earns a place in the system by personally working through the stages of the knowledge in a discipline. Schiller and the others stress more than did Kant the ideal of culture – of *Bildung* – as the defining purpose of the university. *Bildung* names the intellectual process whereby tradition and the life of the people are infused with the spirit of rational enquiry and grounded in an understanding of the unity of all knowledge. As a synthesis of custom and reason, the ideal of *Bildung* is partly a reaction against a radical, abstract and Jacobin rationalism, associated with the French wars and conquest. 'Culture', then, and often since, named a reformist notion of the gradual development of customs and forms of consciousness, the reconciliation of reason and history. The institution is simultaneously the embodiment of culture (*Bildung*) as an archive or repository and the agent of *Bildung* as the process of individual and communal self-development and clarification.

These German ideas of culture are familiar to anyone who has studied the history of criticism. For a very long time the dominant claim to legitimacy of literary study was parallel to a traditional claim made for the institution as whole. This was the notion of literature as the site for a liberal education, specialised but not specialist, academic but not narrowly technical, addressed not just to the intellect but to general cultural skills. Such an ideal is analogous to the traditional 'idea of a university' as the central institution of cultural legislation. In Cardinal Newman's lectures on the idea of the university, a liberal education, being addressed to 'the whole person', is simultaneously a process of self-edification and self-empowerment.[9] It is held to open and refine the mind in ways that enables self-command, self-understanding, and self-esteem.

The idea that literature can be the centre of a scheme of liberal education was a tempered and watered down English translation of the German ideals of *Wissenschaft* and *Bildung*, filleted of anything so difficult as transcendental philosophy, except in the heavily disguised and simplified form of the notion of the 'the imagination'. Literature was offered as a unique form of knowledge not as an object of it, as a defence of the imagination in a world dominated by utilitarianism and political economy, its antagonist being not religion (the implicit antagonist of *Wissenschaft* in the German scheme), but a caricatured view of science as a monstrous calculating machine, murdering to dissect.

For most of the twentieth century literary studies bore the marks of its institutionalisation as part of the nineteenth-century struggle for dominance between two factions of the bourgeoisie – the managerial/technical/utilitarian, and the liberal/humanist. The concept of literature as imaginative writing, a site of humane values and of the creative as a self-evident good, was forged in this struggle. This model of literary education has endured for so long, I think, partly because it met exactly Cardinal Newman's translation of the German *Bildung* into the notion of liberal education. In this sense the legitimacy of English was not that it formed a subset of the research project of the university as a whole, but either constituted its animating centre (as in F. R. Leavis's proposal for an English school) or offered an alternative to it in the form of a non-specialised form of liberal education addressed to the person 'as a whole', rather than as a technician or mere specialist.[10] It was a discipline but also saw itself as supra-disciplinary, a cohesive and redemptively unifying rather than a merely factional form of knowledge. Literary criticism could thus legitimate itself as a discipline opposed both to the dominant values of 'technological-Benthamite civilization' (Leavis) and to the increasing reification and specialisation of the modern university, the decline of ideals of *Bildung* into Clark Kerr's joke 'polyversity' of disparate entrepreneurial faculty heads, united solely by a shared grievance about parking. In this respect, in a muted way, literature took on the role of a unifying principle of *Wissenschaft* and *Bildung*.

We have been then through two ways in which conceptions of the university as a whole have determined the object 'literature'. (1) The ideal of the autonomy of rational enquiry, which in practice becomes the ideal of the autonomy of the discipline, manifests itself in the purist and usually formalist drive to isolate 'literature as literature', or, in the approach still dominant at Oxford, to ignore the question of the distinct nature of the literary altogether and to treat texts as the object of empirical, historical research. (2) The general idea of the university as a site of cultural legislation served to underwrite a vague and expressly anti-theoretical notion of English as a kind of 'meta-subject', centre of a process of liberal education. A great many of the controversies in criticism throughout the twentieth century might be characterised as the oscillation between these two forms of claims to legitimation. New Criticism, for instance, drew on both of them, which may be one reason for its relative durability. In both claims to legitimacy institutional values seem to determine what is taken as literary force.

Such claims to legitimacy have long since collapsed. What is attractive about Young's and Readings's approach to the so-called crisis in English studies is that they see it as to a large a extent a function of a crisis in the concept of the university as a whole. Hence it is that many workers in literary studies now justify their work by seeing it as anti-institutional in some way. Such a stance may embrace people of otherwise opposed views, whether they be intellectuals who see themselves as fighting for the representation in the academy of previously excluded or marginalised groups, or self-proclaimed traditionalists who lament the loss of a once-respected institution to a lot of 'tenured radicals'. The broader cause, then, of many of the issues and disputes in the humanities is not even an academic matter. It is that the idea of the university has collapsed, and the humanities have lost their institutional mission to the ethos of professionalism and the meaningless pursuit of 'excellence', a vacuous term that has become so ubiquitous in university documents that it effectively functions as the modern 'idea of the university'. Arguments, whether on the 'left' or the 'right', that the other side has an unjust hold on the institutions of culture, each presenting itself shrilly as marginalised by the other, mask the deeper issue that the centres of power in contention no longer really function as privileged sites of national cultural self-definition. Young writes:

> Whereas formerly those in the institution could paradoxically claim to see the outside from a privileged point of exteriority more or less unavailable to those who really were outside, the situation has now been reversed. If today's culture is marked by an institutional anxiety about the institution's outside, its effect is to position the latter in the place of knowledge. The history of the institution is made up of these two transcendent impulses: the speculative moment in which the institution itself forms the point of exteri-

ority through which it can comprehend and account for the world [the German idea of the university], and the empiricist counter-movement in which the institution's removal from the world is reversed so that it is posited as an inside which neglects the outside world, which now becomes the point of exteriority.[11]

Young already implies here the third idea of the modern university in Readings's scheme, the modern 'University of Excellence' – an institution that seems geared to no higher idea than its own maximised self-perpetuation according to optimal input/output ratios.

Since English was set up as a result of the struggle for hegemony between two factions of the bourgeoisie during and since the industrial revolution, contemporary debates about literature should not ultimately be seen as a struggle *within the boundaries* of English: they are a contestation of those boundaries and of the terms in which the whole area of intellectual activity was institutionalised. Ultimately, they cannot but be about other parts of the university and the university as a whole.

When traditional critics found themselves having to defend their practice against the neo-utilitarianism of governments since 1979, they had the whole weight of the nineteenth-century defences of the imagination against utilitarianism and political economy behind them. For others the situation was – and is – not so simple. Robert Young writes of the bizarre position in which defenders of literary theory found themselves within their institutions:

> The difficulty for literary theorists, when faced with a new 'technologico-Thatcherite' assault on the humanities, was that the terms by which their subject was established historically, and the only effective ones in which it could still be defended, were those of ... cultural conservatism and humanist belief in literature and philosophy ... When theorists found themselves wanting to protect their discipline against successive government cuts ... they discovered that the only view with which they could defend themselves was the very one which, in intellectual terms, they wanted to attack. You might say that the problem was that the oppositional literary or theoretical mode was not the oppositional institutional one ...[12]

Is then, the notion of literature to be deemed 'past its sell-by date', as many workers in cultural studies would have it? I will devote the second part of this paper to a defence of literature in the university that does not subsume literary force into institutional values, but which offers a far more fluid and uncomfortable account of why literary study can be said to matter in a corporate university whose main terms of legitimation become self-perpetuation at minimum cost.

Literary force

Let me first outline – schematising with all the dangers which that entails – what I understand by the phrase 'literary force'. The relation of literary force and institutional value cannot be one of opposition, but is rather a complicated mutual implication. Part of the force of literature, however, is to be transgressive of institutional boundaries and values. Literary studies is, in its very constitution, a field whose object embraces issues that immediately transcend the competence of any one discipline: like the paradoxical topology of a greater space contained in a smaller. This is not just to say that defining the 'literary' involves interdisciplinary and cross-disciplinary forms of competence, but that the would-be discipline of English cannot define itself (or its object) without consideration of the way its legitimacy as a field is bound up with that of the university as a whole and the very possibility of disciplinarity. In short literary studies has provided and continues to provide an unstable and invaluable place of intersection and contestation between various other disciplines, and spaces outside the academy.

(1) *An aporetic relation between the singular and the universal.* In a late chapter of his *Legislations: The Politics of Deconstruction*, Geoffrey Bennington considers the nature of an 'index'.[13] What is an index, and what sort of considerations are involved in the compiling of one? Bennington refers to the traditional distinction between an *'index nominorum'* and an *'index rerum'* (index of names and index of things). Compiling an index of names is not a particular problem: one could nowadays do it by using the 'find' command on a word-processing program. The problems of self-reference which Bennington considers (of how an author refers to his or her self or work in the text and then index) are not my concern here. This is the peculiar and thought-provoking issues thrown up in trying to compile an *'index rerum'*. An *'index rerum'* is not a concordance. One cannot simply list every word. There are difficult principles of selection:

> Compiling an *index rerum* involves weighty philosophical decisions. It suggests as a basic principle that the compiler is able to distinguish between a purely verbal occurrence of a word, and a thematically or conceptually significant occurrence. It also assumes that the compiler is able to recognize the presence of a concept or theme in the absence of its name. The compiler of the index for the English translation of [Derrida's] *La Vérité en peinture* soon realized that something about that book made it virtually impossible to compile a satisfactory *index rerum*, and wondered why.[14]

The difficulty is that of distinguishing the 'conceptual' from the 'merely verbal', i.e. discerning a concept (which need not coincide necessarily with one specific word or term) as something with a clear organisational role in an account of some overall argument enacted by the text. In a literary text, or a text which deploys literary effects such as Derrida's *La Vérité en peinture*, distinctions of the conceptual and the merely verbal, the significant or insignificant occurrence of a sign, the implicit or explicit work of a concept etc., are all very problematic. It is no accident that while literary texts may have a concordance, usually as a separate publication, they almost never have an index. Imagine trying to compile an index to the first act of *Hamlet*! How could one – for example – talk about 'the poetry as opposed to the ideas' when what is specific is a certain generative undecidability between them.

Such undecidability, I suggest, is one gauge of a text's force. One might say that literary language is not characterised by polysemy, but rather that it puts to work an undecidability about the status of its language which both compels and resists interpretation. One can't talk here about studying 'literature as literature' or distinguishing 'the poetry' from 'the ideas' because it is precisely the impossibility of doing so that is, paradoxically, the distinctive trait of the literary.

It is by skewing the distinctions of the verbal and the conceptual in generative ways that literary language marks an aporetic relation between the singular and the universal. That is to say, any particular mark or sign (say the term 'visage' in *Hamlet* (I, i: 81; II, ii: 554; III, i: 46; III, iii: 47; III, iv: 50)) is the place of a certain undecidability as to whether its occurrence is to be taken under some more general conceptual framework, subserves several distinct concepts, or is relatively insignificant (e.g. that the word 'visage' could be replaced by 'face', or omitted, without significant loss). Literary language has, so to speak, the topology of a greater space contained within a smaller – to repeat the phrase I used earlier to describe the relation of literary studies to the university in general. No procedural rule can be formulated as to how to read it.

(2) *A historicality which is 'to come'*. Because the literary puts to work an aporetic relation between the singular and the universal, its force of undecidability always exceeds whatever may be conceptualised in any one reading or in any one context. This applies even to historicist readings which aim to reconstruct, as fully as possible, the text's original context and hence, supposedly, original 'meaning' or force. Yet, as readers of Derrida know well, such a project is fraught with difficulty. Its conditions of possibility, one says, are also its conditions of impossibility. The fact that *Hamlet* is still legible, with definite semantic effects, long after its inscription, tells us that the historicality of a text is also its ability to function in ways that could never have been programmed or foretold at its composition. The project of delimiting a context is also problematic: when, for example, did the French Revolution end? Is it yet only a thing of the past? Peggy

Kamuf writes:

> A literary work has a historical context, as we call it, but no more or less than
> any document or artifact produced in the past; but the work, if it is still read
> and studied when this 'context' will have subsided into archival compost, has
> a relation as well to a future, by which it remains always to some extent
> incomprehensible by any given present. This is the dimension of the work's
> *historicality*, which is therefore not to be simply confused or conflated with
> historical 'context' ... What we still call literature (but perhaps for not much
> longer) would be one means of this withheld stability of meaning, or to put it
> differently, it would be the *reserve* of every present, instituted meaning and
> thus the possibility of its transformation, that is, the possibility of a future ...
> Despite the fact, therefore, that academic study has largely misrecognized
> this dimension of a, by definition, unknowable future 'literature', the latter
> will nevertheless have been working to transform its own institution.[15]

I will return to Kamuf's last point later.

(3) *Defamiliarisation/fictionalisation*. A literary text not only makes
statements, describes or expresses, it is also always readable as language
that presents or even dramatises itself as so stating, describing or expressing. This putting into inverted commas is always possible. Affirming this
possibility is a familiar strategy of reading. For instance Shakespeare's
Henry V can be read, not as the celebration of an ideal monarch and military leader it appears to be, but as an ironising presentation of such a figure and the kinds of language associated with him, bringing out the way
he constructs or presents himself. Many of Blake's *Songs of Innocence*,
with their childish speakers, can be read 'straight' as expressions of a sentimental Christianity, or as ironic stagings of such views. Exactly the same
sequence of words can be subjected, in effect, to opposite interpretations.
Literature must elude its institution as a bastion of edifying values, for it
can turn their seeming solidity and self-evidence about with an alarming
facility.

(4) *Singular institutionality*. Literary force is a force of instituting, which
is why the relation of literature to institutions is not a simple one. A literary text is a performative singular event that, to the degree that is singular
and sets to work the generative undecidability already described, institutes the rules of its own intelligibility and interpretation. Such a text must
posit certain instituted procedures and codes, it is inventive. Literature is
itself, a 'strange institution', to use Derrida's phrase. He writes:

> [I]t is an institution which consists in transgressing and transforming, thus
> in producing its constitutional law; or to put it better, in producing discur-
> sive forms, 'works' and 'events' in which the very possibility of a fundamen-
> tal constitution is at least 'fictionally' contested, threatened, deconstructed,
> presented in its very precariousness. Hence, while literature shares a cer-

tain power and a certain destiny with 'jurisdiction', with the juridico-political production of institutional foundations, the constitutions of States, fundamental legislation, and even the theological-juridical performatives which occur at the origin of the law, at a certain point it can also exceed them, interrogate them, 'fictionalize' them: with nothing, or almost nothing, in view, of course, and by producing events whose 'reality' or duration is never assured, but which by that very fact are more thought-provoking, if that still means something.[16]

Let me try to put that in terms closer to questions of practice in the university. In institutional terms, the aporetic relation between singularity and generality may mean that it is also undecidable which modes of competence and expertise are applicable to the text. The force of the literary is not inter-disciplinary (if that is understood to imply a space of intersection between constituted fields and competencies), it is *cross-disciplinary* in difficult and undecidable ways. It is easy to agree that *Ulysses* (to return to my opening example) concerns such classical concepts as justice, filiality, nationality. It is far more difficult to state as an argument the precise inflection or revision which the text brings to such things without immediately mistranslating and betraying the force of the text: this is precisely a singular and resistant contamination, generative of the very interpretations it also resists, between the conceptual and general and the idiomatic. It is incontestable that, for instance, one can learn more about nineteenth-century London from the non-realist texts of Dickens, than one can from many straightforwardly constative historical works, or more about Augustan Rome from the *Aeneid* than from a Roman historian, but not perhaps in ways that admit of being institutionalised into a teachable series of statements or propositions.

Literary texts then, may bear a certain *coup de force* in relation to institutionality. They cannot merely be read 'as literature' precisely to the degree that they institute ways of reading and, to that extent, must perform their own reader. For the same reason they cannot simply be parsed for their content or, if you prefer, translated into fully conceptual or philosophical terms. We are thrown into a cross-disciplinary space in which the modes of competence required are multiple and uncertain.

Literary force/institutional values: this is not then an opposition between some affirmed force of the literary and its dubious appropriation in institutions of education, for purposes of acculturation or whatever. That one cannot simply oppose literary force and institutional value is evident in the fact that the most exciting and liberating movements in criticism in the twentieth century have been largely academic. In the institution of formalist and historicist forms of criticism, and their subsequent contestation, one sees the extent to which the history of criticism plays out the inherently unstable economy of relation between institutional value and literary force. Cross-disciplinarity crosses, defines, and constitutes the object 'literature' in such a way that any discipline of literary study cannot but be in a state of continual crisis as to its relations to other disciplines, to the university as a whole, and to the question of criticism's relation to the university's outside.

Such cross-disciplinarity has always functioned in literary study, whether openly or covertly, and has been one reason for its vitality or, if you prefer, its continuing crisis. I have tried to outline, albeit imperfectly, a defence of literary study against the compartmentalising and neutralising professionalism of the 'University of Excellence'. The issues involved in any consideration of this question are so broad, various and incalculable that this has not been an academic paper in a familiar way. It is not a closely defined discussion of issues in which the terms of discussion and the areas of expertise are clearly defined. In saying this, I'm not only making the usual personal apology for incompleteness or lack of expertise. My method here is a calculatedly anti-professional one: my aim has been to trace the exigency by which, time and again, major issues within my supposed field of expertise – English – transgress the boundaries of the very area in which I, for example, feel most comfortable. I suggest that this kind of responsible anti-professionalist procedure is one way in which thinkers can engage in a broadly deconstructive analysis that has immediate institutional, professional implications, and resists the foreclosure of issues in relation to questions of the university as a whole that attends professional specialisation. In effect, one pushes the kind of competence nurtured in a particular discipline to a point of incapacity that calls out for discussion and negotiation from colleagues in other disciplines and from outside the academy. It may do so in ways that necessarily concern the nature of the interrelation of disciplines and the mission or missions of the university as a whole. This last would then become an open point of debate instead of an imposed managerial programme.

Notes

1 See R. Young, *Torn Halves: Political Conflict in Literary and Cultural Theory* (Manchester, 1996), and B. Readings, *The University in Ruins* (Cambridge, Mass., 1996).
2 See F. Court, *Institutionalizing English Literature: The Culture and Politics of Literary Study, 1750–1900* (Stanford, 1992); B. Doyle, *English and Englishness* (London, 1989).
3 P. Kamuf, *The Division of Literature: Or the University in Deconstruction* (Chicago, 1997), pp. 95–6.
4 E. Kant, *The Conflict of the Faculties*, trans. M. Gregor (Lincoln, Nebr., 1992).
5 S. Weber, *Institution and Interpretation* (Minneapolis, 1987), p. 30.

6 *Ibid.*, p. 32.

7 Useful general accounts can be found in E. Shaffer, 'Romantic philosophy and the organisation of the disciplines: the founding of the Humboldt University of Berlin', in A. Cunningham and N. Jardine (eds), *Romanticism and the Sciences* (Cambridge, 1990), pp. 38–54; T. Ziolokowksi, *German Romanticism and its Institutions* (Princeton, 1990), pp. 218–308. The founding documents for the University of Berlin are gathered in W. Weischedel (ed.), *Idee und Wirklichkeit einer Universität: Dokumente zur Geschichte der Friedrich-Wilhelms-Universität zu Berlin* (Berlin, 1960). For an abridged English translation of von Humboldt's proposal, see 'On the spirit and the organisational framework of intellectual institutions in Berlin', *Minerva* 8 (1970), 242–50.

8 F. Schiller, 'Was heisst und zu welchem Ende studiert Man Universalgesichte', in *Sämtliche Werke* (Munich, 1980), vol. 4, pp. 749–67.

9 J. Newman, *The Idea of a University* (Oxford, 1976).

10 See F. R. Leavis, *Education and the University: A Sketch for an 'English School'* (London, 1943).

11 Young, *Torn Halves*, p. 17.

12 *Ibid.*, p. 205.

13 G. Bennington, *Legislations: The Politics of Deconstruction* (London, 1994), pp. 274–95.

14 *Ibid.*, pp. 277–8.

15 Kamuf, *The Division of Literature*, p. 164.

16 J. Derrida, 'This strange institution called literature', trans. G. Bennington and R. Bowlby, in D. Attridge (ed.), *Acts of Literature* (London, 1992), p. 72.

marianne dekoven

THE LITERARY AS ACTIVITY
IN POSTMODERNITY

As John Guillory notes in *Cultural Capital*, 'the several recent crises of the literary canon – its "opening" to philosophical works, to works by minorities, and now to popular and mass cultural works – amounts to a terminal crisis, more than sufficient evidence of the urgent need to reconceptualize the object of literary study'.[1] I take 'reconceptualize' to imply a broadening of the category of the literary as a result of the 'opening' Guillory notes, not its elimination as a meaningful and important term. In this reconceptualisation, 'the literary' would designate not just certain kinds of texts, but also a certain kind of practice in the current social, cultural, political conjuncture: specifically, literary writing as activity.[2]

Current critical discussions generally do not address the question of the literary as practice, as activity. The literary is generally understood as pertaining to objects of consumption and analysis; the valorisation of the literary is seen primarily as a tool of conservative, elitist cultural hegemony, for which literature is the gatekeeper in civilisation's self-defence against barbarism.[3] In place of literary writing, contemporary critical discourses, informed by cultural studies, generally take as their object a broadened, undifferentiated category of text, narrative, or cultural production.[4]

Literary writing as an activity, however, is enjoying great popularity among precisely the nonhegemonic constituencies empowered by the opening of the canon attendant on more general democratisation. Widely acclaimed and successful writers from within those constituencies rely heavily on the literary in their appropriations of cultural capital.[5] Toni Morrison's Nobel Prize for Literature is the most noteworthy recent instance of this phenomenon.[6]

Attacks on the literary frequently depend on a conflation of the literary itself with the dehistoricised, utterly decontextualised literary object of

New Critical reification: what I have described elsewhere, in arguing for the legitimacy of political readings of modernism as critique of twentieth-century culture, as 'the altar of linguistic and intellectual complexity'.[7] It is precisely a *re*-historicised view of the cultural significances of the literary that I am arguing for here. Understanding literature as fully historically contingent – emerging in its general modern form in the Enlightenment and through Romanticism – is not incompatible with understanding the literary as a distinct contemporary discourse which needs to be differentiated from other modes of textuality, narrative, or cultural production. The modern literary did not congeal either at its late eighteenth-century moment of emergence as a bourgeois formation or within its New Critical apotheosis, but has continued to evolve, through the later nineteenth century, modernism, and into postmodernism. The fact that a formation is historically contingent (which of course all social-cultural formations are) does not vitiate its capacity for transformative cultural and political uses, even when a denial of its own historicity has become encoded within some of its self-articulations. The claims for oppositionality made on behalf of the literary by many of its practitioners, by a range of modernist and post-structuralist theorists, and even by the New Critics, may have relevance despite the dehistoricisation and conservative appropriations of 'literature' upon which those claims are often founded.[8]

Complementary or compatible versions of the literary as activity have been developed by a number of contemporary literary writers and post-structuralist theorists. Roland Barthes, in 'Kafka's answer', and other pieces collected in *Critical Essays*, discusses the difference of the literary, of literary signification *as* difference:[9]

> [T]he world [in literature] is a place endlessly open to signification but endlessly dissatisfied by it … literature is no more than an interrogation of the world … it is because signs are uncertain that there is a literature. Kafka's technique says that the world's meaning is unutterable, that the artist's only task is to explore possible significations … [Hence] the essentially interrogative function of literature … it is because the world is not finished that literature is possible.[10]

While these meditations connect clearly to Barthes's allegiance to avant-garde or modernist literary praxis – the literature of multiplicity and indeterminacy (see, for example, *S/Z, The Pleasure of the Text, 'From work to text'*), I would argue they also point toward a more general sense of the literary in the twentieth century as a locus of the *activity* of unanswering interrogation: Barthes's emphasis falls more heavily on acts of writing than on acts of reading. The 'writerly' text Barthes defines in *S/Z* is precisely the text that converts reading, which Barthes dismisses in relation to the 'readerly' text as the passive consumption of bourgeois hegemony, into, or allows it to participate in, the activity of writing.[11]

Writing as activity requires no technology, and very little capital (despite the proliferation of personal computers, they are not *necessary* to writing) yet it still commands a significant amount of cultural capital. One of the best articulations I know of the progressive political significance of literary writing in contemporary America appears in Grace Paley's story 'The expensive moment', in her third collection, *Later the Same Day*, a story about 'cultural exchange' between America and China:

> But the evening belonged to the Chinese artists and writers ... All sorts of American cultural workers were invited. Some laughed to hear themselves described in this way. They were accustomed to being called 'dreamer poet realist postmodernist'. They might have liked being called 'cultural dreamer,' but no one had thought of that yet.[12]

Our literary writers, Paley implies, are inadequately named by both literary critics and leftist cultural analysts; we need a new name that acknowledges the particular kind of progressive political work done by literary writing, and by aesthetic practice in general.

In 'Aesthetics and cultural studies', Ian Hunter makes an important argument, compatible with Barthes and in the spirit of Paley, that the aesthetic, and particularly the literary, has emerged in modern Western culture as a 'practice of the self'.[13] Hunter's argument, like Barthes's notion of the 'writerly text', extends the interrogative function of the literary from the activity of the writer to the activity of the reader practising 'aesthetic criticism'. He differentiates aesthetic criticism from 'philology', considering the latter a form of knowledge and the former an act of self-interrogation and self-construction:

> Philology is a knowledge not because it is somehow infallibly in touch with literary facts but simply because it employs techniques of description, evidential accumulation, and confirmation that brings [sic] its objects into the sphere of the true and the false. In short, it deploys what Foucault calls 'techniques of veridiction' and constitutes a particular 'regime of truth'. Aesthetic criticism on the other hand does not employ such techniques, except incidentally, and forms a different kind of domain ... [Aesthetic criticism is] a practice of self-problematization and self-modification in which literature functions as a device – an object for a practice of contemplation targeted on the self ... It is not that literature is open-ended but that we open its ends, subjecting it to permanent aesthetic surgery as a means of operating on ourselves.[14]

Hunter's argument concerning aesthetic reading applies even more powerfully to literary writing. Writing literature has been viewed loosely throughout modernity as a practice of the self (even if negatively – the era-sure of the self – as in some modernism), and this view has never been more apt than it is now, in light of widespread contemporary practices of autobiographical and poetic writing: poetry, particularly poetry written in the lyrical voice of the 'I', remains the traditional literary genre most closely linked to notions of direct expression of acts of subjective self-con-struction, or 'practices of the self'.[15]

Some of the most extensive and profoundly suggestive poststructural-ist meditations on the literary have been undertaken by Derrida, and my argument here, particularly in its emphasis on literature as activity, has been most materially influenced by Derek Attridge's anthology of Der-rida's work on the literary, *Acts of Literature*.[16] It would be impossible to summarise Derrida's work within an essay such as this; it seems to me most useful to quote one characteristic, suggestive, but by no means defin-itive moment of discussion from Attridge's interview with Derrida, enti-tled 'This strange institution called literature', as a way of gesturing toward some of the dimensions of Derrida's articulations of the literary most rele-vant to my concerns here:

> [L]iterature seemed to me [in youth] ... to be the institution which allows one to *say everything*, [Translator's Note: *Tout dire*, both to 'say everything', with a sense of exhausting a totality, and to 'say anything', i.e., to speak with-out constraints on what one may say.] in *every way*. The space of literature is not only that of an instituted *fiction* but also a *fictive institution* which in principle allows one to say everything ... It is an institution which tends to overflow the institution ...
>
> The institution of literature in the West, in its relatively modern form, is linked to an authorization to say everything, and doubtless too to the coming about of the modern idea of democracy. Not that it depends on a democracy in place, but it seems inseparable to me from what calls forth a democracy, in the most open (and doubtless itself to come) sense of democracy.[17]

'The institution of literature in the West': as Attridge explains in his intro-duction, '[w]hat Derrida emphasises is that literature is an *institution*'.[18] Derrida is always at pains to stress the historically contingent status of the literary. As Attridge argues:

> [Literature] is not given in nature or the brain but brought into being by processes that are social, legal, and political, and that can be mapped his-torically and geographically ... It is worth stressing this point, lest the atten-tion which Derrida gives to literature seem to indicate a perpetual, ahistorical, privileging. That a body of texts called 'literary' can, at a certain historical conjuncture, serve strategic purposes is not the result of any tran-scendent properties these texts possess, any permanent access to truth. Rather, it is an opportunity that can be seized ...[19]

Contemporary writers from nonhegemonic groups have seized the opportunity afforded by this anti-institutional institution of the literary, this practice of the self and unanswered interrogation of the world; they have used this 'authorization to say everything' in literary acts that 'call forth a democracy in the most open (and doubtless itself to come) sense of democracy'. This deployment of the literary as practice is evident in auto-biographical writing by women across a wide spectrum of racial, ethnic, class, and sexual positionalities. The upgrading of autobiography, a previously marginalised genre, into literary legitimacy is itself a more general form of this nonhegemonic appropriation of the literary. Writing of a literary kind is also at the centre of a number of highly influential feminist agendas, of which *écriture feminine* as a general phenomenon is one of the most notable. Hélène Cixous's 'Sorties', an exemplary manifesto of *écriture feminine*, invokes for writing this sort of empowerment of the disempowered:

> I will say: today, writing is woman's. That is not a provocation, it means that woman admits there is an other ...Writing is the passageway, the entrance, the exit, the dwelling place of the other in me – the other that I am and am not ... a feminine one, a masculine one, some? – several, some unknown, which is indeed what gives me the desire to know and from which all life soars ...
>
> Writing is working; being worked; questioning (in) the between (letting oneself be questioned) of same *and of* other ... not knowing one another and beginning again only from what is most distant, from self, from other, from the other within.[20]

For Cixous, writing is the empowerment of a self-alienated subjectivity, the means by which s/he can forge, represent, enact a 'passageway' between the self and the other within the self.[21] I would argue that the literary is such an important arena of empowerment for nonhegemonic subjectivities now precisely because of the way in which it enables the objectified, self-alienated, instrumentalised, reified subject to assume agency in relation to her/his own objectification (self-alienation, instrumentalisation, reification). Alice Walker uses the title of Rebecca Cox Jackson's *Gifts of Power* to discuss Jackson's life and work as a paradigm for 'naming our own experience after our own fashion (as well as rejecting whatever does not seem to suit)'.[22] As Donna Haraway says in her 'Manifesto for cyborgs', perhaps the most frequently quoted and widely anthologised work of leftist American postmodern feminist theory:

> Writing has a special significance for all colonized groups ... Contests for the meanings of writing are a major form of contemporary political struggle. Releasing the play of writing is deadly serious. The poetry and stories of U.S.

women of color are repeatedly about writing, about access to the power to signify ... on the basis of seizing the tools to mark the world that marked them as other.[23]

One of these 'women of color', poet Gloria Anzaldúa, theorises this tool-seizing and world-marking clearly and powerfully in her 'Speaking in tongues: a letter to third world women writers', in language very similar to that of Hélène Cixous. I will quote her at length:

Why am I compelled to write? Because the writing saves me from this complacency I fear. Because I have no choice. Because I must keep the spirit of my revolt and myself alive. Because the world I create in the writing compensates for what the real world does not give me. By writing I put order in the world, give it a handle so I can grasp it. I write because life does not appease my appetites and hunger. I write to record what others erase when I speak, to rewrite the stories others have miswritten about me, about you. To become more intimate with myself and you. To discover myself, to preserve myself, to make myself, to achieve self-autonomy ... The act of writing is the act of making soul, alchemy. It is the quest for the self, for the center of the self, which we women of color have come to think as 'other' – the dark, the feminine. Didn't we start writing to reconcile this other within us? We knew we were different, set apart, exiled from what is considered 'normal', white-right. And as we internalized this exile, we came to see the alien within us and too often, as a result, we split apart from ourselves and each other ... The writing is a tool for piercing that mystery but it also shields us, gives a margin of distance, helps us survive.[24]

A number of successful, widely-read, cultural-capital-rich contemporary American literary texts by nonhegemonic writers, generally the texts onto which I have cathected most deeply, are organised around parables of this self-empowerment.[25] The greatest and clearest is Toni Morrison's *Beloved*, in which the reified, objectified, instrumentalised subjectivity of the African-American slave is retrieved and rewritten, if not redeemed or transcended, by and for an active storytelling and naming subjective agency.

How did the literary become a practice of the self in postmodernity? This shift in the historical trajectory of the literary can be traced to the general extension of democratisation in the 1960s, as called for by Derrida; a development coincident with the emergence of postmodernity. 1960s texts in general were characterised by a simultaneity of dominant modern with emergent postmodern paradigms.[26] William Burroughs's works of the 1960s provide an excellent case study of this simultaneity, and reveal at the same time the emergence of the literary as activity in postmodernity.[27]

Burroughs develops a number of formal techniques associated with the historical avant-gardes of modernity, and works within the legacy of high modernism as well, particularly influenced by Eliot and the Symbolists – he lists *The Waste Land*, Tzara, and the 'Camera eye' sequences in Dos Passos's *USA* as his crucial formal antecedents.[28] His word juxtapositions, evident in the titles of his major 1960s tetralogy (*Naked Lunch, The Soft Machine, The Ticket That Exploded, Nova Express*), hark back to Gertrude Stein, one of his primary influences.[29] At the same time he writes, as do fully postmodern writers, from within particular, situated subcultures (gay and drug subcultures, in his case) without universalising them. Also, like postmodernists and unlike modernists, Burroughs deploys elements of various kinds of genre fiction without assimilating or transforming them to a unique, high-literary voice or style. Most important for my argument here, it is on the pivot of Burroughs's 1960s democratising egalitarianism that modernist utopian transformation – the revolution of the word – becomes postmodern empowerment of the 'minoritarian and ex-centric', in Linda Hutcheon's terms, through the literary as practice.

William Burroughs's 'novels' of the 1960s are at once modernist/avant-garde and also thoroughly implicated in such popular genres as science fiction, hard-boiled detective fiction, pornography, horror, and superhero comic.[30] Unlike high modernist/avant-garde works by Conrad, Joyce, Eliot, or Stein, which draw on popular modes but absorb, transform, sublate them within a self-consciously unique or individual, transformatively innovative style, Burroughs leaves the popular genre material more or less intact, only exaggerating it through parody and skewing it toward his own obsessions. This opportunistic deployment of popular modes within the literary is characteristic of postmodern writing.[31] For Andreas Huyssen, it is precisely the breakdown of the modernist 'divide' between 'high' and 'low' cultures, and the pastiche incorporation of the popular, that defines postmodernism.

Burroughs's quasi-satirical, apocalyptic gay pornographic sequences, especially those involving hanging, for example 'A. J.'s annual party' in *Naked Lunch*, are well known. (Burroughs has claimed that these sequences constitute an argument against capital punishment.) The tetralogy is full of science fiction/horror film figures, from junkies who morph into blob-like protoplasm to absorb heroin, to 'Uranian Willy', 'The Heavy Metal Kid', the evil 'Divisionists', 'Liquefactionists', and the criminal 'Nova Mob' itself. Many of his characters are satiric versions of superheros of the comics, especially Inspector J. Lee of the Nova Police, Burroughs's primary narrative persona. Burroughs's tone often simultaneously reproduces and mocks that of the hard-boiled narrator, as is evident in the opening of *Naked Lunch*:

> I can feel the heat closing in, feel them out there making their moves, set-
> ting up their devil doll stool pigeons, crooning over my spoon and dropper
> I throw away at Washington Square Station, vault a turnstile and two flights
> down the iron stairs, catch an uptown A train ... And right on time this nar-
> cotics dick in a white trench coat ... hit the platform.[32]

At the same time, Burroughs's work in many ways looks stylistically no
different from a high modernist/avant-garde text, making allowances for
the sci-fi, hard-boiled, porn, comics-inflected content. In a television news
obituary for Burroughs on the day of his death, *Naked Lunch* was
described as a 'stream-of-consciousness novel', thereby marking it with a
prime code or metonym for experimentalist high modernism. Here is a
sequence from *Nova Express* that is characteristically avant-garde/experi-
mental:

> Could give no other information than wind walking in a rubbish heap to the
> sky – Solid shadow turned off the white film of noon heat – Exploded deep
> in the alley tortured metal Oz – Look anywhere, Dead hand – Phosphores-
> cent bones – Cold Spring afterbirth of that hospital – Twinges of amputation
> – Bread knife in the heart paid taxi boys – If I knew I'd be glad to look any-
> place – No good myself – Clom Fliday – Diseased wind identity fading out
> – Smoke is all – We intersect in the dark mutinous door – Hairless skull –
> Flesh smeared – Five times of dust we made it all – consumed by slow metal
> fires ... [33]

Burroughs's obsessions are evident here, particularly in the pervasive
presence of certain forms of gay sex ('paid taxi boys' and 'five times of dust
we made it all', which is a transformation of 'made it five times', a recurring description of a sexual encounter), sci-fi-tinged apocalypse, and idiosyncratic lore of the drug subculture ('Clom Fliday', a recurrent motif
throughout the tetralogy, refers to a sequence in *Naked Lunch* where
the narrator explains that '[i]n 1920s a lot of Chinese pushers around
found The West so unreliable, dishonest and wrong, they all packed in, so
when an Occidental junky came to score, they say: "No glot ... C'lom
Fliday ..."').[34]

Despite the presence of this subcultural material, more characteristic
of the postmodern than the modern, this passage, in its formal structure, is
representative of Burroughs's positioning within the modernist/avant-
garde/experimentalist tradition. It is constructed of loosely, associatively
linked fragments comprising poetically suggestive verbal juxtapositions,
in a characteristic modernist experimental manner. These links and juxtapositions are constructed by means of a technique Burroughs calls 'cut-up
and fold-in', which in itself stands as a marker of the simultaneity of the
modern and the postmodern in 1960s texts. Fold-in harks back to Steinian

experimental writing and the modernist cult of the Barthesian 'writerly'. At the same time, cut-up/fold-in looks forward to the democratising, deau-thorising imperatives of postmodernity.

Cut-up/fold-in aims for a modernist authenticity that Burroughs unashamedly calls the 'Truth': '[n]o one can conceal what is saying cut-up ... [sic] You can cut the Truth out of any written or spoken words//'.[35] Yet at the same time, the cut-up/fold-in method works through postmodern pas-tiche, based on the deauthorisation of the author, the vitiation of the uniqueness of the authorial literary voice, and therefore of the authentic-ity upon which modernism depends.

In Steinian experimental writing, as in Burroughs's 'cut-up and fold-in' method, conventional word associations, syntactical patterns and literary sequences are broken apart to make room for new modes of thought. These literary methodologies aspire to change the world by opening out new possibilities of thought-in-language on the assumption, common in 1960s countercultural ideologies, that revolution must come not through politics alone but through an accompanying, or even preceding, changed consciousness as well (see, most notably, Marcuse). This experimentalism, characteristic of a good deal of 1960s culture, was the essence of the mod-ernist/avant-garde revolution of the word; the logical endpoint of what Vir-ginia Woolf calls, in *A Room of One's Own*, 'breaking the sentence' and 'breaking the sequence'. Art is transformative, potentially redemptive, in this ideology, in its unique ability to reinvent the world through reinvent-ing thought-in-language.

As Burroughs develops its ideology, however, the cut-up and fold-in method is more actively democratic, egalitarian, and participatory than modernist/avant-garde experimentalism. While modernist aesthetics wanted to transform consciousness in order to rescue it from the degrada-tions of the mass 'culture industry', depending on the power and unique genius of the imaginative artist who can effect this transformation, cut-up/fold-in can be used immediately by anyone, working on any sort of cul-tural material, to liberate themselves from the stranglehold of authoritarian 'control'. Cut-up/fold-in works though pastiche and univer-sal accessibility to deauthorise the artist-genius and to undercut unique-ness and authenticity. Burroughs invites all *'peoples of the earth'* to 'cut the enemy beam off your line'.[36] The open, accessible, participatory nature of Burroughs's method marks it as characteristic of the prime 1960s political ideology of participatory democracy and as the site of emergent postmod-ern valorisation of the popular, particularly, for my purposes here, the val-orisation of the literary as practice.

In *The Job*, a series of interviews conducted by Daniel Odier in the late 1960s supplemented by Burroughs with excerpts from a range of his other

publications, Burroughs elaborates at some length his cut-up/fold-in technique, and its cultural-political-ideological implications. In these discussions, Burroughs moves back and forth between characteristically modern
and characteristically postmodern paradigms. In the section titled 'Jour-
ney through time-space', the opening section of the original version of *The
Job*, Burroughs gives the fullest account of cut-up/fold-in available in his
works. This account is prefaced with a question and answer that vividly
demonstrate the simultaneity of the modern and the postmodern in Burroughs's work (the following sequence opens this section of the book):

> Q: *Your books, since* The Ticket that Exploded *especially, are no longer 'nov-
> els'; a breaking up of novelistic form is noticeable in* Naked Lunch. *Toward
> what end or goal is this break-up heading?*
> A: That's very difficult to say. I think that the novelistic form is probably out-
> moded and that we may look forward perhaps to a future in which people do
> not read at all or read only illustrated books and magazines or some abbre-
> viated form of reading matter. To compete with television and photo maga-
> zines writers will have to develop more precise techniques producing the
> same effect on the reader as a lurid action photo.[37]

Odier's question about the breaking up of novelistic form draws on the
assumptions, characteristic of high modernism and avant-garde experimentalism, that traditional genres must be dismantled and redefined.[38]
Odier is locating Burroughs within this tradition, expecting from him, presumably, a reply about the inadequacy of traditional genres to represent
modernity.

Burroughs, however, gives a very different sort of reply. He doesn't
invoke the Woolfian distinction between realism's 'series of gig lamps sym-
metrically arranged' and the 'luminous halo or envelope' of modernist fiction. He does not sound any call to a realer realism of the twentieth
century, true to its fragmentation, mechanisation, alienation, reification,
commodification, self-consciousness, or depth psychologies. While he
agrees that 'the novelistic form is probably outmoded', he does not think it
needs to be replaced by a truer, realer prose fiction that at once represents
and transforms the twentieth century (the modernist credo). Instead, it
needs to be replaced by 'more precise techniques producing the same
effect on the reader as a lurid action photo'. The reflex effect on the reader
of a lurid action photo, invoking passive, pre-packaged, visceral responses
rather than consciousness-altering engagement in the invention of new
meanings, is precisely what the modernist/avant-garde ideology of the
writerly intends to blast apart. Burroughs looks directly here, along with
MacLuhan though with far less utopian optimism, at the end of the
'Gutenberg Galaxy': the advent of postmodern post-literacy. Burroughs's

tone is neutral – he neither welcomes nor abhors this paradigm shift. Rather, he hopes to use it to the advantage of his liberatory aesthetics.

Odier moves quickly to a set-up question, designed to allow Burroughs to explain his alternative to the outmoded novel form: '[w]hat separates Naked Lunch from Nova Express? What is the most important evolution between these two books?'[39] This question initiates Burroughs's discussion of cut-up/fold-in, which, of course, is what separates Naked Lunch from Nova Express – he evolved the technique in the post-Naked Lunch books of the tetralogy. As Burroughs explains, 'the simplest way [to do a cut-up/fold-in] is to take a page, cut it down the middle and across the middle, and then rearrange the four sections'.[40] (His deployment of the technique became much more elaborate than that, involving piecing together fragments of a range of literary and non-literary texts, as well as of tape recordings made at different times and places, along with similarly cut up and rearranged fragments of his own writing.)

Burroughs immediately swerves away from postmodern post-literacy, locating his literary practice firmly within modernist/avant-garde aesthetics. He adverts to the Steinian sentiment, derived most immediately from the artist Brion Gysin, his collaborator, that:

> '[W]riting is fifty years behind painting'. Why this gap? Because the painter can touch and handle his medium and the writer cannot. The writer does not yet know what words are. He deals only with abstractions from the source point of words. The painter's ability to touch and handle his medium led to montage techniques sixty years ago. It is to be hoped that the extension of cut-up techniques will lead to more precise verbal experiments closing this gap and giving a whole new dimension to writing. These techniques can show the writer what words are and put him in tactile communication with his medium.[41]

Burroughs invokes here the long tradition of modernist/avant-garde self-referentiality – the focus on the medium itself, on the plasticity of language, the need to make language as directly, concretely, immediately expressive as daubs of paint or notes of music. This focus is a primary impetus of experimental writing.

Burroughs follows Stein again in insisting on the conscious artistry of the cut-up/fold-in process (Stein explained, in a 1946 interview conducted just before her death, that her seemingly random or arbitrary experimental word juxtapositions were in fact carefully chosen). Odier asks him '[w]hen you have arrived at a mix or montage, do you follow the channels opened by the text or do you adapt what you want to say to the mix?' Burroughs's reply becomes a classic defence of the experimental method from within a traditional definition of artistic practice: 'I would say I follow the channels opened by the rearrangement of the text … It's not unconscious at all, it's a very definite operation … It's quite conscious, there's nothing of automatic writing or unconscious procedure involved here'.[42] Stein repudiated in very similar terms the notion that her writing was in any way automatic or unconscious.[43] Discussing cut-up/fold-in of tape recordings, Burroughs says 'you get very interesting juxtapositions. Some of them are useful from a literary point of view and some are not'.[44] Again: '[a]s to the sequences and rhythms organising themselves, well, they don't. The cut-ups will give you new material but they won't tell you what to do with it'.[45] Note the emphasis on 'sequences and rhythms' here, core concerns of the 'literary point of view'. Burroughs finds 'texts which try to describe the visions offered by drugs … for the most part dull. The writer has forgotten that he is a writer'.[46] Burroughs praises Conrad and Ford; 'Beckett and Genet I admire without reservation'.[47]

In an answer to a question about Burroughs's desire for clarity, he locates himself firmly within the representational ideology of the modernist/avant-garde tradition:

> When people speak of clarity in writing they generally mean plot, continuity, beginning middle and end, adherence to a 'logical' sequence. But things don't happen in logical sequence and people don't think in logical sequence. [Remember Woolf's 'luminous halo or envelope' replacing the falsifying 'series of gig lamps symmetrically arranged']. Any writer who hopes to approximate what actually occurs in the mind and body of his characters cannot confine himself to such an arbitrary structure as 'logical' sequence. Joyce was accused of being unintelligible and he was presenting only one level of cerebral events: conscious sub-vocal speech. I think it is possible to create multilevel events and characters that a reader could comprehend with his entire organic being.[48]

We are in a different universe, here, from the post-literary anti-aesthetics of the lurid action photo.

However, in 'Prisoners of the earth come out', in response to Odier's provocative question '[h]ow do you feel about human beings?', Burroughs switches readily to that postmodern, post-literary orientation:

> Nothing basically wrong with the human beings themselves, but they certainly will have to take a very basic forward step in evolution … I think the next step will have to be beyond the word. The word is now an outmoded artefact. Any life form that gets stuck with an outmoded built-in artefact is doomed to destruction. The dinosaurs survived because they were large and then they got larger and larger and this ultimately of course led to their extinction. The present form of human being quite possibly results from words, and unless they get rid of this outmoded artefact, it will lead to their extinction.[49]

This simultaneity of irreconcilable modern and postmodern modes of self-positioning is vividly apparent in Burroughs's theorisations of language itself. On one hand, he believes that the word is not only an 'outmoded artefact' but also the primary vehicle of what he calls 'control', the seamless domination of the world by various linked, interchangeable repressive forces, which encompass the standard 1960s villains – capitalism, imperialism, the military, the police, organised religion, sexual repression, the family, the nation, the law; 'power in all its forms', as Daniel Odier says. Burroughs says, 'you must leave the old verbal garbage behind: God talk, country talk, mother talk, love talk, party talk. You must learn to exist with no religion no country no allies'.[50]

Q: *What is the importance of power, in all its forms, in the machinery of destruction?*
A: The exercise of power for power's sake is precisely the machine of destruction. This would seem to be something we have had throughout history … [but] to confuse this old-style power with the manifestation of control madness we see now on this planet is to confuse a disappearing wart with an exploding cancer …
Q: *And what of money, ownership, property?*
A: Vested interest of power and/or money is perhaps the most potent factor standing in the way of freedom for the individual.[51]

Even in theorising the end of 'the word', then – the postmodern end of the Gutenberg Galaxy – Burroughs constructs a revolutionary/redemptive scenario derived from central paradigms of modernity. In this paranoid ideology, characteristically modern in its binaristic totalisation of domination and resistance, 'the word' or 'word-and-image' stand as the vehicle of domination, and 'silence', beyond the word, is the utopian mode of resistance: '[y]ou must learn to live alone in silence'.[52] Yet at the same time, as we will see, Burroughs believes contradictorily that, through cut-up and fold-in's liberation of the word or word-and-image from its conventional 'association tracks', language itself can effect its own rehabilitation, if not redemption. Further, the 'message of resistance', as he calls it, involving destruction of all conventional language, is, at times in Burroughs's work, only a partial, compromised message. When asked directly, he says he does not believe in the possibility of pure or total resistance, and this statement accords with many of his fictional representations of compromised modes of resistance. As he says in the introduction to *Nova Express*, '[t]o speak is to lie – To live is to collaborate'.[53] This is a quintessential postmodern position, rejecting the utopian hope of modernity for a total liberation, a position outside or beyond the history of social-political determinations. This position is linked to what is variously described by postmodern theorists as 'complicitous critique' or 'resistance from within'. These contradictory modern and postmodern relations to liberatory possibility coexist within Burroughs's work.

Burroughs rails regularly against the forces of control, of which the most important and pervasive is language: '[t]he word of course is one of the most powerful instruments of control as exercised by the newspaper and images as well ... Now if you start cutting these up and rearranging them you are breaking down the control system'.[54] (Other vehicles, embodiments or metaphors for control are heroin ['junk'], virus, Mayan thought control, the Nova Mob. Word-and-image, junk, virus become interchangeable, metonymic for one another and for control itself). Again, this is a classic modernist/avant-garde position, in which conventional language is seen as the tool of the bankrupt, oppressive status quo, the mass culture industry, and experimental writing as its antidote, bringing the possibility of freedom, authenticity, truth. Burroughs differs from these avant-garde, experimentalist language theories (of which language poetry is the most recent incarnation) only through the extreme literalness of his view of linguistic mechanisms of control, in which certain word-and-image combinations exert the same sort of direct biological power as addictive drugs, holding the word-junkie (all of us) in the same sort of absolute vice.

The language of control, tool of the world enforcers of power – as in some 'jewels gathered from one of the periodicals admittedly subsidised by the CIA' – is 'blind prose. It sees nothing and neither does the reader. Not an image in a cement mixer of this word paste'.[55] Cut-up/fold-in can both expose the deadness and manipulativeness of this prose, and substitute a mode of language capable of releasing us from it, connecting us with the true, authentic expression of the free human imagination:

> As a literary exercise I pick up the Penguin translation of Rimbaud and select images to place in congruent juxtapositions with this colorless vampire prose which having no color of its own must steal color from the readers such contractually accessible linguistically structuralized preparations on blue evenings I shall go down the path in a dream feeling the coolness on my feet starved of direction or vector by derivationally confluent exasperations five in the evening at the Green Inn huge beer mug froth turned into gold by a ray of late sunshine perspective of illiterate human beings would traduce or transfigure fecundate with orifices potential the Watchman rows through the luminous heavens and from his flaming dragnet lets fall shooting stars and precisely reciprocal latent consensus ...[56]

Burroughs regularly exhorts his readers to resist these forces of control through an apocalyptic refusal or negation, which he generally calls 'silence', or 'the message of resistance':

Q: *Is the introduction of what you call 'the message of resistance' the most important thing in the montage? Why?*
A: Well, yes, I would say it's a very important factor in the montage because it does tend to break down the principal instruments of control which are word and image and to some extent to nullify them.[57]

This modest, tentative, qualified reply belies the apocalyptic tone of Burroughs's call to his readers in his fiction:

What scared you all into time? Into body? Into shit? I will tell you: *'the word'*. Alien Word *'the'*. *'The' word* of Alien Enemy imprisons *'thee'* in Time. In Body. In Shit. Prisoner, come out. The great skies are open. I Hassan i Sabbah *rub out the word forever* ... And what does my program of total austerity and total resistance offer *you?* I offer you nothing. I am not a politician. These are conditions of total emergency ... cut the enemy beam off your line. Apomorphine and silence. I order total resistance directed against this conspiracy to pay off peoples of the earth in ersatz bullshit.[58]

Note the modernist ideology of transcendence here – we are exhorted to leave the body behind, through total austerity and total resistance; we are offered nothing in return but freedom, purity, liberation from the ersatz universe of capitalist commodity culture. Burroughs advocates the totalised, apocalyptic revolutionary scenario of modern/1960s redemptive ideologies, in which the realisation of utopia must be preceded by wiping the contaminated slate clean.

Contrary, postmodern paradigms are just as pervasive in Burroughs's work as the paradigms of modernity discussed above.[59] Cut-up/fold-in may liberate us from the obsessional association tracks of control, but it also introduces postmodern pastiche, deauthorising and deconstructing the unique individual free human spirit of the literary author:

A writing machine that shifts one half one text and half the other through a page frame on conveyor belts ... Shakespeare, Rimbaud, etc. permutating through page frames in constantly changing juxtaposition the machine spits out books and plays and poems – The spectators are invited to feed into the machine any pages of their own text in fifty-fifty juxtaposition with any author of their choice any pages of their choice and provided with the result in a few minutes.[60]

The result evidently is quintessential postmodern pastiche. Further, 'the spectators are invited': anyone can participate in this process; anyone can use the cut-up/fold-in method. The priest-like power of the modernist artist, the transcendent greatness of imagination and highly evolved artistry, are annihilated here. Literature becomes a site of 1960s participatory democracy that opens directly onto postmodern egalitarian ideologies of the popular and of the literary as practice.

Writing for Burroughs was an act of self-reconstruction that he wanted to share with the world. Concerted writing and emerging from heroin addiction were concomitant for him, and he saw them as linked manifestations of one process. Since 'junk *is* image', liberating himself from the control of heroin was equivalent to liberating language (word-and-image) from the control of its oppressive conventional structures of association and meaning.[61] He says in the Introduction to *Naked Lunch* that:

> I awoke from The Sickness at the age of forty-five, calm and sane, and in reasonably good health except for a weakened liver and the look of borrowed flesh common to all who survive the Sickness [sic] ... Most survivors do not remember the delirium in detail. I apparently took detailed notes on sickness and delirium. I have no precise memory of writing the notes which have now been published under the title *Naked Lunch*.[62]

Yet in *The Job*, in answer to the question '[w]hat does the discovery of apomorphine represent in your life', he says '[t]he turning point between life and death. I would never have been cured without it. *Naked Lunch* would never have been written'.[63] He distinguishes between notes taken in the 'delirium' of heroin addiction, an apparently non-volitional activity, and the active, volitional 'writing' of *Naked Lunch*. Notes were taken during his heroin addiction, of which he has no precise memory; though these notes somehow became *Naked Lunch*, they do not inhabit the same universe as the *writing* of *Naked Lunch*. Writing as an activity represents to him the sign, manifestation, embodiment of agency – the opposite of addiction, which is a state of utter passivity, in the grip of junk's control.

Further, this act of self-construction in the act of writing, in the literary as practice, is not limited to the artist, to one who has been set apart and elevated as a practitioner of a demanding, difficult, redemptive calling, as in the modernist ideology of the artist as cultural saviour. It is potentially available to everyone, as we have seen. Burroughs repeatedly calls on his reader to try cut-up and fold-in, to try splicing together tapes of ordinary life to produce new meaning. He repeatedly, in fact, gives fairly detailed instructions for how to do it, developed within elaborate comic scenarios of saturnalia invading humdrum office or subdivision life:

> [R]ecord your boss and co-workers analyze their associational patterns learn to imitate their voices oh you'll be a popular man around the office but not easy to compete with the usual procedure record their body sounds from concealed mikes the rhythm of breathing the movements of after-lunch intestines the beating of hearts now impose your own body sounds and become the breathing word and the beating heart of that organisation become that organisation ... why not give tape recorder parties every guest arrives with his recorder and tapes of what he intends to say at the party

recording what other recorders say to him it is the height of rudeness not to record when addressed directly by another tape recorder ...[64]

Satire aside, Burroughs sees the egalitarian diffusion of the power of word-and-image, the appropriation of cut-up/fold-in to tape splicing by 'millions of people', as a powerful subversive force. In 'Playback from Eden to Watergate', a 1973 piece that prefaces the revised edition of *The Job*, Burroughs fantasises the disruption of the political forces of control epitomised by the Nixon presidency ('tape recorder three', which plays back spliced-together pieces recorded separately on tape recorders one and two, is the crucial factor both in control and in Burroughs's plan for subverting it):

> The basic operation of recording, pictures, more pictures, and playback can be carried out by anyone with a recorder and a camera. Any number can play. Millions of people carrying out this basic operation could nullify the control system which those who are behind Watergate and Nixon are attempting to impose. Like all control systems, it depends on maintaining a monopoly position. If anybody can be tape recorder three, then tape recorder three loses power. God must be *the* God.[65]

Millions of people, playing in the fields of the literary as activity, might no longer, in postmodernity, be imagined to be able to nullify the control system, but they do, at least, 'seize the tools to mark the world that mark[s] them as other.'

Notes

1 J. Guillory, *Cultural Capital: The Problem of Literary Canon Formation* (Chicago, 1993), p. 265.
2 In her unpublished working paper, 'The witness of poetry', Harriet Davidson discusses the wide proliferation of poetry writing among her own students, including those who say they do not read or even like poetry, and throughout the American populace in general: 'never, I would like to argue, have so many people written poetry' (Davidson, 'The witness of poetry', p. 10).
3 In articulating this position, theorists of cultural studies are not beating any dead Arnoldian horse. Promulgators of the conservative position are vocal, numerous, and well funded. One need only think of the Right's heroes of the culture wars, such as William Bennett, Allan Bloom, Dinesh D'Souza, and E. D. Hirsch.
4 Exemplary in articulating this position are John Beverley, in *Against Literature* (Minneapolis, 1993), and Antony Easthope, in *Literary Into Cultural Studies* (London, 1991). It seems to me that film studies occupies an ambiguous position within this shift from, as Easthope puts it, 'literary into cultural studies', because of its (at least) dual emphases on the aesthetic practices of filmmakers and on the position of film within (particularly popular and mass) culture.
5 The phrase 'cultural capital' is taken, of course, from the crucial work of Pierre Bourdieu, and refers as well to John Guillory's uses and extensions of Bourdieu in *Cul-*

tural Capital. Guillory's work has particular relevance to my argument here, as will be apparent.

6 Linda Hutcheon, in *A Poetics of Postmodernism: History, Theory, Fiction* (New York, 1988) argues that what she calls 'minoritarian and ex-centric' writing is characteristically postmodern.

7 M. DeKoven, *Rich and Strange: Gender, History, Modernism* (Princeton, 1991), p. 12.

8 For John Beverley, the oppositionality of the literary which drew him to the profession (the Beats and the literary 1960s) was a false god, discredited by the revelation of literature's complicity in maintaining hegemony by venting and recontaining potential opposition. See particularly Chapter 2, 'The formation of the ideology of the literary (from Garcilaso to Greenblatt)', in *Against Literature*, pp. 25–46.

9 For an extended treatment of the notion of literary writing as locus of difference, see Derek Attridge, *Peculiar Language: Literature as Difference from the Renaissance to James Joyce* (Ithaca, 1988).

10 R. Barthes, 'Kafka's answer', in *Critical Essays*, trans. Richard Howard (Evanston, 1972), pp. 135–7.

11 R. Barthes, *S/Z*, trans. R. Miller (New York, 1974), p. 4: '[w]hy is the writerly our value? Because the goal of literary work (of literature as work) is to make the reader no longer a consumer, but a producer of the text'. Note Barthes's indebtedness to Sartre here. I emphasise the issue of unanswered interrogation because it differentiates literary writing most materially from non-literary writing such as this, which, though it might edge toward various other literary freedoms, still has the primary purpose of making arguments and therefore of proposing determinate answers to the questions it raises. That primary purpose has a pervasive effect on the shape and texture of the writing, inextricable from the impact of the whole array of conventions (shifting but powerfully enforced) of critical style.

12 G. Paley, 'The expensive moment', in *Later the Same Day* (New York, 1985), p. 189. The suggestive power of Paley's phrase, 'cultural dreamer', raises the enormous question of the position of psychoanalysis and the unconscious within the field of inquiry mapped out by a juxtaposition of the literary with cultural studies. I cannot begin to do justice to the ramifications of this question here. I can only stipulate the truisms that the unconscious is profoundly implicated in artistic practice, that psychoanalysis, particularly Lacanian psychoanalysis, has been crucial to our understanding of divided or split or self-alienated subjectivity, that much twentieth-century artistic practice is derived from or coincident with psychoanalytic insight into dream structure, and that both dream-work and psychoanalysis are, or can be, practices of the self very similar to the activity of literary writing as I am articulating it here (the clearest instance of this contiguity would be Anne Sexton).

13 I. Hunter, 'Aesthetics and cultural studies', in L. Grossberg, C. Nelson, and P. Treichler (eds), *Cultural Studies* (New York, 1992), pp. 347–72, p. 363. Again, I would note here the connection to psychoanalysis as a 'practice of the self'.

14 *Ibid.*, pp. 364–5. This argument is highly reminiscent of, and indebted to, the Roland Barthes and Susan Sontag of the 1960s.

15 Harriet Davidson's work on 'The witness of poetry' is particularly relevant here.

16 J. Derrida, *Acts of Literature*, ed. D. Attridge (New York, 1992). Derek Attridge's introduction, 'Derrida and the questioning of literature', pp. 1–29, is especially useful.

17 *Ibid.*, pp. 36–7 (emphases as in the original).

18 *Ibid.*, p. 23.

19 *Ibid.*

20 H. Cixous, 'Sorties: out and out: attacks/ways out/forays', in H. Cixous and C. Clément, *The Newly Born Woman*, trans. B. Wing (Minneapolis, 1986), pp. 63–132, pp. 85–6. 'Writing' has the same force here, I would argue, as 'the literary'. Like Barthes and Derrida, the advocates and practitioners of *écriture féminine* are primarily interested in avant-garde modes of literary writing, and use the term '*écriture*' to designate those modes. I would also note here *écriture féminine*'s close connection to and rootedness in psychoanalytically informed analyses of language and/or culture. Cixous has been a prime target of the repudiation of French feminism and *écriture féminine* by academic (post)feminists because of its essentialism. As this passage makes clear, however, essentialism is far from thoroughgoing or consistent in Cixous's work.

21 Cixous, multiply other as are many of these writers, is a Jew who grew up in Algeria.

22 A. Walker, 'Gifts of power: the writings of Rebecca Cox Jackson', in *In Search of Our Mothers' Gardens* (New York, 1983), pp. 71–82, p. 82.

23 D. Haraway, 'A manifesto for cyborgs: science, technology, and socialist feminism in the 1980s', in L. Nicholson (ed.), *Feminism/Postmodernism* (New York, 1990), pp. 190–233, p. 217.

24 G. Anzaldúa, 'Speaking in tongues: a letter to third world women writers', in G. Anzaldúa and C. Moraga (eds), *This Bridge Called My Back: Writings by Radical Women of Color* (New York, 1981), pp. 165–73, pp. 168–9. Yvonne Yarbro-Bejarano discusses Anzaldúa's *Borderlands/La frontera* in very similar terms: '*[m]estiza* consciousness is not a given but must be produced, or "built" … It is spatialized … racialized ("*mestiza*"), and presented as a new mythology, a new culture, a non-dualistic perception and practice … In *Borderlands*, this new consciousness is created through *writing*; Anzaldúa's project is one of discursive self-formation' ('Gloria Anzaldúa's *Borderlands/La frontera*: cultural studies, "difference", and the non-unitary subject', *Cultural Critique* 28 (Fall, 1994), 5–28, p. 13 (emphases as in original)).

25 I may appear to be using literary texts by black women and other women of colour to 'flesh out' white theory, literally to be the body for the white mind, the concrete example of white abstraction, a practice dissected brilliantly by Valerie Smith in 'Black feminist theory and the representation of the "Other"', in C. Wall (ed.), *Changing Our Own Words: Essays on Criticism, Theory, and Writing by Black Women* (New Brunswick, 1989), pp. 38–57, and by Margaret Homans in 'Women of color, writers and feminist theory', *New Literary History* 25 (1994), 73–94. However, these are in fact the contemporary American literary texts I care about most, and that, in addition to my own literary writing, motivated this essay. The white male theory that gets so much attention here has in fact set the terms of the debate over the literary within cultural studies. The question of where the exemplary literary texts appear in the essay, when this placement is governed by the overall structure of argument rather than by an unconscious deployment of racist critical practice, strikes me as of little material significance.

26 'Residual, dominant and emergent' come from Raymond Williams. I take 'text' to include film, theatre and 'happenings' as well as the printed text.

27 'Throughout the 1960s, Burroughs' works were seen by attackers and defenders alike as somehow emblematic of the times' (R. Lydenberg and J. Skerl (eds), *William S. Burroughs at the Front: Critical Reception, 1959–1989* (Carbondale, 1991), p. 6). Also, the blatancy of self-contradiction in Burroughs's work and thought makes him an ideal marker of transitionality.

28 W. H. Burroughs and B. Gysin, *The Third Mind* (New York, 1978), p. 3.

29 What I have called, in *A Different Language: Gertrude Stein's Experimental Writing* (Madison, 1983), Gertrude Stein's 'lively words' style – the radical experimental style of works such as *Tender Buttons*, written between 1911 and 1914 – is premised on precisely such unlikely, disjunctive but resonant, polysemous word juxtapositions. The phrase 'heavy metal' that appears in *Nova Express* can be considered such a juxtaposition. The uncertain origination of this phrase has been attributed by some to Burroughs, though others dispute this attribution (thanks to Marcia Ian for this information).

Most Burroughs critics consider *Naked Lunch* distinct from the three subsequent novels, designating those three a trilogy and *Naked Lunch* a novel unto itself, because Burroughs used cut-up/fold-in only in the 'trilogy' and not in *Naked Lunch*. Nonetheless, all four novels were drawn from the same notes and occupy roughly a continuous imaginative universe, so I choose to consider the four works a tetralogy.

30 Burroughs adds the Western to this repertoire in his later work – see D. Glover 'Burroughs' Western', in Lydenberg and Skerl (eds), *William S. Burroughs at the Front*, pp. 209–15.

31 See DeKoven, Hutcheon, Huyssen, et al.

32 W. S. Burroughs, *Naked Lunch* (New York, 1959), p. 2. The writing in the rest of the tetralogy, deploying Burroughs's cut-up and fold-in method, is far less conventional but frequently preserves the narrative tone and referential universe of hard-boiled detective fiction evident here.

33 W. S. Burroughs, *Nova Express* (New York, 1964), p. 86.

34 Burroughs, *Naked Lunch*, p. 144. The racist orthography is characteristic of Burroughs's satire, which is broad, utterly uninhibited, and no respecter of any kind of persons, particularly himself.

35 Burroughs, *The Third Mind*, p. 73.

36 Burroughs, *Nova Express*, p. 14.

37 D. Odier, *The Job: Interviews with William Burroughs* (New York, 1974), p. 27.

38 Friedberg points to the Dada antecedents of cut-up/fold-in: '[i]n one of the dadaist manifestos, Tristan Tzara commands: "Take a newspaper / Take some scissors". He then directs the making of a dadaist poem: A newspaper article is cut into its constituent words. The words are placed in a paper bag. The paper bag is shaken. The poem is "constructed" by copying the words in the order they are pulled from the paper bag' (A. Friedberg, '"Cut-ups": a synema of the text', in Lydenberg and Skerl (eds), *William S. Burroughs at the Front*, pp. 169–73, p. 169).

39 Odier, *The Job*, p. 27.

40 *Ibid.*, p. 29.

41 *Ibid.*, pp. 27–8.

42 *Ibid.*, p. 29.

43 As an undergraduate at the 'Radcliffe Annex', star pupil of William James, Stein had participated in experiments concerning the relation of attention to writing; critics subsequently used this fact to characterise her experimental work as automatic writing. Stein always adamantly denied any such connection, nor did she associate herself in any way with Surrealist versions of this practice. Burroughs is aligning himself with Stein here.

44 Odier, *The Job*, p. 28.

45 *Ibid.*, p. 32.

46 *Ibid.*, p. 160. Tanner emphasizes Burroughs's 'control over' the language of 'ugliness' through 'constantly regurgitating all the foul material' by means of the cut-up/fold-

in method (T. Tanner, 'Rub out the word', in Lydenberg and Skerl (eds), *William S. Burroughs at the Front*, pp. 105–13, p. 111).

47 Odier, *The Job*, p. 55. 'Any appreciation of Burroughs has to answer the question: does he belong in a major literary tradition. I believe that the preceding analysis aligns Burroughs with novelists, such as Kafka and Beckett, whose major theme is ambivalence and indeterminacy' (N. Oxenhandler, 'Listening to Burroughs' voice', in Lydenberg and Skerl (eds), *William S. Burroughs at the Front*, pp. 133–47, p. 145). Zurbrugg locates Burroughs alongside Beckett and Proust in their 'diverging – and at times incompatible – approaches to the image of the self' (N. Zurbrugg, 'Beckett, Proust, and Burroughs and the perils of "Image Warfare"', in Lydenberg and Skerl (eds), *William S. Burroughs at the Front*, pp. 177–88, p. 186).

48 Odier, *The Job*, p. 35.

49 *Ibid.*, p. 98.

50 *Ibid.*, p. 21.

51 *Ibid.*, pp. 59–60.

52 *Ibid.*, p. 21.

53 Burroughs, *Nova Express*, p. 15.

54 Odier, *The Job*, p. 33.

55 *Ibid.*, p. 104.

56 *Ibid.*, pp. 104–5.

57 *Ibid.*, pp. 34–5.

58 Burroughs, *Nova Express*, pp. 12, 14. Hassan i Sabbah is one of Burroughs's many narrative aliases – others are Inspector J. Lee of the Nova Police, and Uranian Willy or Willy the Rat. Apomorphine is a chemical derivative of morphine that successfully ended fifteen years of heroin addiction for Burroughs – again, Burroughs conflates drug addiction with language as control.

59 Solotaroff compares Burroughs to both Lenny Bruce and T. S. Eliot; Lydenberg and Skerl encapsulate this transitional status, describing Burroughs as 'the grand old man of the avant-garde and the pioneer of the space age' (Lydenberg and Skerl (eds), *William S. Burroughs at the Front*, p. 8). They see his career as straddling modernism and postmodernism: '[m]any earlier critics had compared Burroughs either favorably or unfavorably to the high modernism of writers like Kafka or Joyce. In this decade [the 1980s], instead of criticizing Burroughs as a failed modernist for his lack of continuity and organic wholeness, some critics celebrated his breakdown of conventions, his dissolving of individual indentity and voice, as a postmodern victory' (p. 11). Burroughs moved fully into the postmodern in his later work.

60 W. S. Burroughs, *The Ticket That Exploded* (Paris, 1962), pp. 53–4.

61 Burroughs, *Nova Express*, p. 17.

62 Burroughs, *Naked Lunch*, p. xxxvii.

63 Odier, *The Job*, p. 145.

64 *Ibid.*, p. 163.

65 *Ibid.*, p. 20.

thomas docherty

THE QUESTION CONCERNING LITERATURE

Polemical

The question concerning literature is complex, in that it involves at least three separable strands of inquiry. In the first place, we have a question of definition, of course ('what is literature?');[1] secondly, ghosting the question of definition is a concern regarding the place or places in which we read and study ('what is the nature of literary *studies* and, by extension, what is the function of the *university*, as the place in which we study literature, in our time?'); and, further, there is the question of what literature might have to do with the linguistic – and, through the linguistic, finally, the *national* – identities of human citizens or subjects (that is, what is the status of 'English' literature or literary study with respect to English people or to the category of Englishness as an ethnic marker; and, by extension, what is the nature of a subject's or citizen's *participation* in the national via the linguistics and literacy that govern the literary?).[2] One reason for rehearsing the question concerning literature in our time is that, despite recent controversies within literary departments or national cultures, debate has circled and, indeed, circumvented what is at stake in posing the question.

In 1983, at the height of the 'theory wars', it all seemed so simple; and it was presented in a cunningly simple fashion by, for a highly typical instance, Terry Eagleton. In his very influential textbook primer, *Literary Theory*, Eagleton poses the question 'what is literature?' with his characteristic rhetorical flourish, knowing all the while that to present the question concerning literature in this simple fashion is to ensure that no satisfactory answer will be available; and, consequently, he will therefore be able to divert attention from the question to some other matters. To look for a definition of 'literature' that will be necessary and sufficient to all cases in such a way as to allow perfect, clear and distinct typological or taxonomical classification for all instances of writing is a search doomed to failure – which is why Eagleton asks it in the first place. The very notion of having a 'clear and distinct idea' of the *essence* or *being* of something that is continually evolving or *becoming* is ill-judged and misplaced; and to draw inferences, as Eagleton does, regarding politics and power from the fact that certain individuals subscribe to the notion that 'literature' is a usable and workable term, is an exercise in the purest rhetoric, and one that will not stand scrutiny in any serious critical fashion.

Eagleton has little difficulty in dismissing those who argue that literature can be defined through its supposed distinction from 'factual' writing. Empirical evidence itself, he remarks, deals with this, when we reflect on the fact that '[s]eventeenth-century English literature includes Shakespeare, Webster, Marvell and Milton; but it also stretches to the essays of Francis Bacon, the sermons of John Donne ... [and] might even at a pinch be taken to encompass Hobbes's *Leviathan* or Clarendon's *History of the Rebellion*'.[3] (What Eagleton means, of course, is that these writings have been often taught in university 'English' curricula; and not that they 'are' or 'are not' intrinsically 'literature' – that is what he is allegedly trying to define in the first place.) He has much more difficulty when he tries to dismiss the notion of there being some peculiar uses of language that mark out characteristically distinct moments in writing or reading. What he has to accept is that the Russian Formalists – who broadly subscribe to this view – did not themselves try to define literature as such, but rather confined themselves to noting the instances or happenings of 'literariness'. Eagleton then insists that: '[a]nyone who believes that "literature" can be defined by such special uses of language has to face the fact that there is more metaphor in Manchester than there is in Marvell. There is no "literary" device – metonymy, synecdoche, litotes, chiasmus and so on – which is not quite intensively used in daily discourse'.[4]

Yet the Formalists did *not* define 'literature' in this way; rather, they acknowledged precisely the kinds of anxiety displayed by Eagleton, and restricted themselves to the attempt to define 'literariness', or moments when the aesthetic function in writing asserted a specific kind of autonomy. The sloppy misrepresentation of their argument allows Eagleton to knock down a straw-person and imply that anyone who subscribes to a *value-system* that would see more literary worth in 'Marvell' than in 'Manchester' is fundamentally mistaken, or that he or she is doing so on shaky philosophical grounds. (Let us leave aside the clear implication or invitation to consider a value-system that would see more worth in Manchester than in Marvell; it is this particular kind of rhetorical jolt that Eagleton seeks, not committing himself to any such position, but implying an allegiance to those who might scorn or feel threatened by Marvell or by their ignorance of Marvell). The point at issue, however, has not (yet) to do with value, but rather with the difficulty of proposing some stable definition for something that develops historically and culturally.

As Eagleton knows, to ask 'what is literature?' is a bit like asking 'what is a sofa?' When Cowper, in the early 1780s, was invited by Lady Austen to 'write on this sofa', he immediately made the phrase itself into the base for his great poem, 'The Task'. Playing on the double sense of 'on', he wrote *on* the sofa, *about* the sofa; and, at the start of the poem, he gave his brief cultural history of the development of the sofa and what we might call its standing in England. Cowper displays a number of items on which people have sat, from the three-legged joint stool on which King Alfred sat, through to the more stable four-legged version, then, with the arrival of cane from Indian trade, the lattice-chair, on through to the simple chair, then the arm-chair, contrived by 'an alderman of Cripplegate', until eventually we reach, after many variants, the sofa itself. He writes:

> So slow
> The growth of what is excellent; so hard
> To attain perfection in this nether world.
> Thus first necessity invented stools,
> Convenience next suggested elbow chairs,
> And luxury the accomplish'd Sofa last.[5]

These lines, full of innuendo (the 'nether' world, the necessity of our passing 'stools' in our progress), and following on from the obvious political implications regarding England's trading position in the world (the cane from India), describe the slow evolution of a single item from its variant models or sources. To define a sofa by the fact that one might sit or lie comfortably on it is, clearly, not an adequate definition; since there are so many other items satisfying this description. Each different form of seat has a different historical and cultural position, clearly; but are we to infer from this simple fact that it is now impossible to accept the existence of the sofa as such? After all, Cowper is in the process of demonstrating the worth of writing about it (just as the critic might demonstrate the worth of writing about something called literature). Are we to say, in acknowledgement of the fact that sofas are not naturally occurring phenomena, and that we have appropriated a word for them, that they are 'merely' an arbitrary construct and therefore not to be treated differently from other kinds of furniture?

The fact that we 'merely' linguistically describe certain items as 'sofas' does not, of itself, invalidate the claim that there may be a distinguishable something called a sofa, and that its *being* a sofa is somehow independent of my – or *my* community's – strategic or tactical desire to call it such. Nor does it follow that my acceptance that there *is* something called a sofa – or, by analogy, literature – implies some fundamental essentialist or monotheological or unhistorical or damningly elitist view of the world on my part. Rather, all that is implied in accepting that there *is* a category called 'literature' is that I agree to participate in meaningful discussion of the topic. To push the argument by analogy further, I can accept that there is a useful category of those called 'men', which will allow me to talk meaningfully of gender. I can even accept that the notion of maleness or of masculinity might be constructed. Yet the fact that transsexuals exist and that gender is located on a spectrum, rather than on one side or other of some absolute barrier, will not disallow my conversation or prove it to be inherently sexist, vacuous or, worse, elitist. On the contrary, without such a category, talk of transsexuals, even talk of gender – or, by analogy, talk of 'boundary cases', even of texts, in the category of literature – would itself be meaningless and thus lacking in any interest.

Further, although we may have culturally 'invented' literature or constructed it as a concept, it does not follow from this that *anything* can become literature. Sure, many things – especially written artefacts or events involving language – can be treated *as if* they were literature; but such a view is functionalist, reductivist, and fails to acknowledge the facts of cultural or aesthetic difference. Although some universities may use television programmes as raw material in a literature course, television programmes are not literature; nor are films or advertisements or comicstrips or the semiotics of body-piercing and so on, however interesting these things may or may not be. It follows, polemically but also logically, that although one may legitimately study such phenomena, they have no place as legitimate, fundamental objects of study in a university literature programme.

I shall put this argument polemically at this outset. There are some who will argue that one of the consequences of the introduction of 'theory' into English literature programmes has been to propose a more inclusive approach to legitimate culture. There are some who argue that the introduction of 'theory' into English literature programmes has served a positive political purpose, in that it has led to the necessity of our describing curricula that are more 'representative' of social groups who did not previously figure in an older curriculum; and, further, that the *inclusion* of that which had previously been excluded has served the purpose of *legitimising*, culturally and socially, those who had allegedly been excluded or unrepresented in 'English'.[6] Such an argument, ethically and politically attractive, is worth examining. Catherine Belsey is among those who have claimed that, with theory, 'the discipline of studying English literature comes to embrace a form of cultural history and cultural analysis that takes us beyond the handful of "great works" that used to be selected for study in order to preserve good taste'.[7] Well, she must have pretty big hands. My own undergraduate programme (in the University of Glasgow, 1973-78, typical of the kind that Belsey would regard as unhelpful) required that I had some knowledge of, at a conservative estimate, the works (usually multiple, rarely if ever anthologised) of at least ten, and usually around twenty, writers from each of six centuries; and that I would be able to write ably about these texts up to four years after I had studied them in classroom situations. Compare this with a contemporary 'modular' system, driven in the UK by 'quality assessment/control', which forbids an examiner legitimately requiring knowledge of what has been taught anything later than about a month after it has been studied; explicitly requires that no knowledge 'outside' of that which has been taught be examined; and requires that students of literature should only be asked to read minimal quantities, usually anthologised and 'selected' beyond recognition. The simple, if polemical, question is this: 'have we genuinely expanded the possibilities for the realisation of a rational social democracy by extending the literacy of students; or, on the other hand, have we been forced, however unwillingly, to capitulate to a set of "market-forces" that have driven quality steadily ever downwards, that have allowed us to preserve the forms of education while emptying those forms increasingly of content, and that have served the purpose of pushing a hoped-for participatory democracy further and further into the receding distance?'

In the same piece from which I have already quoted her, Belsey is rightly pleased that '[t]o be worth reading, texts written by women, members of the working class or colonial and post-colonial authors no longer have to be measured by standards of taste established a generation ago in white, patrician and patriarchal senior common rooms'. My own contention, however, is that we are *not* reading these texts, *nor* even the older, allegedly 'exclusivist' curriculum; we teach *neither* of these, but rather a banalised form of 'cultural semiotics' that blandly homogenises *all* writing, such that we are fundamentally unable now to distinguish *texts,* not to mention texts *by* women, say. The reason for this is, I allege, simple: we have lost the category of the literary; and, in the particular ways in which we have tried to achieve something politically through the university, we have thrown the baby of political change out with the bathwater of 'traditional' studies of 'literature'.

It will be clear from the foregoing that, in this piece, I shall be mounting a defence of literature as the 'proper' object of study for a university English department and its students. This position, I believe, is not reactionary or conservative; and I stress at the outset that I do not endorse in any way the by now familiar rantings of the conservatives – the Blooms (both Allen and Harold), Hirsch, D'Souza, Bennett, for random examples – in the so-called 'culture wars' that have deflected many within the American academy from its proper work. That said, I argue in what follows that it is time that we reconsider the 'question concerning literature' in terms of the complexity that lurks within that question. I shall explore slightly more fully, therefore, the questions of definition and the rhetorical gestures of 'theory' in the debate; following which, I shall consider the place of literature in the university and the place of the university in our communities; and finally, I shall outline what we might call 'the persistence of the literary' as our proper object of study; and in this, we will see that 'the question concerning literature' is, in fact, the question – and, perhaps troublingly, the questioning of – democracy.

Rhetorical

In *Cultivating Humanity* (1997), Martha Nussbaum follows the general tendency according to which anything can become a legitimate object of inquiry in a literature programme. The ethical (and also political) argument behind this has to do with giving voice to the previously unheard or delegitimised within our societies. Having argued for the positive ethico-political values of including Richard Wright's *Native Son*, or Ralph Ellison's *Invisible Man* (a development, she argues, of Sophocles' *Philoctetes*) in our contemporary literary curricula on the grounds that they encourage what she calls 'the compassionate imagination', she then writes that:

> These works are all written in a conventional literary language, a fact that explains their relatively easy acceptance into the realm of 'literature' despite the radical character of their subject matter. It can also be argued, however, that literary art most fully fulfills [sic] its Whitmanesque mission of acknowledging the excluded when it allows the excluded to talk as they really talk, to use a daily language that is nonliterary and that may shock our sensibilities.[8]

The example she gives of such a text is James Kelman's *How Late It Was, How Late*, 'a novel of working-class life in Glasgow, Scotland', which 'uses throughout the working-class Scots dialect that [its Glaswegian protagonist] would actually speak, and includes all the words that such a character would be likely to use in thought and speech'.[9] Nussbaum's argument, which she thinks aligns her with Kelman, is that Kelman is giving a voice to those who had typically been excluded, rendered invisible, by the dominant literary forms; and that this is a positive thing in itself, on the grounds that a democracy must inherently be able to encompass cultural difference and a multiplicity of diversities.

The notion of democracy that lurks behind this is one based, as I believe Nussbaum herself would accept, upon the rather imperfect models offered by the ancient world, upon which we can only improve. The ancient model is that of the *agora*, the public sphere or arena in which deliberation takes place and in which there is an exchange of voices or views. Through debate in this public sphere, it becomes possible to align oneself with one specific voice or speaker rather than with another: to make what is now a choice within and for the *polis* in which one identifies oneself with what is spoken by another, or in which one finds one's own voice adequately represented in the speech of another. Thus, *voicing* can be seen to be cognate with *voting* (as it is in Latin); and what we now call 'representative democracy' occurs. Central to this is the notional primacy of discussion, and specifically of oral debate, to any proper democracy. For democracy to work in an ethical fashion, it is incumbent on all participants that they strive to hear the voices of those who, for whatever reasons, do not figure in the *polis*, the excluded or 'those outside'.[10] It is by giving voice to those dispossessed of the usual forms of legitimised speech that we can enact an ethical version of representative or 'deliberative' democracy. Nussbaum's arguments for the inclusion of many new works into the curriculum of literature departments rest precisely on this ethical ground: an inclusive democracy must correct the tendency to monolingualism or to authoritarianism or even just to the coercions of social normativity, by attending to the voices of those who have been silenced in the past.

There are problems with this notion of democracy, one fundamentally indebted to the Marxian idea that 'these people are not represented. It is vital to represent them'. This much-cited *dictée* from Marx's *Eighteenth Brumaire* might usefully be placed alongside a lengthier passage from that same work in which Marx argues that ...

> the democrat, because he represents the petty bourgeoisie ... imagines himself elevated above class antagonism generally. The democrats concede that a privileged class confronts them, but they, along with all the rest of the nation, form the *people*. What they represent is the *people's rights*; what interests them is the *people's interests*. Accordingly, when a struggle is impending, they do not need to examine the interests and positions of the different classes. They do not need to weigh their own resources too critically. They have merely to give the signal and the *people*, with all its inexhaustible resources, will fall upon the *oppressors*.[11]

Some might find this a more or less adequate description of the kind of 'democracy' understood by leftist literary theory in the last three decades of the twentieth century. What is at issue in it is primarily the concept of cultural 'representation'. To 'represent' those who have not been represented, it is first necessary to 'invent' them, in the sense that it is first of all necessary to consider them *abstractly*, as a homogenised class with shared qualities or properties.

An anecdotal example of this might suffice to show the point. In a public debate in Cambridge in March 1998, Wlad Godzich and Margaret Anne Doody defended this kind of ostensibly admirable 'democratic' line of argument. A counter-argument was proposed, in which a participant in the debate alluded to the case of his relatively uneducated mother, a woman who had left school at the age of thirteen, with no qualifications, limited literacy, and absolutely no 'cultural capital' in that she had no knowledge whatsoever of what counted in her society as legitimate culture. All she knew was that it was not for her; and that, as a consequence, she was the poorer in every sense. The woman was described as an avid reader, but of low-grade romance-stories and of court-room detective stories. Her son suggested that critics such as Godzich and Doody were failing in their ethical and social responsibilities: they had the opportunity to give this woman cultural capital that would enrich her life and her social standing, but, by pretending to 'legitimise' culturally the low-grade books that she more or less partially read (for the most part books that they themselves would not read, they themselves preferring 'high culture'), they were effectively simply saying to her that where she stood was in itself already 'legitimate', requiring no further education (and all the while keeping the riches of cultural capital – literature – away from her). In response, Doody said to me (for it was, of course, my mother) that it was so typical of a male critic that he should stigmatise *woman* for her low levels of literacy and that he should so negatively dismiss the kinds of reading done by *women*. This manoeuvre won the predictable applause, despite the fact that Doody had simply effaced all presence thereby of this particular and singular woman. Why, I inquired, should the audience applaud Margaret Anne Doody's incapacity, as a supposed feminist, to fail to see the specifics of a particular case; why applaud the failure to see a specific woman, submerging her historical being under the wraps of an abstraction? This was not applauded, equally predictably. Yet it is this failure to see specificity that is the direct result of the kind of 'representative democracy' – fundamentally a bourgeois concept, as Marx points out – that makes me wonder why a critic such as Doody bothers to teach at all. My point was – *is* – that it is the responsibility of the critic to make some judgements, even in the absence of universalisable criteria; and that the failure to make a judgement that says, for example, that *Middlemarch* is more edifying than, say, the novels of Georgette Heyer or of Danielle Steele, is a total abnegation of responsibility, and one that has potentially dire social, ethical, and political consequences. To validate equally *everything* that is read in 'cultural' terms – that is, in terms of its capacity for enabling a participatory democracy and for establishing the autonomy of human citizens or subjects – is to validate nothing, and to render fragile the link that obtains between literature, or literacy, and freedom.

In relation to this, I introduce here what appears to me to be a potentially devastating intervention. In his examination of 'The expressive force of language: on the function of rhetoric in gaining knowledge', Gadamer indicates at the outset that there has been a shift in the operations of rhetoric whose consequence cannot be stressed enough:

> In modern civilization the topic of rhetoric is no longer what it was at its ancient origin, nor is it the same as the 'rhetoric' that has attended our cultural tradition for so many centuries. For us, the change has to do with converting the art of talking into the art of writing and the art of reading .... This at once makes clear a problem hidden behind this whole range of topics: the dissociation of writing and reading, which brings about a fundamental modification of understanding. How to bridge the distance between the meaning fixed by the writer and that understood by the reader is the basic question of hermeneutics. For modernity, this is also its pre-eminent problem.[12]

In this, Gadamer draws attention to the fact that it is inappropriate to 'translate' a form of polity based on the primacy of the immediacies of spoken dialogue and debate into the extremely heavily mediated forms of communication that are central to a literate culture without significant modification. As he argues, talking always takes place within the immediate relations between a speaker and a definite addressee; and both speaker and addressee are identifiable – defined – through the polity that arises from the conversation. Writing, too, requires an addressee, but in this case, the addressee is necessarily indefinite, and the temporal immediacies of speaking – which allow for the classical construction of democracy as that based on a spatial consciousness (democracy as applied in the *agora*, establishing a *polis*) – give way to the *problem* of establishing a democracy that is guided and characterised by time or by *mediation*. As Gadamer says, '[i]t cannot be sufficiently emphasized that today what is at issue is not speakers but writers. Here, in literary aesthetics ... lie many as yet unsurmounted problems'.[13] The problems, as I shall argue here, are not simply problems relating to stylistics or aesthetics, but also relating to precisely the forms of democracy that we might relate to the question concerning literature.

Democratic

I have remarked above that the posing of the question of literature in the form of the simplicity of 'what is literature?' was a rhetorical gesture. For a theorist such as Eagleton, the rhetoric drew attention to questions of power supposedly inscribed in any act of definition, with the clear implication that such an assertion of power was unwarranted, suspect, and (usually, and by implication only) anti-emancipatory. The reason for this is that any act of definition must, *by* definition, *exclude* from its ambit those elements – in this case, writings – that do not satisfy the terms of the definition; and such categorical, but *linguistic*, exclusion is then rhetorically treated as if it were *social* exclusion, the exclusion of certain people from access to political power or social standing. Behind the analysis here (which is either extremely weak intellectually, or extremely cunning – or both) there lies a serious issue; and that is the question of the relation of literature to politics, especially under the sign of autonomy. How might literature relate to the production of autonomous human individuals, subjects, citizens?

Alongside this, one might usefully consider the history of literary studies in the academy or university. I do not intend to rehearse here the by now dispiritingly familiar story of 'the rise of English studies' as a story punctuated by the names of Arnold, Eliot, Leavis, Williams, and culminating in our present predicaments. Rather, I take a slightly wider scope for the question, allowing us to see the stakes of the rise of national literary studies in various locations. To begin with, however, I explore the implications of noting that what we now call 'English' in university departments is a mutation from something that used to be known, perhaps more technically, as 'rhetoric'.

When Hugh Blair was appointed to the Chair of Rhetoric and Belles Lettres in the University of Edinburgh in 1760 (it becoming the Regius Chair in 1762, and Blair the first holder of that royally-endowed and influential, if still politically sensitive, position), he proposed an annual series of lectures on the topic of rhetoric, exemplifying the tropes and figures of rhetoric through analyses of a significant number of passages from some works that we have come to treat – either positively or negatively – as among the 'canonical' texts of English literature. One of Blair's great themes is the superiority of spoken over written forms of communication. For Blair, speech is sensible, immediate: it gives the present act of communication its full presence as the *content* of a specific material experience. Writing, by contrast, may be powerful; but in its lack of immediacy, its necessary capacity for abstraction, it gives but the *form* of experience without the specific content that would be there in the immediacy of a speech or dialogue situation. As Gadamer would have it, there is a dissociation of the act of reading from that of writing, such that the rhetorical encounter is necessarily muted or mediated; and the consequence – with which the whole trajectory of reader-response literary criticism has always tried to deal – is that the 'experience' of the reader is always somehow merely formal, vicarious, distanced from the self of the reader. In such a state of affairs, it is clear that there is a particular sense in which the 'experience' of the reader is 'inauthentic', in that there is a dissociation of the reading-subject from itself such that, unable to be 'present-to-itself', it cannot genuinely be present to the site of the textual dialogue either; and consequently, it is not fully participating in the great democratic project of dialogue or conversation itself.

Blair, in following this line suspicious of writing is, as we all know after Derrida, simply one thinker among many in this regard. More important for present purposes is that, for Blair, as for Vico some sixty years previously in Naples, speech had an intimate relation to the social, and eloquence or rhetoric were to be placed at the heart of a university education. It is through the proper inhabiting of a language (and, in the European post-medieval universities, this is increasingly a vernacular language) that we will be able to assert our autonomy, to distinguish sense from sensibility, and to prioritise reason in our construction of the social itself, at the cornerstone of which is the intellectual life. If our societies – and our linguistic communities or nations – are to persist at all, they must be based on reasonable and reasoned grounds; and if we are to have reasoned grounds, we must master rhetoric.

The culmination of this kind of thinking is to be found in Humboldt's report on the founding of the University of Berlin in 1810. There, as Bill Readings pointed out, we find an articulation of the 'university of culture'. The University such as this is an institution that, in Readings's words,

> draws its legitimacy from culture, which names the synthesis of teaching and research, process and product, history and reason, philology and criticism, historical scholarship and aesthetic experience, the institution and the individual. Thus the revelation of the idea of culture and the development of the individual are one. Object and process unite organically, and the place they unite is the University, which thus gives the people an idea of the nation-state to live up to and the nation-state a people capable of living up to that idea.[14]

In Humboldt, the function of the University is to address and even to constitute a national culture, thereby making the nation *available* to, or *inhabitable* by, its people; such people become specific citizens, able now to live the nation-state empirically or to embody it in their actual practices. It is these practices that we can now call culture – and, in the case of Berlin, the culture in question is specifically that which emerges, at this early moment of the nineteenth century, as 'German' culture, forged through the literature of Schiller and Goethe, and the philosophy – in particular the aesthetics – of Kant, Hegel and Schopenhauer.

In all of these thinkers, as in Newman too in Ireland, the centrality of grammar and rhetoric to a university education is unquestionable. It is axiomatic that one can *participate* culturally and socially as a citizen only to the extent that one can participate adequately in meaningful dialogue. However, as Gadamer points out, that dialogue is not voiced as such in modernity, but rather it is the case that information is primarily a matter of written documentation. It is here, quite simply, that the link of literacy to democracy is forged: to participate within a modern democracy, one must be literate; and, further, one must have so mastered rhetoric that one is able to speak in different voices, in different registers, in order to assert one's autonomy. For every participant in such a polity, *prosopopoeia* is fundamental. That is to say, in certain circumstances, I, as a working-class speaker of a Glaswegian dialect, must learn how to speak precisely in the person of a Glaswegian; yet, if I am to participate in other social relations, I must also master other forms of speech or rhetoric. Thus the speaker herself becomes not just dialogical (able to engage in dialogues with others unknown to her or different from her); but also multivocal, plural in her voicings, and thus able to *think* or to speak to herself. This is the real consequence of following the Wittgensteinian line regarding the impossibility of a private language: one must always be speaking in and through borrowed voices if one is to 'hear/understand' oneself at all. If I speak 'authentically', that is, always in the pure presence of my own 'proper' voice, then, quite simply, I do not speak (or think) at all. A linguistic difference – and a *persona* or act of personification – is necessary if I am to be able to represent things to myself or to think.

It is not the case, therefore, that Kelman, say, 'gives a voice' to those who have been unheard. Does Nussbaum really think that upper-class snobs have no awareness of the voices of Glasgow? Is it really the case that middle-class students will herald a new revelation when they 'hear' or read Kelman? 'Oh, so this is how the Glaswegian working-class male speaks'. It may come as a surprise to those who agree with Nussbaum, but there is no such thing as *the* Glaswegian working-class male; there are only singular people, speaking in singular fashions, sometimes denied access to the centres of culture, and sometimes delegitimised by others, and especially by those who feel able to categorise them as an abstract, if homogeneous, type. If we are to read Kelman in a university literature syllabus (as we should), it is assuredly *not* primarily because he 'represents' some class that has typically been excluded from cultural forms of representation; it is rather because his work is *literature*.[15]

In conclusion, then, we must reconsider the claims for the supposed intrinsic link between literature and democracy. At the core of this, as Badiou has recently argued in his *Petit manuel d'inesthétique*, is the troubling link between art and philosophy. Badiou proposes that the link between art and philosophy has traditionally been thought in one of three ways. In the first way, which he calls *didactic*, it is proposed that art is incapable of truth, yet that it offers the semblance of truth; and accordingly, philosophy's task, here, is either to correct art, or to banish it, or to treat it in a purely instrumentalist fashion. The second way, called by Badiou the *romantic*, claims that it is *only* art that is capable of the truths that philosophy can merely hint at or suggest or imply; thus art, here, is a kind of *incarnation* or realisation of a truth that can be felt, lived, or experienced *only* through the medium of art. The third way, the *classical*, accepts that art does not propose the truth, but doesn't feel any concern at this fact; for it says, following Aristotle, that the purpose of art is therapeutic; and thus, its domain is not that of truth but rather of *vraisemblance*, and of probability. In this classical schema, art is not to be described as a kind of thinking or 'thought' at all; rather, it has its being fully in its enactment or in its public service in rendering pleasure. These three schemes, argues Badiou, have dominated throughout the twentieth century; but the consequence of such domination has been the effacing of a third term that should properly hover between art and philosophy: education.

In the face of this impasse, Badiou asserts that we might re-think the relations of art – and from now on I shall limit this to literary art, *literature* – and philosophy (or criticism). In doing this, we should note first of all that literature is itself what Badiou calls 'une procédure de vérité':

> L'art est une pensée dont les oeuvres sont le réel (et non l'effet). Et cette pensée, ou les vérités qu'elle active, sont irréductibles aux autres vérités, qu'elles soient scientifiques, politiques ou amoureuses. Ce qui veut dire aussi que l'art, comme pensée singulière, est irréductible à la philosophie.[16]
>
> (Art is a thought for which the works [of art] constitute its [the thought's] reality (not its effect). And this thought, or the truths that it activates, are irreducible to other truths, be they scientific, political, or amorous. Which means to say, further, that art, as a singular thought, is irreducible to philosophy.)

In this, to be literature, a specific literary text will demonstrate both 'immanence' and 'singularity'; by which we can claim that the literature is 'rigorously coextensive with the truths that it propagates' (immanence) and that 'these truths are given nowhere else' except in the specific literary text (singularity).[17] In this state of affairs, Badiou would ask what becomes of the third term in our set of relations, that is, the educational function of art. For him, art is educative simply because it produces truths, and: '[c]e pour quoi l'art eduque n'est rien d'autre que son existence. Il ne s'agit que de *rencontrer* cette existence, ce qui veut dire: penser une pensée'[18] (That for which art educates is nothing other than its own existence. It is only a question of *encountering* this existence, which means to say: to think a thought).

The distinguishing characteristic of literature, thus, is that through an encounter, it forces the thinking of a thought. Yet, as I remarked earlier, following Wittgenstein, such 'thinking' cannot take place within the realms of a private language. It thus requires the reader of literature to be always other than herself, to be *essentially* 'hypocritical', in the sense of that term given by its etymology. The 'hypocrite lecteur' is, as it were, an *actor*, one who can inhabit various voices and who can, thereby, 'speak' to herself and, simultaneously, 'hear/understand' herself *without this being an immediate – unmediated – encounter*; that is, this reader is one who occupies not the *space* of the *agora* but rather the *time* of becoming. That is to say, literature is literature precisely to the extent that it produces a reader who, of necessity, is 'inauthentic'. Such a reader will not be distinguished by finding some adequate representation, in the text, either of herself (i.e., allowing the text to speak 'for her', or 'identifying' with its characters or ethos) or of an other (that troubling 'Glaswegian', say, whose dialect is not usually transcribed in the history of the texts we have thus far encountered, but whose being I can now 'locate', 'identify', or homogenise).

Literature, in this way of thinking, is that which renders somewhat problematic the easy or straightforward relation that would suggest that an increase in autonomy and democracy is proportionate with an increase in literacy. To put this simply: it is folly to hope that we will establish autonomous democracy by representing classes, 'races', genders, sexualities and so on in our curricula, as if we were trying, like Borges, to imagine a map that describes perfectly and totally the world it supposedly only represents: such a map would have to *be* the reality it supposedly represents, in some kind of Cratylean fantasy. The error of some recent theory has been to believe that one can easily translate from the representation to the real; that to imagine the world differently is to make it so.

Now, what happens to democracy in this? Badiou suggests that there should be a 'co-responsibility' of art and philosophy ...

... une coresponsabilité de l'art, qui produit des vérités, et de la philosophie, qui, sous condition qu'il y en ait, a pour devoir, et tâche très difficile, de les montrer. Les montrer veut essentiellement dire: les distinguer de l'opinion. En sorte que la question d'aujourd'hui est celle-ci, et nulle autre: y a-t-il autre chose que de l'opinion, c'est-à-dire, ... y a-t-il autre chose que nos 'démocraties'?[19]

(a co-responsibility of art, which produces truths, and of philosophy which, on the condition that there is any [art], has for its calling, and a difficult task this is, to demonstrate these truths. To demonstrate them essentially means: to distinguish them from opinion. Such that the question today is this, and none other: is there anything other than opinion, or in other words … is there any thing other than our 'democracies'?)

Given its propensity for establishing an 'authentic democracy', those versions of contemporary theory that dispose of the exclusivist category of 'literature' manage to circumvent the complexity of the relations between literature or literacy and politics. In particular, they depend upon a simplistic version of 'identity-politics' in which the task is to legitimise an authentic identity for the reader. Yet, as I argue here, such 'authenticity' is itself that which exerts a *limitation* on the possibilities of democracy; for a democracy such as that desired by our Left – a genuinely historical or participatory democracy – requires that specific form of inauthenticity that I called above *hypocrisy*. The version of authenticity espoused by inadequately considered Leftist criticism is one in which authenticity is guaranteed by the supposedly adequate representation, in a text, of certain voices (homogenised as those of specific classes, or 'races' or genders and so on). The version of 'democracy' espoused, likewise, is that rather bourgeois one which is nothing other than the triumph of 'opinion', in the multiple voicings of what Marx satirised as 'the people'; and, further, it is a notion of democracy that, while it may possibly have been adequate to non-literate cultures, is simply inappropriate for the highly developed cultures within which we have literature at all.

Notes

1 It is worth noting, at the outset, the difference between two questions: 'what is literature?', which invites a rather open response ('this' is literature, or 'that' is; and so on); and 'literature is what?', which invites a closed response, a strict definition. It is this latter question that has usually been addressed by a criticism that wants to 'explode' the boundaries or category of the literary.

2 On these two questions, see, respectively, B. Readings, *The University in Ruins* (Cambridge, Mass., 1996); and T. Docherty, *Criticism and Modernity: Aesthetics, Literature and Nations in Europe and its Academies* (Oxford, 1999).

3 T. Eagleton, *Literary Theory: An Introduction* (Oxford, 1983), p. 1.

4 *Ibid.*, pp. 5–6.

5 W. Cowper, 'The Task' in *The Poetical Works of William Cowper* (1852), p. 251.

6 For how this is understood in the American academy, see R. Rorty, *Achieving our Country* (Cambridge, Mass., 1998), where Rorty points out that the 'excluded' in this situation is itself a category that excludes those who are the 'wrong' types of victims in society (i.e., those for whom a fully-fledged 'theoretical' understanding of their victimhood has not yet been formulated in the academy – such as the unemployed).

In many cases, argues Rorty, the cultural left's 'futile attempts to philosophize one's way into political relevance are a symptom of what happens when a Left retreats from activism and adopts a spectatorial approach to the problems of its country. Disengagement from practice produces theoretical hallucinations' (p. 94). In relation to this, see also M. Nussbaum, *Cultivating Humanity: A Classical Defense of Reform in Liberal Education* (Cambridge, Mass., 1997), which I discuss in more detail below.

7 C. Belsey, 'All texts are our province', *The Higher* (30 January 1998).

8 M. Nussbaum, *Cultivating Humanity* (Cambridge, Mass., 1997), p. 98.

9 *Ibid.*

10 It is worth noting how this notion of a 'deliberative democracy', one based on verbal deliberation, persists within the thought of those Marxists such as Habermas whose work took a 'linguistic turn', according to which the primacy of rational argument or *Diskurs* can determine the possibilities of the establishment of a democratic – rational – state of affairs. Additionally, it is worth indicating that the ethics of this position can fundamentally be related to a neo-Christian theology, in that 'those outside' were also precisely the people who represent a problem-case for the Christian understanding of parables. In relation to this, see F. Kermode, *The Genesis of Secrecy* (Cambridge, Mass., 1979), itself dedicated to 'those outside'.

11 K. Marx, *The Eighteenth Brumaire of Louis Bonaparte* (Peking, 1978), pp. 50–1.

12 H-G. Gadamer, *Praise of Theory*, trans. C. Dawson (Newhaven, 1998), p. 123.

13 *Ibid.*, p. 124.

14 Readings, *University in Ruins*, p. 65.

15 This, clearly, is a different position from that advanced by Rorty, say, in *Achieving our Country*. There, Rorty points out how, following some of the reforms in education that are sneered at by the Right as merely 'politically correct', the change in the way that (educated) Americans treat one another is enormous, and for the better (though he concedes, of course, that it is still possible to be sexist, homophobic, racist, misogynistic, and so on; but it is not quite so easy to be these things as it was some forty years ago). This change, he argues, 'is largely due to the hundreds of thousands of teachers who have done their best to make their students understand the humiliation which previous generations of Americans have inflicted on their fellow citizens. By assigning Toni Morrison's *Beloved* instead of George Eliot's *Silas Marner* in high school literature classes … these teachers have made it harder for their students to be sadistic than it was for those students' parents' (p. 81). I agree with this; but this is not yet a sufficient reason for assigning Morrison. My view, simply, is that we assign Morrison because *Beloved* is literature; and we know it to be literature precisely *because* of its edifying effects.

16 A. Badiou, *Petit manuel d'inesthétique* (Paris, 1998), p. 21 (translation mine).

17 *Ibid.*

18 *Ibid.*

19 *Ibid.*, p. 29.

john frow

LITERATURE AS REGIME
(MEDITATIONS ON AN EMERGENCE)

1

At the beginning of Joseph Roth's novel *The Radetzky March* a young infantry lieutenant, seeing the Emperor accidentally put himself in danger in the course of the battle of Solferino, pushes him to the ground and receives the bullet intended for the Supreme War Lord. Many years later, now a captain and ennobled, Joseph Trotta finds in his son's school reader an account of this incident. What he reads, however, is a quite different story, in which the Emperor 'had ventured so far forward among the enemy in the heat of battle that suddenly he found himself surrounded by enemy cavalry. At this moment of supreme danger a young lieutenant, mounted on a foaming chestnut horse, galloped into the fray, waving his sword. What blows he inflicted on the backs and heads of the enemy horsemen'.[1]

This mythical lieutenant is then pierced by an enemy lance, but is protected from further harm by 'our young and fearless monarch'.[2] Reading this exemplary fiction Trotta is outraged – perhaps particularly at his reassignment to the cavalry; he complains to the Emperor and retires from the army; the story is expunged from the textbooks, but not before Trotta has come to understand 'that the stability of the world, the power of the law, and the splendour of royalty are maintained by guile'.[3]

This incident repeats that moment in Part II of *Don Quixote* in which the hero discovers the existence of a spurious account of his adventures, and expresses his fears 'that if the author of that history of my exploits, which they say is now in print, chanced to be some enchanter hostile to me [*algún sabio mi enemigo*], he has probably changed one thing into another, mingling a thousand lies with one truth, and digressed to narrate actions out of the sequence proper to a faithful history'.[4] Two contrary movements are at play in these passages. On the one hand, by being opposed to the spurious fiction which misrepresents Trotta's or Don Quixote's life, the prior and encompassing fiction is raised to the power of truth. On the other, this 'faithful history', now manifestly unable to control the penetration of (novelistic) life by secondary fictions, becomes even more intensely a fiction, fiction to the second degree, more true because more fictive; the narrative of a resistance to literature has itself become a work of literature. When, later in this second part of the novel, Don Quixote discovers a spurious Part II (the really existing forged continuation of Cervantes's novel by Avellaneda), and indeed encounters characters from it, the novel's theme of the unreality of the literary is further undone: it is now only at a great ironical remove that this initial demystificatory step can be taken. It is in this double movement – merely adumbrated in Roth's novel, but worked out in its full complexity in Cervantes's – that the emergence of the literary can be traced: an emergence which is not only a punctual event (the initiation of 'literature' as a category of modernity) but a repeated structure of thematised reflexive reference.

Now consider a second such moment of emergence. At a certain point in Balzac's *Lost Illusions* the provincial poet and man of letters Lucien Chardon (now calling himself Lucien de Rubempré) writes a review of a play in which a leading role is played by the actress Coralie, to whom he has offered 'the virginity of my pen'.[5] The review is a piece of puffery; Adorno describes it as 'the birth of the feuilleton', and says of it that its '"for the first time" quality gives that contemptible form a conciliatory charm'.[6] Like the passages from Roth and Cervantes, this embedded text represents a moment of reflexivity, since it explicitly thematises journalistic corruption. Adorno thus understands this feuilleton as 'the work of art's reflection on itself. The work becomes aware of itself as the illusion that the illusory world of journalism in which Lucien loses his illusions also is. Semblance is thereby elevated above itself'.[7] The literary text is at once like and unlike the piece of mass-produced journalism, sharing its commodified status but transcending it by virtue of an ability to recognise this status and to take a critical distance from it.

But another and less redemptive way of reading this moment would be to see it as the crystallisation of a set of tensions that run through this novel, the first major European literary text to explore in a detailed and systematic way the commodity production of books. Two contradictory structures of value, centred on the relation between Lucien and his friend David Séchard, organise the book. In the first, the literary (exemplified by the poetry of Chénier and of Lucien himself, and by the historical novels of d'Arthez, a self-portrait of Balzac) is counterposed to the corrupt world of journalism and of the book trade to which it nevertheless belongs. This world is governed by the figures of prostitution and of commercial calculation. For the cynical Lousteau, the literary world is a place of bribery, of 'spiritual degradation', and of the buying and selling of reputations, a place in which venal journalists viciously attack work of merit and publishers treat books as short-term capital risks.[8] As one 'wholesale bookseller' puts it to an anguished author, 'Walter Scott's novels bring us eighteen sous a volume, three francs sixty for the complete works, and you want me to sell your rubbishy books for more than that?'[9] But the category of literature is undercut not so much by its immersion in this world, to which it is at least morally superior, as by its merely honorific status in the text: all the intensity of writing is to be found in the nether world of venal prose, not in the higher realms of apparently autonomous literary production. And this focus of the novel's energy corresponds to the way in which, in a second structure of value, its fascination with David Séchard's ambitions is developed. David is an inventor seeking a process for making cheap, good-quality paper from vegetable pulp. At a time of rapid increase in the production and marketing of books and newspapers it was, says the anonymous narrator:

> vitally necessary to adapt paper-making to the needs of French civilization, which was threatening to extend discussion to all subjects and to take its stand on a never-ending manifestation of individual thought – a real misfortune, for the more a people deliberates the less active it becomes. And so, curiously enough, while Lucien was getting caught in the cogwheels of the vast journalistic machine and running the risk of it tearing his honour and intelligence to shreds, David Séchard, in his distant printing-office, was surveying the expansion of the periodical press in its material consequences. He wanted to provide the means for the end towards which the spirit of the age was tending.[10]

The contradiction is straightforward, but between that moralising 'real misfortune' and a 'spirit of the age' (*l'esprit du Siècle*) driven by technological advance and capital investment the novel's sympathies are fully engaged with the latter. The 'literature' that emerges from this play of forces and values is neither the transcendent stuff of poetry and the 'high' historical novel, nor the mere corruption of journalism, but a writing which is torn between the two and whose defining character is its status, and its dissatisfaction with its status, as a thing to be bought and sold.

Let me finally propose a third moment of emergence of the literary. I find it in one of the canonical sites of (post)modernist lyricism, Frank O'Hara's 'The Day Lady Died', which is built around an opposition between two incommensurate temporalities.[11] The first is the mundane time of a chronicle of disconnected events. This chronicle (O'Hara's 'I do this and I do that' genre) sets up several different ways of describing what time it exists in, and veers between them since none seems satisfactory:

> It is 12.20 in New York a Friday
> three days after Bastille day, yes
> it is 1959 ...

The poem then moves into the empty punctuality of a train timetable ('I will get off the 4.19 in Easthampton/ at 7.15'). The 'I' of the poem gets a shoeshine, buys a hamburger and malted, buys some books: this is a 'flat literalism', a recording of surfaces.[12] The books that the speaker buys or thinks of buying – a copy of *New World Writing* ('to see what the poets/ in Ghana are doing these days'), an illustrated Verlaine, Hesiod, Behan, Genet – are of the same order as the liquor and cigarettes he buys, packaged writing. It is only with the mention, five lines from the end of the poem, of buying 'a NEW YORK POST with her face on it', a reference to the unspoken death of Billie Holiday (the 'Lady Day' whose name is inverted in the singsong rhymes of the title), that the turn to the poem's other temporality begins. This turn is completed in the final quatrain:

> and I am sweating a lot by now and thinking of
> leaning on the john door in the 5 SPOT
> while she whispered a song along the keyboard
> to Mal Waldron and everyone and I stopped breathing

The sweat is because it's a muggy day (line 7), but it also perhaps accompanies the 'thinking' that initiates the poem's second plane, that of a remembered time which breaks the episodic time of the previous stanzas and is their underlying reality. This is not the time of Holiday's death (that too belongs to the episodic present) but of the song 'whispered ... along the keyboard' so that everyone 'stopped breathing', in a kind of death which does and does not resemble hers.[13] The lyrical stasis of this time is generated above all by the ambivalent syntax and rhythms of the final line, which reads in three different ways:

> to Mal Waldron and everyone | and I stopped breathing

or:

> to Mal Waldron | and everyone and I stopped breathing

or, in an unavoidably synthetic reading which, since the syntax is perfectly undecidable, combines the other two:

> to Mal Waldron | and everyone | and I | stopped breathing.

The first of these readings moves the song out along the keyboard from the pianist to the whole audience, and then rests on the isolated response of the speaker ('I stopped breathing'). The second, with its isolation of the pianist as the recipient of the song and its simultaneous immersion of the speaker in the audience and separation of him from it ('everyone and I') slows the line right down at the end as the speaker takes part in a shared experience. The third, which I think is the only possible way of reading the line, is a 'torn' reading in which 'everyone' goes both ways at once (and in which 'I' perhaps functions ungrammatically both as a quasi-dative – the third recipient of the song – and as the subject of the verb). Again, this reading is slowed right down (we should probably add a further caesura between 'stopped' and 'breathing'), miming the loss of breath which meets the whispering of the song. The 'emergence' of the literary that I find here is the effect of this shift of planes from the mundane to the epiphanic moment of memory, and from the book as packaged writing to the breathed authenticity of the voice as it intimates death and its transcendence.

2

Each of these three different modes of emergence of the literary – as epistemological reflexivity; as sociological reflexivity; and as a shift from mundane time to the ecstatic moment – validly affirms a mode of its being (which is to say a mode of reading, and the forms of textual complexity that correspond to it). But the concept of literary emergence, as I have tried to indicate, specifies a dual temporality: on the one hand, it refers to the literary as an event that occurs within (or *as*) an act of reading; on the other, it refers to a structure of historical value which is variably consolidated in an institutional form. These two configurations of value are always potentially contradictory, since the stability of the latter threatens the status of the former as a momentary and always historically fragile achievement. It is surely clear enough that consolidated canonical formations are historically variable: the continuous reception of 'Homer' or 'Shakespeare' is a matter of constant reinvention within discontinuous frameworks of value and for changing social uses, rather than the constant recognition of a timeless worth. But it is equally the case that the sense of the literary as fleeting realisation, with its ruptural relation to the ordinary time of writing, cannot be assumed to have a transhistorical force, since it is itself the achievement of a postromantic regime of reading. Thus when Thomas Keenan defines literature not as a collection of poems and novels but as 'our exposure to the singularity of a text, something that cannot be organized in advance, whose complexities cannot be settled or decided by "theories" or the application of more or less mechanical programs', he ignores the extent to which reading is indeed always organised in advance by the institutions of genre and by norms of semantic determinacy (including norms of indeterminacy).[14]

To posit 'the literary' in these three rather different forms is not to posit a common structure, be it that of the self-awareness of language, of the embedding of social function in complex patterns of writing, or of a passage to redeemed authenticity; it is, rather, to pose the question as to whether there can be any ontological or functional unity to the category of the literary as I have used it here. The difficulty is not that the question 'What is Literature?' cannot be answered, but that many perfectly valid answers are possible. In almost all cases these answers are normative: the literary constitutes a distinct, unitary and special language game recognised contrastively in its relation to one or another non-literary languages, or non-literary uses of language, or non-literary levels of organisation of language, or indeed to canonical literary language itself. It is the opposite of scientific or philosophical statement (Richards, Lacoue-Labarthe), or the opposite of everyday language (Shklovsky); it is language of high intensity (Arnold) or of a high level of semiotic complexity (Eco); it is performative rather than constative language (Burke), language as aporia rather than communication; it is language aware of its own rhetorical status and its inherent liability to error (de Man), or a generalised principle of reflexivity, or it is its own impossibility. There is none of these definitions that does not embody a particularistic structure of value (if only because of the assumption of literacy or of the ability to thematise formal structure). Any attempt now to define the literary as a universal or unitary phenomenon necessarily fails to account for the particular institutional conditions of existence which underpin its assumptions, and falls thereby into the fetishism of a culture of social distinction and of the marketing regime which it supports.

For, far from being a problem, Literature is alive and flourishing in the great world. Think of the John Keating character played by Robin Williams in *The Dead Poets Society*, tearing pages of formalist and 'official' criticism out of the poetry textbook in order to teach his boys that poetry is life, passion, authenticity, humanity. Think of *Educating Rita*, with its alignment of Literature with working-class feminist vigour pitted against a burnt-out academicism. Think of the valorisation of the literary in *Shakespeare in Love*, or *Orlando*, or *Shadowlands*, or any of the recent Jane Austen adaptations. Think of the way the full romantic concept of authorship continues to flourish in the brand-naming of popular authors or in the production of literary biographies or on Oprah, but also in the legal system, where authorship and originality continue to be the major support of copyright. In the cafe culture of upmarket book-shops, in the cultural promotion apparatus of festivals and chat-shows and prizes, and in Hollywood's version of the art movie, Literature remains a timeless product of genius and feeling, directly apprehended in the heart by the empathetic

reader. None of this is at all far from Harold Bloom's reverential resuscita-
tion of the Bard, or Lentricchia's profession of an untheorisable love of literature, or what Sedgwick calls 'the organisation of liberal arts education
as an expensive form of masterpiece theatre'.[15] Indeed, the literary canon
never went away: it was always there as negative theology in deconstruction, and the *Norton Anthology* has simply got fatter. Literary criticism
remains an important part of a marketing system and of a highbrow taste
culture which it blindly serves.

3

There are no texts, readers, meanings or values separate from the institutional framework that determines their place, their use, their very mode of
being.[16] Texts and readers are in the first instance not entities but functions,
values within a system, and texts and readings count as literary or non-literary by virtue of protocols which govern this distinction and specify the
processes (the routine recognitions and the leaps of the heart) by which it
is ongoingly realised. These protocols may require the reader to apprehend
a text (or rather certain kinds of text and not others) as revealed religious
truth, or to scrutinise it for layers of allegorical significance, or to treat it as
the basis for a practice of ethical self-perfection, or to actualise rather than
restrict its full informational potential. Mircea Marghescou calls this
semantic code regulating the informational potential of the linguistic code
the *regime* of a text, and writes that 'only a regime designating the textual
function through opposition to its linguistic function and above all to other
possible semantic functions could give form to this virtuality, transform the
linguistic form into information'.[17] In adapting this concept I take it to designate a semiotic apparatus that inspires and regulates practices of valuation and interpretation, connecting people to textual objects or processes
by means of normative patterns of value and disvalue.[18] But if it is not to be
understood merely as a semiotic relation, the concept of regime must be
more broadly defined as a social apparatus, the structured articulation of a
set of knowledge institutions (the school, the church, the theatre), a more
or less professionalised custodianship of literary knowledge, a designated
set of proper social uses, and a more or less supportive relation to hierarchies of caste or class, of gender, of ethnicity, and so on. Ontologically
impure, the literary regime in this broader sense is composed at once of
codes, practices, organised bodies of texts, physical spaces (libraries, book-
shops, bedrooms), modes of authority, and people and things interacting (all
at once) physically, semiotically, and socially.

In thus cutting the ontological knot, the concept of regime shifts attention from an isolated and autonomous 'reader' and 'text' to the institutional

frameworks which govern what counts as the literary and the possible and appropriate manners of its use and valuation; it asks, not 'what is this thing and what does it mean?', but 'under what conditions and to what ends does this thing come into being, and what operations can be performed upon it?' It describes relations rather than substances. The danger is that in this shift of focus this purely relational concept can itself come to be objectified as a static and final cause – as though values and interpretations could simply be read off from this prior and determinant structure as its necessary effects, and in such a way that the details of any textual engagement could be predicted in advance. It is against this kind of mechanical determinism that Keenan's argument that we should not understand reading as the *application* of a code or programme is directed. The literary regime has no reality beyond the shape it gives to acts of reading. It can be 'recognised' only by means of an interpretation; it must itself be read, and indeed its force resides entirely in its reinforcement (or its modification) in every act of reading. There is no 'system' separate from its actualisations.

To speak of a literary regime is to posit that it is one regime amongst others, existing in a relationship of overlap and difference with regimes of popular reading, of film, of television, of visual culture, of all the domains of activity that make up the realm of cultural practice and cultural value. No special privilege attaches to a literary regime except in so far as such a privilege can be enforced by political means; although it may define itself as different and superior to the regimes of popular culture (for example), in fact it is only different. This difference is not, however, that of one social group from another (not, at least, in complex modern societies); cultural regimes are relatively autonomous from social groups, and do not represent them in the sense of bearing or expressing their essential interests. Although they may recruit preferred constituencies, they are normally not reducible to them. Nor – to make a final qualification to the model of relational difference that I have proposed here – should any of this be taken to imply an absolute relativism, such that no regime either overlaps with or contests the values of another; on the contrary, the principle of relationality requires that we think in terms of a relative relativism, an articulation not of pure differences between fully self-identical formations but of partial, incomplete and constantly contested differences between formations which are themselves internally differentiated and heterogeneous. We ourselves are always positioned, and it is only as a necessary methodological abstraction that we can posit that all regimes should be considered to be axiologically equal. A literary regime is thus neither simply detached from other regimes, nor a homogeneous structure of value; it is a regulatory manifold which makes possible the free exercise of judgement within a limited but disparate range of interpretative possibilities.

4

If this attempt to rethink the status of the categories of the literary, the text, and reading is to have any value other than as a taxonomic exercise, it will be to the extent that it can help to redefine and to redirect what goes on in a good practice of reading. What it suggests, I hope, is that an informed and reflexive reading will find it both possible and necessary to *notice* different kinds of structure: the plane of its vision will move from a focus on a 'text' with 'meanings' to the relation between a text and the set of framing conditions that constitute its readability. In this relation, the 'text' is at once a closed aesthetic space, with lines of force radiating inwards from the framing conditions that establish its closure, and a space of opening which begins to merge with its edges, its borders with the non-textual or the hetero-textual. This is not, however, a relation between an 'inside' and an 'outside' or between a 'text' and its 'context', since the framing conditions are rather the margin that at once carries and unsettles that distinction. As the literary regime changes in its interaction with other systems it constantly modifies the valency of the framing conditions and of the textuality they govern; conversely, new readings or uses of a text become incorporated as structural conditions in the textual regime and thus gradually alter the 'context' of the text.

One way of imagining reading in this perspective is as a series of regressions, from 'content' to 'form' (at increasing levels of abstraction), to the level of 'technique' determining the decision to read in this way, to the 'literary' order that specifies these 'technical' decisions and the objects on which they will work, to the structure of value within which this order is hierarchically ordered, and so on. A series of decisions about how and what to read is thus framed by this regression of frames, and it is this series itself that then becomes an object of attention. But it does not yield itself to a sociological or literary-historical description: the framing conditions of textuality are not to be thought as general and objectively transposable structures which can be apprehended in their own right; they are extrapolations, from an act of reading, of a prior order that can be defined only a posteriori. Textuality and its conditions of possibility are mutually constitutive and can be reconstructed only from each other in a kind of hermeneutic bootstrapping which precludes conclusion and the perspective of a total understanding. This is the methodological implication of Paul de Man's reminder that 'what we usually call literary history has little or nothing to do with literature and that what we call literary interpretation – provided only it is good interpretation – is in fact literary history'.[19]

'History' is the other major dimension of this interpretative focus on constitutive relations. I use the word here to designate very specifically the discrepancy between the conditions of writing and the conditions of reception of a text, either because of a temporal passage or because of translation from one regime to another. Any text which continues to be read over an extended period of time or beyond the bounds of its own culture will in some sense not be the 'same' text; its value and standing, the interpretative possibilities it is seen to offer, its intertextual relations, its social or affective force and the uses to which it can appropriately be put all shift unstably in this passage. At least two sets of framing conditions must then be included in the act of reading, in such a way that interpretation is governed neither by a moment of origin nor by an unreflected application of contemporary relevances, but rather sets itself the task of mediating these two moments. A reading of O'Hara's 'The Day Lady Died', for example, would attend both to the moment of the New York 'School' (itself however a retrospective construct), with its dual relation to high-modernist painting and to a camp aesthetic rooted in certain forms of popular culture, and to the canonisation of that 'third generation' of postwar American poetry (which I in turn would read in part through its influence on Australian poets like John Tranter and John Forbes) and its relation to the problematically marginalised place of poetry in contemporary culture. The mediation of these two moments would then give rise to a restricted set of thematic possibilities (is this a New York poem? A poem about the blues, about African-American culture, about gay culture? A poem about art and its relation to death?) and to choices between them governed by particular, partly definable structures of interest.

This model of a relational reading corresponds, I want to argue, to the project of cultural studies, which I define in shorthand as a concern with the social relations of textuality. The concept of regime expresses one of the fundamental theses of work in cultural studies: that no object, no text, no cultural practice has an intrinsic or necessary meaning or value or function; and that meaning, value, and function are always the effect of specific (and changing, changeable) social relations and mechanisms of signification. The exclusion of the literary from cultural studies in favour of the devalued practices of popular culture was a strategic delimitation of the field against an older and more prestigious discipline which was perceived to be deeply committed to a fetishised object of study. But there is no reason of principle why this exclusion should continue to be sustained, and the time has now perhaps arrived for a rapprochement in which literary studies would learn to attend in a more routine manner to the social relations of signification, and cultural studies would in its turn be reminded of the constitution of its major explanatory categories in practices of reading.

5

To attend to the specific historical, social, and semiotic conditions of existence of the literary is to open the way to the relativisation of the literary in relation to other cultural regimes. With this detachment from final grounds, the structures of value organising each formation now lose their claimed universality: internally more or less coherent, they are nevertheless incommensurate and perhaps incommensurable with the axiologies governing other formations. In one sense what this aporia requires of us is an indefinite deferral of the moment of substantive engagement with literary texts as we seek, in a necessarily perpetual prolegomenon to literary studies, to define and account for those prior conditions governing the status, the relevance, the very possibility of the literary. In another, however, that moment has of course always already arrived, and it carries with it critical uncertainties about what can and should constitute literary study.

The moment of 'theory' in Anglophone literary studies was, almost in the same breath, the promise and the undoing of the possibility of a systematic poetics. The post-structuralist complication of that project failed – for complex political and conjunctural reasons – to work as its continuation, and in its wake the discipline of literary studies has been split between a barely theorised 'ethical' criticism, the idiot scion of the classical and neo-classical pedagogies of literary precept, which generates an endless stream of thematic commentary around the category of the (unified or disunified) 'self'; a deconstructive criticism now enfeebled and demoralised since the disgracing of de Man – an event, however, which perhaps only confirmed an exhaustion that had already firmly set in; a 'political' criticism whose routine practice is grounded in the category of identity and for which textuality is deemed to have an expressive or instrumental relation to race or gender or sexual preference; and a historicist criticism, now more empiricist than Foucauldian, for which the literary archive has a merely documentary value. In one sense, the discipline of literary studies is flourishing as never before; in another, it has become lost in irrelevance.

These are not just issues about disciplines, of course; they have to do with the structure of socially valued knowledge, with hierarchies of cultural value in an era of mass visual literacy, and with the transformation of the ends of the University. At a mundane level, the most important questions for literary studies – the questions that go to the heart of its connection to the world – have to do not with research and the higher reaches of disciplinary development but with undergraduate teaching and the question of what might count as useful knowledge for a literary propaedeutics. The answer to that question is, I believe, less the imparting of systematic information than the teaching of a practice – of 'reading' in the broadest sense – which would meet three conditions: it must be at once continuous with and richer than untutored practice; it must have a theoretical foundation which can be generalised; and it must be able to be extrapolated from 'literary' texts to other discursive kinds. It would be at once a practice of intense scrutiny and intense connection, and it would be integrated with directly practical rhetorical skills of writing and arguing.

Those requirements for theoretical grounding and for a reach to non-literary discourses of course suppose a certain model of disciplinary coherence. Yet, while literary studies has provided an enduringly powerful paradigm of the rhetorical analysis of texts, it continues to find itself in almost complete disarray over the principles that would constitute its integrity as what Northrop Frye called 'an impersonal body of consolidating knowledge'.[20] This disarray means that it is not possible to contemplate redeeming a sense of disciplinary wholeness and purpose by means of a theoretical programme. Indeed, disciplinary coherence may not after all be as desirable a goal as the alternative values of theoretical openness and heuristic richness. It may be that the category of the literary itself is an obstacle both to the formation of a systematic knowledge of texts, and to that interdisciplinary dynamic and that sense of exploratory creativity that has characterised literary studies at its best in the decades since the 'moment of theory'.

It is for this reason that I have stressed the ambivalence of the notion of an emergence of the literary. If that emergence is at every moment a hard-won achievement of the text, it is also what most fully problematises the category of the literary. Its dual temporality institutes a tension and perhaps a necessary contradiction between the interlocking dimensions of instituted value and of reflexive awareness. Take the cases, first, of *The Radetzky March* and *Don Quixote*. In Roth's novel, the very order of the world (*der Bestand der Welt*) is maintained by a fiction, *Schlauheit* – 'guile' or 'cunning' – in which both the bureaucrats of the Ministry of Culture and Education and the Emperor himself, a servant of that order, are complicit.[21] In *Don Quixote* this order is two-fold. On the one hand, the order of life is above all a simulacrum of that of the book: if Sancho has happened to bestow on Don Quixote the title of Knight of the Sad Countenance, this is because 'the sage [*sabio*] whose task it is to write the history of my deeds must have thought it right for me to take some title'; Don Quixote's deeds are governed by an already existent future for which the present has the closure of a past.[22] On the other hand, the order of the world is an essence lying beneath the enchanted surfaces of reality; this enchantment is again the work of 'sages' who turn giants into windmills. But what if this order and this false order are the same? This is the conclusion to which Don Quixote is forced when, learning that the history of his deeds is already in print, he surmises that 'the author of our history is some sage enchanter'[23] (*debe de ser algún sabio encantador el autor de nuestra historia*). We too, however, are drawn to reach this conclusion, since the disenchantments performed by Part I of the novel themselves become a myth to be disenchanted by a further act of literature. Writing never escapes enchantment; enchantment and guile transform it into a universal principle of untruth.

Similarly irreconcilable tensions inform the other two texts which I took to exemplify an emergence of the literary. *Lost Illusions* condemns the commodity production of literature at the very moment in which intellectual property rights – *droits d'auteur* – are becoming entrenched as the basis of the trade in writing, and it does so in a language whose rhetorical force is entirely engaged with the dynamics of contract and money. And 'The Day Lady Died', moving between the packaged writing, the 'little Verlaine/ for Patsy with drawings by Bonnard', and the nameless song of the dying singer, reaches its breathtaking final moment in a line which cannot be read in a grammatically or rhythmically coherent manner. I would say that literature, 'the literary', refuses itself, if this formulation did not repeat so closely the essentialising definitions that derive a general and ahistorical order from particular instances. These texts tell very different histories of the institution of the literary, but the refusal that is specific to each of them can be taken as a figure for the institution of a reading that would at once display and displace the literary regime and the relations of reading it enables.

Notes

1 J. Roth, *The Radetzky March*, trans. E. Tucker and G. Dunlop (London, 1932, 1974), p. 7 (J. Roth, *Radetzkymarsch, Werke 5: Romane und Erzählungen 1930–1936* (Cologne, 1990), p. 145).

2 *Ibid.*

3 *Ibid.*, p. 10 (Roth, *Radetzkymarsch*, p. 149).

4 M. de Cervantes Saavedra, *The Adventures of Don Quixote*, trans. J. M. Cohen (Harmondsworth, 1950), p. 516. (M. de Cervantes Saavedra, *Don Quixote de la Mancha, Obras Completas, Vol. II*, ed. A. Valbuena Prat (Madrid, 1970), p. 1516).

5 H. de Balzac, *Lost Illusions*, trans. H. J. Hunt (Harmondsworth, 1971), p. 302 (H. de Balzac, *Illusions perdues, La Comédie Humaine V* (Paris, 1977), p. 393).

6 T. W. Adorno, 'On an imaginary feuilleton', *Notes to Literature*, trans. S. W. Nicholsen (New York, 1992), vol. 2, p. 34.

7 *Ibid.*, pp. 35–6.

8 Balzac, *Lost Illusions*, p. 251 (Balzac, *Illusions perdues*, p. 348).

9 *Ibid.*, pp. 200–1 (Balzac, *Illusions perdues*, p. 301).

10 *Ibid.*, pp. 489–90 (Balzac, *Illusions perdues*, p. 560).

11 F. O'Hara, 'The Day Lady Died', *The Collected Poems of Frank O'Hara*, ed. D. Allen (New York, 1972), p. 325.

12 M. Perloff, *Frank O'Hara: Poet Among Painters* (New York, 1977), p. 125.

13 Billie Holiday 'whispered' because at the end of her life her voice had almost gone. For background on the poem, cf. B. Gooch, *City Poet: The Life and Times of Frank O'Hara* (New York, 1993), pp. 327–8.

14 T. Keenan, *Fables of Responsibility: Aberrations and Predicaments in Ethics and Politics* (Stanford, 1997), p. 1.

15 E. K. Sedgwick, *Epistemology of the Closet* (Harmondsworth, 1994), p. 51.

16 The following section draws on concepts elaborated in my *Marxism and Literary History* (Cambridge, Mass., 1986), pp. 182–7, and *Cultural Studies and Cultural Value* (Oxford, 1995), pp. 144–51.

17 M. Marghescou, *Le Concept de littérarité* (The Hague, 1974), p. 47 (my translation).

18 Cf. T. Bennett, 'Texts in history: the determinations of readings and their texts', *Bulletin of the Midwest Modern Language Association*, 18:1 (1985), p. 7.

19 P. de Man, *Blindness and Insight: Essays in the Rhetoric of Contemporary Criticism* (Minneapolis, 1983), p. 165.

20 N. Frye, *The Anatomy of Criticism: Four Essays* (New York, 1965), p. 8.

21 The word *Kultus* refers both to culture and to religious observance.

22 Cervantes, *Don Quixote*, p. 147 (Cervantes, *Don Quixote de la Mancha*, p. 1289).

23 *Ibid.*, p. 484 (Cervantes, *Don Quixote de la Mancha*, p. 1497).

peggy kamuf

'FICTION' AND THE EXPERIENCE OF THE OTHER

for derek attridge, in answer to a question

How can we take fiction seriously? The question may be either serious or not-so-serious, an urgently real question or a dismissively rhetorical one. In this form and without any context, it sets up an undecidable oscillation between its grammar and its rhetoric, as Paul de Man might have noted.[1] On the one hand, it asks, seriously, to know how to take fiction seriously, thus also implying that this is something we must or should do, while, on the other hand, it says that we cannot take fiction seriously, that it is not to be taken seriously, that it is even the name of everything which must not be taken seriously.

Let this undecidable grammar stand for the doggedness of the problem we have taking fiction seriously. The question (or statement) resonates to its full, oscillating extent perhaps only in the place where it is already supposed that one *can* take fiction or literature seriously: in that wing of the literary institution housed in the university. Throughout its brief history, academic literary studies will never have had all that much difficulty achieving its standing as a serious undertaking in that institution.[2] In the last decade or so, however, it appears that the discipline of literary studies has begun to negotiate a transition or a displacement into the almost unlimited domain of cultural studies, media studies, communications, and so forth. This development may well indicate that a growing number of practitioners in this domain has renounced the project of taking literature seriously, at least under that name. In any case, it signals some displacement there that affects literature as the name of something to be taken seriously, in a disciplined manner.

This development might be seen as the most recent outcome of the long-standing misunderstanding between the university, as a project of knowledge, and literature, that object about which no essential knowledge is possible. Literature's inclusion among the divisions of knowledge has always been highly ambivalent and incomplete. This ambivalence is such that it can never be finally resolved, only provisionally relieved.[3] A construction that provided some relief for a time was what came to be called literary theory – a misnomer if there ever was one. But the misnomer was no accident; rather, it satisfied the requirement of the discourse of knowledge. And for a while it seemed to bury the ambivalence in a title (and in innumerable course titles in university catalogues), one whose ambiguity could then be forgotten. For the title 'literary theory' may be understood grammatically in at least two ways: as a theory *of* literature, and literary theory, that is, theory *qualified as* literary or *modified by* the literary. In the first sense, the phrase implies that literature is an *object* of theoretical knowledge like any other, while in the second sense, it implies some qualification or modification of theoretical knowledge itself, perhaps even a transformation of its whole basis. 'Literary theory' was thus able to absorb the fundamental ambivalence into these two, not necessarily compatible ideas. Eventually the *mésentente* would have to resurface and would do so in the obvious place, around the question of the literary qualifier or modifier. For indeed, what is literary about literary theory?

This is, as always, a very good question, but it is also irresolvable as soon as it is posed as an ontological question – *what is*, e.g., the literary, literariness, literature? Literature is essentially nothing, essentially nothing but its name. The name of literature has always been peculiarly full of emptiness. This has something to do with why it will have been so easily displaced. But precisely because it is empty of substance, literature is also tied to and dependent on its name. It exists in name only, we could say. This does not mean that the particular name literature, itself, is irreplaceable. Of course it is not, as its history would easily confirm. The name is replaceable; it is even effaceable, at least in theory, although one has to concede that, for quite practical reasons, 'literature' is not about to be effaced from the general archive any time soon. Which is fortunate, because that means we still have time to figure out what, if anything, should be saved from the ruins.

I am going to argue here that it is a certain notion of *fiction* or the fictional operation that, above all, ought not to be dispensed with. In the inaptly named literary theory, it is the irreducible possibility of fiction that is brought to bear in such a way as to shift the ground on which any theoretical discourse may claim validity. Essentially, literary theory takes *fiction* seriously. By this I mean simply that it prizes literature's display of the fictional operation and isolates it as a lever with which to shift a number of familiar theoretical assumptions. Although these have classically found their place in a strictly philosophical tradition and have even defined that

157

tradition to a certain extent, they are certainly not confined to formal philosophy. Philosophy, however, in order to formalise its system, has had to rely on certain assumptions concerning what the fictional operation is or does, assumptions that not coincidentally allow one to proceed *as if* the possibility of fiction had been eliminated, *at least in theory*. It is thus assumed that one need not take fiction or the possibility of fiction into account in order to construct a valid theory of how truth is to be made, known, or recognised. On the contrary, one of the most consistently recurring gestures of philosophical discourse makes out literary fiction in particular but all so-called representative art in general to be essentially dependent or parasitical on, therefore secondary to the whole presumed realm of 'non-fiction'.

Let us take an example, which will be familiar to many. In *How to Do Things with Words*, J. L. Austin writes that, when spoken on stage or in a poem, language is 'in special ways – intelligibly – used not seriously, but in ways *parasitic* upon its normal use – ways which fall under the doctrine of the *etiolations* of language'. This determination is meant to set up and indeed to justify the exclusion that the next sentence performs: '[a]ll this we are *excluding* from consideration'.[4] In his reading of this passage, which would figure prominently in a subsequent dispute with the philosopher John Searle, one can see how Derrida executes very precisely with a series of questions what I described above as a shift of the theoretical ground:

> What is the status of this *parasitism*? In other words, does the quality of risk admitted by Austin *surround* language like a kind of *ditch* or external place of perdition which speech could never hope to leave, but which it can escape by remaining 'at home', by and in itself, in the shelter of its essence or *telos*? Or, on the contrary, is this risk rather its internal and positive condition of possibility? Is that outside its inside, the very force and law of its emergence? In this last case, what would be meant by an 'ordinary' language defined by the exclusion of the very law of language? In excluding the general theory of this structural parasitism, does not Austin ... pass off as ordinary an ethical and teleological determination ... ?[5]

These questions are provoked by Austin's easy acquiescence to philosophical doctrine as regards the status of the literary or fictional object. By defining that status as parasitical on ordinary language use, the doctrine Austin uncritically endorses encloses theory, for example the theory of speech acts, within the limited and finally untenable space from which its own conditioning possibility has been excluded. Instead of elucidating the theorised object's real possibilities, the theory truncates them so as to uphold 'an ethical and teleological determination' of the object. At this juncture at least, it closes the door on a general theory that can account in the same terms for all speech acts, without recourse to a prior determination of what constitutes 'serious' or 'non-serious' speech.

Thus, the shift onto a more general theoretical terrain has to put in question what Austin calls here the 'doctrine of the etiolations of language'. Doubtless this doctrine would identify many kinds of 'etiolations' other than the literary. Yet, it is certainly not by chance that, to illustrate the sort of utterance he has in mind, Austin goes to the storehouse of literature, as broadly defined: 'a performative utterance will, for example, be *in a peculiar way* hollow or void if said by an actor on the stage, or if introduced in a poem, or spoken in soliloquy'.[6] Theatre and poetry are cited precisely because they are exemplary of the hollowing or voiding of utterance that we recognise as the consequence of fiction's operation. Although, as Austin acknowledges, such hollowing out can happen to utterance anywhere and not just in a poem, on a theatre's stage, or in a novel, these more or less generic categories serve to *announce or mark* the work of fiction by calling it poem, play, novel, story, soliloquy. In this way, the categories *marked out* as fiction seem to offer themselves as example, whenever one needs one, of a *general* operation of fiction that, as Austin puts it, can 'infect *all* utterances'.[7]

What, however, is literature exemplary of, exactly? What does the fictional operation do? Before going much further trying to take fiction seriously, shouldn't we be clear at least about what it is that solicits such serious concerns? Or rather, not what it *is* but what it *does*? The question concerning fiction is not: what is it? but rather, what does it do? This form of the question is dictated at least in part by the word itself, deriving as it does from the Latin past-participle root *fict-* of the transitive verb *fingere*: to shape, fashion, make, feign, contrive, invent; (cf. *fictor, fictoris*: a fashioner, counterfeiter). Fiction would be a kind of doing, then, even though the word is most often used now as a noun. As a substantive, however, it names something without substance, hollow, false, or, as Austin preferred to say, void. ('Is not a statement', he asked, 'which refers to something which does not exist not so much false as void?')[8] A fiction refers to nothing that exists. It refers, but to nothing in existence. Thus, the fictional act or operation consists in making reference but also in suspending the referent. It is a referential operation that does something with or to reference.

Let us try to specify further the nature of this referential operation. As we've just seen, literary fiction, because of its peculiar hollowness, is left out of consideration by Austin in his elaboration of a theory of speech acts. Despite that, he shows persistent interest in the general question of how the referent may be, as he calls it, voided by a statement, that is, by a constative utterance. He takes up this question in a section of the second lecture, right before the passage already cited, where he is wondering whether the sort of 'infelicity' that characterises performative utterances can also affect the way a *statement* does what it is supposed to do, which is to refer, reliably, to a true or real state of affairs.

> Lastly we may ask – and here I must let some of my cats on the table – does the notion of infelicity apply to utterances *which are statements*? So far we have produced the infelicity as characteristic of the *performative* utterance, which was 'defined' (if we can call it so much) mainly by contrast with the supposedly familiar 'statement'. Yet I will content myself here with pointing out that one of the things that has been happening lately in philosophy is that close attention has been given even to 'statements' which, though not false exactly nor yet 'contradictory', are outrageous. For instance, statements which refer to something which does not exist as, for example, 'The present King of France is bald'. There might be a temptation to assimilate this to purporting to bequeath something which you do not own. Is there not a presupposition of existence in each? Is not a statement which refers to something which does not exist not so much false as void?[9]

When Austin specifies that a statement may be outrageous without being either false or contradictory, he makes clear that such infelicity is a matter neither of faulty logic, nor of some kind of falsehood: a lie, a misstatement, or a misapprehension of facts. It thus has some other source that he will proceed to elucidate, first by assimilating or equating the sample statement to an infelicitous performative and then by transferring the infelicity of the performative utterance to the constative one.

One sees that Austin is interested above all in the way in which a statement may also do something, like a performative. Yet, it is difficult to determine, in the analogy he makes between the 'The present King of France is bald' and a false promise, just how far one can take the assimilation of constatives to performatives. Does it go so far as to transfer moral outrage to the statement for referring to what does not exist? This is unclear. According to Austin, the statement's outrageousness arises from a 'presupposition of existence' that one makes upon hearing such a statement, no less than one supposes a benefactor to own what he promises to bequeath. In the case of the promise, the presupposition is easy to grant: because the promise will have been made in some situation of address, the presupposition takes the form of a presumption of the other's good faith. Moreover, the addressee and potential legatee has every interest in presupposing the existence of the other's property, since he stands to inherit it. But in the situation of the so-called statement, why does Austin suppose that it presupposes existence?

This would seem to be because the utterance 'The present King of France is bald' is understood as uttered here, now, by someone addressing me, or else it is a statement that I, or some 'I', have just now made to another. Yet, the situation of present address is only one among an incalculable number of others imaginable in which the same statement might be said, even in all seriousness, without necessarily appearing outrageous. One does not need to invoke theatre or poetry (for Austin would have us consider only serious speech) in order to imagine many other contexts in which the same statement, 'The present King of France is bald', would be altogether banal, hardly outrageous, without being either false, contradictory, or fictional, at least in the literary sense: if made, for example, in the memoirs of a royal wigmaker. Austin thus supposes the utterance fully in the present, where a speaker is present to a listener, in time if not in space. This presence of the speech situation is the condition of the particular presupposition of existence that Austin makes here. Under that condition, a statement, to be fully felicitous, ought to be full of this presence, rather than the empty vehicle of a voided referent. That is the outrage. It is an outrage to presence, to the present reference, because it voids or suspends it.

This presupposition of presence has everything to do, of course, with the exclusion from serious discourse of fictional modes of speech, where all 'speakers' are radically absent, that is, with an absence that has never been present. And yet, Austin's analysis of the 'statement which refers to something which does not exist' situates quite precisely the standing possibility of fiction as a suspended or voided relation to the referent. He has not, however, in the least foreclosed that possibility (for how could he?). He has, however, limited the scope of the question 'what do such speech acts do?' He looks for an answer there where language does something other than state what is the case, but he ends up assimilating fiction to a moral (or immoral) action. This is what Derrida identified, in the passage cited above, as 'an ethical and teleological determination'.

Yet, clearly Austin's fictional example of a fiction also exceeds this determination. That is, it does something more (or less) than that to which it is being compared. It also *marks and lets be remarked* the voiding of the referent, which is why it can be taken as an example of an outrageous statement in the first place. Such marking is not at all necessary for the false promise; indeed, if it wants to achieve rather than annul the effect of a promise, the speech act will have to avoid remarking and thus making known the non-existence of the referent.

Fiction, the excessive mark of fiction, suspends the sign as sign of a referent, which otherwise, without the mark, would be presupposed. As such a mark, it has its 'being' only by virtue of an act of reading, whereby its mark gets remarked. It is thus less the name of an entity than the name of an *experience*. What does it mean to call fiction, literature, experience?

This term can be used here only with considerable caution, for one must take care not to understand, as one commonly does, the 'lived' or 'life' experience of a subject, the sum of adventures or occurrences to which some subject will have been present as conscious witness and participant.[10] It is true that literature, in the modern sense, has been massively assimilated to this notion of experience, hence to the subject. The appropriation by the subject has been mounted from at least two directions. First, when it is thought to record, represent, or report the lived experiences of a writer, literature, and above all lyric poetry, is made to stand for or refer to the full presence to itself of this subject's consciousness. Secondly, and this is above all the case for narrative fiction, when literature is thought to make available the experience of 'characters', which can be assumed vicariously or virtually by the reader as his or her subjective experience for the duration of the reading. I wish to evoke, however, an experience of literature, fiction, or poetry, that, on the contrary, takes place outside and before any subject, an extreme experience, therefore, because from beyond the circle within which the subject appropriates experience as its own. The extreme experience of literature recalls, as both Jean-Luc Nancy and Philippe Lacoue-Labarthe have done, that the Latin *ex-periri* at its root associates crossing with danger, risk, *periculum* at the perimeter.[11] Fiction, poetry, would be experience only on the condition that we understand: experience of the other.

But is there any other kind? What would an experience be without any intervention of difference? How could there be an experience of the same, an experience without experience, in sum, because without any difference from itself? This is the serious question that fiction keeps open, on the condition that one continues to take seriously the ways in which its excessive, extreme mark resists assimilation to and appropriation by a subject's 'own' experience of presence to itself.

It is this resistance that would be remarked by 'literary theory', that is, by a thinking that does not enclose itself within the presupposed existence, to recall Austin's language, of its objects or its referents. At the edge of the philosophical thesis of existence, literature offers philosophy the experience of the suspended thesis of existence, which is why it can in no sense be simply opposed to the experience of philosophy that it also makes possible or even provokes. This 'force of provocation' is discerned by Derrida in what he calls a neutralised or neutralising 'philosophical' experience:

> Even if they always do so unequally and differently, poetry and literature
> have as a common feature that they suspend the 'thetic' naivety of the tran-
> scendent reading. This also accounts for the philosophical force of these
> experiences, a force of provocation to think phenomenality, meaning, object,
> even being as such, a force which is at least potential, a philosophical *dynamis*
> – which can, however, be developed only in response, in the experience of
> reading, because it is not hidden in the text like a substance. Poetry and lit-

erature provide or facilitate 'phenomenological' access to what makes of a thesis a *thesis as such*. Before having a philosophical content, before being or bearing such and such a 'thesis,' literary experience, writing or reading, is a 'philosophical' experience which is neutralized or neutralizing insofar as it allows one to think the thesis; it is a nonthetic experience of the thesis, of belief, of position, of naivety … But it is true that … the phenomenological language in which I'm presenting these things ends up being dislodged from its certainties (self-presence of absolute transcendental consciousness or of the indubitable *cogito*, etc.) and dislodged precisely by the extreme experience of literature, or even quite simply of fiction and language.[12]

Literary experience is a neutralised or neutralising 'philosophical' experience inasmuch as it suspends thetic referentiality, thereby allowing one to think that thesis as such. But this neutralisation is never completely effective – it is, in a sense, itself neutralised – since, as Derrida goes on to remark, the suspension of the referent is also, irreducibly, a suspension *from* or dependence on the referent. Literature, that is, does not effect an absolute suspension of the referent, which would destroy its structure ('a literature that talked only about literature or a work that was purely self-referential would immediately be annulled').[13] Thus, whereas 'literature's *being-suspended* neutralizes the "assumption" which it carries', this capacity remains 'double, equivocal, contradictory, *hanging on* and *hanging between*, *dependent* and *independent*, an "assumption" both assumed and suspended'.[14] That which I am calling the experience of fiction, then, would be essentially equivocal, hanging as it does between the suspension of the referent, as signalled by fiction's mark, and the persistence of the assumption of referential language, whereby fiction also always exceeds itself toward something other.

Derrida's analysis of this equivocation presents a problem, however, for our own reliance on the term 'fiction' up to this point. For fiction itself is an equivocal term, indeed a 'terribly equivocal' one, as we are reminded here: '[t]he terribly equivocal word *fiction* (which is sometimes misused as though it were coextensive with literature) says something about this situation. Not all literature is of the genre or the type of "fiction", but there is fictionality in all literature. We should find a word other than "fiction"'.[15]

The point is certainly well taken and we would do well to recall the terrible equivocation 'fiction' shares with the Greek *pseudos* (both poetic fiction and falsehood, lying), which Plato, for example, exploits to the full in Books 2 and 10 of the *Republic*. This equivocation can always superimpose itself on the necessarily ambivalent suspension of the fictional operation. And because this double suspension is irreducible, the equivocation really is terrible, that is, terribly equivocal. Fiction is also terrifying, terrorising, or terribilising so long as it can be taken to name those acts called lying, perjury, misleading statement, or, as in Austin's example, false promise. That is perhaps why one should try to find another name and reserve it for 'fictions' that we consent to experience as neither true nor false, innocent nor guilty, 'beyond good and evil', the interpretation or, more exactly, the experience of a world without substance and without subject.

To call for another name for this 'fiction' does not, however, call for the end of the equivocation as such. Rather it would displace that name with and to another name. In other words, it cannot be a matter of putting an end to equivocation, but of calling upon a plurality of names, and thus a plurivocity, more precisely a *heteronomy*. Heteronomy – the law of more than one law – preserves equivocity in another name, the name of the name, 'Literature' or 'fiction'.

We are tempted to call out, as Juliet did into the night: Oh be some other name! The cry would echo that of every reader whose experience takes place at the limit, the extreme limit of this heteronomy. It calls into Being, it is the calling of being at the limit of everything that is, the whole world as it is presumed 'to be', in Hamlet's phrase. Derrida, who has also been known to recite both *Romeo and Juliet* and *Hamlet*, puts it in these terms in the interview we've been following:

> Experience of Being, nothing less, nothing more, on the edge of meta-physics, literature perhaps stands on the edge of everything, almost beyond everything, including itself. It's the most interesting thing in the world, maybe more interesting than the world, and this is why, if it has no defini-tion, what is heralded and refused under the name of literature cannot be identified with any other discourse.[16]

Almost beyond everything: this is the equivocation and it is irreducible. 'Fiction' remains irreducibly suspended between the world of presup-posed referents, which it can never fully suspend, and this same every-thing-of-the-world, everything-in-the-world from which it hangs suspended. It suspends the world: everything hangs from it. It is the pos-sibility of world, of possible, virtual, fictional worlds, of other worlds.

As to finding a word other than fiction, one might look to the recurrence in this analysis of the figure of a certain neutralisation. Reference is made to a 'neutralised or neutralising' philosophical experience. Neutralisation is said to be the effect of the literary or the fictional on philosophy. Rather than an experience of fiction, then, would one do better to evoke an expe-rience of neutralisation, neutrality, the neuter, or the neutral? 'The neu-tral': this term (if it is one and only one, without equivocation) has perhaps a certain force to dislodge what philosophy poses as thesis, which is always the thesis of some subject. What would be neutralised by 'fiction' is the thesis, the position of the subject.

In a section or fragment of *The Infinite Conversation* from which, unless I am mistaken, the word fiction has entirely disappeared, Maurice Blanchot deploys a notion of 'the neuter' or 'the neutral'[17] as what it becomes possible to read in the wake of Kafka's writing:

> In the meantime Kafka wrote … What Kafka teaches us – even if this formulation cannot be directly attributed to him – is that storytelling brings the neutral into play. Narration that is governed by the neutral is kept in the custody of the third-person 'he', a 'he' that is neither a third person nor the simple cloak of impersonality. The narrative 'he' [*il*] in which the neutral speaks is not content to take the place usually occupied by the subject, whether the latter is a stated or an implied 'I' or the event that occurs in its impersonal signification. The narrative 'he' or 'it' unseats every subject just as it disappropriates all transitive action and all objective possibility.[18]

Notice that Blanchot is describing here an experience that is undecidably one of writing and reading. It is an experience of narration governed no longer by a subject and an organising subjective point of view, all of which has been neutralised from somewhere outside the circle of narrated/narrating subjects. This narration, in other words, is governed in all its aspects by the neutral, which because it is external to language, can receive no simple name. Characterless, featureless, it is consigned or, as Blanchot writes, 'kept in the custody of the third-person "he",' that is, of the neutral pronoun *il*, not only 'he' but 'it', and thus 'neither a third person nor the simple cloak of impersonality'. Blanchot here is signalling an essential difference with the impersonal narration achieved by Flaubert, where 'the ideal is still the form of representation of classical theatre' and where impersonality is that of aesthetic distance.[19] Flaubert's achievement of impersonal narration, in other words, leaves altogether intact, according to Blanchot, the Kantian, disinterested subject of aesthetic contemplation and enjoyment. It is this subjective theatre of visibility and disinterested distance that Kafka's writing displaces, and displaces definitively for whoever now takes 'fiction' seriously.

With Kafka, 'fiction' takes itself seriously, that is, it takes seriously the demands made by an exteriority that can no longer be seen as set up for the subject's pleasure, indeed that can no longer be *seen* at all. But Kafka's writing of 'the neutral, the "he/it"' also comes after a long sequence of displacements of the passage from 'I' to 'he/it' that, as Blanchot recalls near the beginning of the essay, he had earlier identified as the essential gesture of writing: '[i]f, as has been shown (in *The Space of Literature*), to write is to pass from "I" to "he"'.[20] For Blanchot, in other words, the pronoun shift marks all writing; it is even what writing essentially is or does. Literature, 'fiction', is the space, however, in which this gesture is remarked in and as narrative. The narrative possibility will have been repeatedly affirmed, throughout literary 'history', by the different displacements of the 'he/it'. Through these displacements, the neuter pronoun can be traced as the marker of 'the unlighted event that occurs when one tells a story'.[21] If the event is 'unlighted', *inéclairé*, that is because what is taking place is a telling and not a showing, a writing and not a pointing to objects as they already are in the world. Blanchot will quickly sketch here some of these displacements: from epic story, to the disenchantment of story in *Don Quixote*, where the neutral 'he/it' becomes 'everyday life without adventure: what happens when nothing is happening, the course of the world as it escapes notice, the passing of time, life routine and monotonous'.[22] And, he continues, it is through this 'banality of the real' that 'realism seizes on the form of the novel that for a long time to come will be the most effective genre of the developing bourgeoisie'. This ideological seizure finds a sturdy handle in the 'he' to the extent it also …

> … marks the intrusion of the character: the novelist is one who foregoes saying 'I,' but delegates this power to others; the novel is peopled with little 'egos' – tormented, ambitious, unhappy, although always satisfied in their unhappiness … the novel's narration, that of individuality, is already marked … by an ideology to the extent that it assumes that the individual, with his particular characteristics and his limits, suffices to express the world: it assumes, in other words, that the course of the world remains that of individual particularity.[23]

It is this whole ideologically marked construction of narrative that yields, deconstructs, when, in the meantime, Kafka wrote. In Kafka's texts, as already noted, the '"he" of narration in which the neutral speaks is not content to take the place usually occupied by the subject, whether this latter is a stated or implied "I" or the event that occurs in its impersonal signification'. There is thus a shift of the essential 'fictional' gesture, whereby 'I' passes into 'he'.

As Susan Hanson has remarked in the introduction to her translation of *The Infinite Conversation*, this text should be read as continuing but also breaking with Blanchot's thinking of the 'space of literature' in the earlier work by that title. She remarks:

> This break is signaled most clearly by the emergence of the problematic of *autrui* – by the *address* of *autrui* as Blanchot responds to it throughout the text. While the carefully worked through terms of the question of reflection that Blanchot brings out in his earlier critical writings in fact prepare the space of encounter with *autrui*, the thematization of *autrui* in this collection signals the intrusion of otherness with an urgency that is not heard [earlier].[24]

One may find a confirmation of this observation at the juncture we are examining, where, after recalling his own earlier formulation of the essential gesture of writing in the pronoun shift, Blanchot goes on to raise a fundamental question and to take it as the one to which this essay will endeavour to respond:

> If, as has been shown (in *The Space of Literature*), to write is to pass from 'I' to 'he,' but if 'he,' when substituted for 'I,' does not simply designate another me any more than it would designate aesthetic disinterestedness – that impure contemplative pleasure that allows the reader and the spectator to participate in the tragedy through distraction – what remains to be discovered is what is at stake when writing responds to the demands of this uncharacterizable 'he'.[25]

That is, what is at stake when writing no longer portrays or relays the interests of subjects? Or when it no longer pretends to *show* a spectacle to the reader's disinterest? When the question is later addressed specifically to Kafka's texts, the notion of subjective interest/disinterest is going to be displaced into the strange figure of a concern with what does not concern one and indeed concerns no one directly. But already here in this general formulation of the question, what is said to be at stake and in play is writing (or reading, still undecidably one and the other) as possibility of *response* to demands that come from some other who or which is radically uncharacterisable: the neutral. Blanchot's articulation of the stakes is very precise: 'what remains to be discovered is what is at stake *when writing responds* to the demands of this uncharacterizable "he"'. Writing responds, to the demands of the neutral other. Perhaps, then, it is simply the possibility of response – to what concerns me without concerning me – that is at stake?

This is suggested when the vocabulary of the stake, of what is *en jeu*, recurs a few pages later. The passage in question is describing the marked austerity of Kafka's narratives, which should not be confused with the austerity of Flaubertian impersonality and distance. Kafka's distance, in effect, puts something altogether other in play, *en jeu*.

> The distance – the creative disinterestedness (so visible in Flaubert inasmuch as he must struggle to maintain it) – which was the writer's and the reader's distance from the work and authorized contemplative pleasure, *now enters into the work's very sphere in the form of an irreducible strangeness* … this distance is the medium of the novelistic world, the space in which the *narrative experience* unfolds in its unique simplicity – *an experience that is not recounted but that is in play* [en jeu] *when one recounts*. This distance is not simply lived as such by the central character who is always at a distance from himself … this distance keeps him aloof from himself, removing him from the centre, because it is constantly decentring the work in an immeasurable and indiscernible way, while at the same time introducing into the most rigorous narration the alteration occasioned by another kind of speech or by the other as speech (as writing).[26]

Although the italics added to these sentences ought to suffice for commentary, since Blanchot's language is, as always, so precise, let us nevertheless attempt, not paraphrase, but something more like another, looser translation. It is a matter of a distance that no longer holds the work at a distance, from writer or reader, because it now *enters* the work as 'irreducible strangeness'. Distance is, as it were, brought closer. What does it mean to say distance enters the work? It means that distance is now in play, at stake, *en jeu* in what the passage calls the narrative *experience* (the word is repeated), which is glossed as 'the experience that is not recounted but that is in play [*en jeu*] when one recounts'. This description, then, is of the *entry* of distance or something distant into the experience involved 'when one recounts'. And what enters alters, for distance introduces 'the alteration occasioned by another kind of speech'. Narrative experience puts in play the experience of distance and alterity.

As the description continues into a new paragraph, the term *enjeu* (now used as a composite noun) will recur once more, indicating that one is still endeavouring to respond to the question of what is at stake in this writing. But shouldn't the question also be: how can anything come to be at stake there at all? What has happened to turn writing, that space of the disinterestedness of aesthetic distance, into the space of an *enjeu*, and even perhaps (upping the ante),[27] the space of all possible *enjeux*? I continue the citation:

> One consequence [of this sort of change], immediately evident, is noteworthy. As soon as the alien distance becomes the stake [*enjeu*] and, in a sense, the substance of the story, the reader can no longer be disinterested in it; he who up to now has been identifying from afar with the story in progress (living it, for his part, in the mode of contemplative irresponsibility), *can no longer take a disinterested pleasure in it*. What is happening? What *new exigency has befallen the reader*? It is not that this concerns him: on the contrary, it concerns him in no way, and perhaps concerns no one; it is in a sense the *non-concerning* [Blanchot's italics], but with regard to which, by the same token, the reader *can no longer comfortably take any distance* since he cannot properly [*d'une manière juste*] situate himself in relation to what does not even present itself as unsituatable. How, then, is the reader to set himself or herself apart from the absolute distance that seems to have taken all distance up into itself? Without any bearings, deprived of the interest of reading, *he is no longer allowed to look at things from afar, to keep between things and himself the distance* that belongs to the gaze ...[28]

This time, with the added italics, I would bring out all the ways these sentences are defining a heteronomous law to which reading is submitted once distance enters into the narrative experience, once distance can no longer be kept at the comfortable distance of a disinterested distraction. It is this relation of aesthetic distance that will always have been irresponsible; more precisely, it irresponsibilises the reader, who has no call to respond to anything set before him or her because distance remains the distance between the reader and the object of contemplation. But when distance *enters into* the narrative experience, when it involves that experience in the stakes of distance, when distance, as we've just read, 'becomes the stake and, in a sense, the substance of the story', thereby displacing the narrative 'substance' or substrate that is the subject, well, then, something happens to the reader and to the reader's experience. Remarking Blanchot's language closely, one reads that the reader *falls under* a new demand or necessity. This affirmation comes in the form of a question: '[s]ous quelle exigence nouvelle [le lecteur] est-il tombé?' The experience of reading is governed here by a law of distance, a heteronomy, which both falls upon it, compels it, and touches it but *as* distance. The experience of the reader thereby comes to involve a new exigency that befalls it. Above all, what is new is the possibility of response that this exigency or demand confers upon this act – reading/writing – which, up until then, has been left to its disinterested irresponsibility. The narrative experience enters the age of its responsibility and this is marked by the necessity of somehow *responding* to distance. The description insists on the new constraint that falls upon the reader, who 'can no longer take a disinterested pleasure in it', who 'can no longer comfortably take any distance', and who is 'no longer allowed to look at things from afar'. This new demand, in other words, demands what, for the self-interested subject, can only seem to be a paradoxical response: to concern oneself with the non-concerning. More precisely, not to keep one's distance from it, even as one has no longer any measure with which to determine the proper distance. The reader's response to this demand cannot take its bearings 'since he cannot properly [*d'une manière juste*] situate himself in relation to what does not even present itself as unsituatable'. There is thus demand and impossibility of responding to the demand 'd'une manière juste'. What is now impossible is any calculation of the *proper* distance in one's relation to the other, since the other's distance is such that it does not present itself as situatable or even unsituatable in a space no longer oriented by vision or point of view, that of some subject or other. It does not come from a subject, yet the demand remains a demand, the necessity to respond to the other 'd'une manière juste': *in a proper or correct way*, but also *in a just manner*, which is to say, to respond justly, in the manner of justice.

Nothing less, therefore, than the demand of justice is at stake in the narrative experience, which is the experience of a distance and a strangeness, the experience of a relation that is *not yet* or *no longer* between subjects. Justice is at stake in this relation because it alone would speak, *if that were possible*, the neutral or neutralised language transcending language, from somewhere outside language, as other than language. What is at stake and in play in the narrative experience is always the *possibility* of the relation to the other who *just is* different from all the concepts and names by which language situates otherness within its own limits.

It is this possibility that is carried or borne by the form of writing Blanchot calls *récit*, the word that can be read as displacing, with great economy and precision, the term 'fiction'.[29] This displacement is very closely traced in the final pages of the fragment we're reading, which ought to be cited *in extenso* and commented upon endlessly, 'were there world enough and time'. But as we're reaching the limit of what can be said in this brief essay, let us once again resort to the silent commentary of italics on a long final quotation from 'The narrative voice, the "he", the neutral'. I will simply underscore, in these rapidly telescoped lines, certain active verbs or phrases indicating an action, be it the strange 'action' of *attraction* or of *tendency*, or yet again, a certain force of *obliqueness* that turns language toward an outside, if not inside out, emptying or voiding it, as Austin might have said, of its power to pose or express being, to do what is called, in the lines I'll cite, the work of being. It is this kind of action or attraction (the attraction not of sameness nor finally of strangeness, but of the neutral that withdraws from even this difference), that, we read, *may be* at stake in *récit*, that is, 'in recounting (writing)'. Although there is no further recurrence in the lines we'll cite of the term *enjeu*, the mode of this 'might be', 'may be', or 'maybe' locates all the same something that is still in play and therefore at stake in *récit* or writing. It is the mode of possibility, which neither affirms nor negates but, as Blanchot writes, *donne à entendre*, gives to be heard the possibility of all that can be understood through affirmation and negation. The neutral *récit*, then, would be – might be, maybe – the possibility of putting anything at all at stake in language. As such, it has an irreducibly *critical* function, in an almost-Kantian sense of the term. It criticises, one might say, all that language presumes to name; that is, it both sets and lifts the limit of language, keeping thus *at stake*, in possibility, the opening to the other.

> The narrative 'he' [or 'it', *il*], whether absent or present, whether it affirms itself or hides itself, and whether or not it alters the conventions of writing – linearity, continuity, readability – thus *marks* the intrusion of the other – understood as neutral – in its irreducible strangeness and in its wily perversity. The other speaks. But when the other is speaking, no one speaks because the other ... is neither the one nor the other, and the neutral that indicates it withdraws it from both, as it does from unity, always establishing

it outside the term, the act, or the subject through which it claims to offer itself. The narrative (I do not say narrating) voice derives from this its aphony ...

Although it may well borrow the voice of a judiciously chosen character, or even create the hybrid function of mediator (the voice that ruins all mediation), it is always different from what utters it: it is the indifferent-difference that alters the personal voice. Let us (on a whim) call it spectral, ghostlike. Not that it comes from beyond the grave, or even because it would once and for all represent some essential absence, but because it always *tends* to absent itself in its *bearer*...

Tacit, the narrative voice *attracts* language indirectly, *obliquely* and, under this attraction of an *oblique* speech, allows the neutral to speak ... [I]t may be that recounting [*récit*] (writing) *draws language into a possibility* of saying that would say being without saying it, and yet without denying it either. Or again, to say this more clearly, too clearly: it would establish the centre of gravity of speech elsewhere, there where speaking would neither affirm being nor need negation in order *to suspend the work of being* that is ordinarily accomplished in every form of expression. In this respect, the narrative voice is the most critical voice that, unheard, might give to be heard. That is why, as we listen to it, we *tend* to confuse it with the *oblique voice* of misfortune, or of madness.[30]

Although commentary must break off here, a few words in conclusion about this last remarked tendency, the tendency to *confuse* narrative voice with another voice. Given that both are said to be 'oblique', it cannot be a matter so easily of avoiding the confusion between the one and the other, between narrative voice and the voice of 'misfortune, or of madness', between, that is, a neutral other or exteriority, which knows neither fortune nor misfortune, reason nor madness, and the other who will already have come to stand before me suffering from all the marks these differences make. Therefore, one should not read any simple admonition here to distinguish what we tend to confuse. *Perhaps even*, and on the contrary, it is through the inevitability of this confusion that one can still hear the call to respond to the other, in other words, the call to or toward justice.[31]

Perhaps – a final perhaps – this call for response brings its answer to the terribly equivocal question with which I began: how can one take fiction seriously? For now we might even be able to reply, after Derrida, Blanchot, Kafka, and quite a few others have written: there is nothing that could or should have a more *serious*, *critical* claim on our attention than 'fiction'.

- 'Fiction'?

- No. No 'fictions', never again.

- Oh be some other name.

Notes

1 'The grammatical model of the question becomes rhetorical not when we have, on the one hand, a literal meaning and on the other hand a figural meaning, but when it is impossible to decide by grammatical or other linguistic devices which of the two meanings (that can be entirely incompatible) prevails' (P. de Man, 'Semiology and rhetoric', in *Allegories of Reading: Figural Language in Rousseau, Nietzsche, Rilke, and Proust* (New Haven, 1979), p. 10).

2 On the relation of literary studies to the modern scientific university, see my *Division of Literature: Or the University in Deconstruction* (Chicago, 1997) and B. Readings, *The University in Ruins* (Cambridge, Mass., 1996).

3 On this ambivalence as an irreducible feature in the 'humanities', see S. Weber, 'Ambivalence: the humanities and the study of literature', in Weber, *Institution and Interpretation* (Minneapolis, 1987).

4 J. L. Austin, *How to Do Things with Words*, ed. J. O. Urmson and M. Sbisà (Cambridge, Mass., 1975), p. 22 (italics in the original).

5 J. Derrida, 'Signature event context', *Glyph*, 1 (1977), pp. 190–1.

6 Austin, *How to Do Things with Words*, p. 22.

7 *Ibid.*, p. 21.

8 *Ibid.*, p. 20.

9 *Ibid.*

10 For a very interesting discussion of experience and poetry, see W. Benjamin, 'On some motifs in Baudelaire', in Benjamin, *Illuminations*, trans. H. Zohn (New York, 1969). Benjamin's interpretation of Baudelaire's experience pays particular attention to the distinction between *Erlebnis* and *Erfahrung*, that is, between a lived moment and experience that enters memory. For a clarification of this distinction in Benjamin's thought, see Benjamin, 'Central Park', trans. L. Spencer, *New German Critique*, 34 (Winter 1985), p. 57.

11 See, for example, J-L. Nancy, *L'Expérience de la liberté* (Paris, 1988), p. 25, and P. Lacoue-Labarthe, *La poésie comme expérience* (Paris, 1986), p. 30. See as well my 'Experience of deconstruction', *Angelaki*, 4:3 (2000).

12 D. Attridge, 'An interview with Jacques Derrida', in Attridge (ed.), *Acts of Literature* (New York, 1992), pp. 45–6.

13 *Ibid.*, p. 47.

14 *Ibid.*, p. 49.

15 *Ibid.*

16 *Ibid.*, p. 47.

17 Both translations have been given of Blanchot's term: 'le neutre'. There are in fact three extant English translations of this essay: 'The narrative voice (the "he", the neuter)', trans. L. Davis, in Blanchot, *The Gaze of Orpheus and Literary Essays* (Barrytown, 1981); 'The narrative voice or the impersonal "he"', trans. S. Rabinovitch, in *The Sirens' Song: Selected Essays by Maurice Blanchot* (Bloomington, 1982); and most recently, 'The narrative voice (the "he", the neutral)', trans. S. Hanson, in M. Blanchot, *The Infinite Conversation* (Minneapolis, 1993). We will follow Susan Hanson's translation and will therefore refer more consistently to 'the neutral'.

18 Blanchot, 'The narrative voice', pp. 383–4.

19 *Ibid.*, p. 382.

20 *Ibid.*, p. 380.

21 *Ibid.*, p. 381.

22 *Ibid.*

23 *Ibid.*

24 *Ibid.*, pp. xxv–vi.

25 *Ibid.*, p. 380.

26 *Ibid.*, pp. 383–4 (italics added).

27 On this phrase as marking the anteriority of response in relation to any knowledge, see S. Weber, 'La surenchère (upping the ante)', in *Le passage des frontières: Autour du travail de Jacques Derrida*, ed. M-L. Mallet (Paris, 1994), p. 147.

28 Blanchot, 'The narrative voice', p. 384 (italics added, and translation modified).

29 The term *récit* means narrative, story, recounting. But it also carries the mark of repetition, of citation. It thus conjoins the remarking of the mark with the citation of some other speech. On the question of the *récit* in Blanchot, a question that is more precisely a demand, see J. Derrida, 'Survivre', in *Parages* (Paris, 1986), esp. pp. 130–52.

30 *Ibid.*, pp. 385–7 (italics added). These last words of the text are followed by the signal for a final footnote, which begins: '[i]t is this voice – the narrative voice – that I hear, perhaps rashly, perhaps rightly, in the narrative by Marguerite Duras that I mentioned [*Le ravissement de Lol V. Stein*]'. The note then proceeds to justify in a few lines this reference to Duras's novel. But it also might be taken to suggest that we read the final lines of the text precisely in the sense of such an admonition to avoid confusing narrative voice with the voice of some character, Lol V. Stein, for example, whose 'oblique voice' would be that of 'misfortune, or of madness'. Read in this sense, the final sentence of the text wards off the sort of psychological criticism that has been the mainstay for so long of writing about narrative fiction, including Duras's fiction.

31 In *Altered Reading: Levinas and Literature* (Chicago, 1999), Jill Robbins concludes her very fine and thorough study with a brief section devoted to Blanchot, whose narrative writing earns it the status of exception, along with very few others, to Levinas's otherwise consistently negative judgement concerning the ethical force of literary discourse. She points out that 'Levinas acknowledges very precisely the possible convergence and the limits of such a convergence between the alterity of the ethical and the alterity of the literary when he describes the literary work of art in Blanchot as an "impersonal speech, without a 'you'", without interpellation, without vocative, and at the same time distinct from "a coherent discourse" manifesting universal Reason, both discourse and Reason belonging to the order of the Day'. This is to say that at issue in the literary work of art in Blanchot's analysis is not an ethical speaking but nonetheless a kind of speaking that is distinct from the totality. It is the outside or an exteriority that speaks' (pp. 152–3). Robbins points as well to 'a certain circularity' in the thought of Blanchot and Levinas, which must be kept in mind when one reads the one beside the other. Thus if a certain *récit* of Blanchot's can be read as 'an instance in which a literary work is genuinely commensurable with the level of Levinas's ultraethical discourse' it is no doubt because Blanchot's text has 'relayed itself through Levinas's ethical philosophy' (p. 152). And vice versa, of course, although Robbins will not argue that Levinas's ethical philosophy relays itself through Blanchot's *récit*. She is doubtless correct when she concludes that 'on the basis of reading Blanchot, Levinas has modified somewhat his understanding of the work of art', but then adds: 'any question of how much Levinas may have learned from Blanchot in the interim must also acknowledge that Levinas remains unconvinced about the capacity of art to signify transcendence' (p. 154). There is no question, however, that one of Blanchot's foremost interlocutors in *The Infinite Conversation* is Levinas.

adrian page

CONSTRUCTING XANADU: TOWARDS A POETICS OF HYPERTEXT FICTION

As Jerome McGann has written, '[t]he change from a paper-based text to electronic text is one of those elementary shifts – like the change from manuscript to print – that is so revolutionary we can only glimpse at this point what it entails'.[1] This chapter will consider the nature of hypertext and ask on what grounds it can be seen as a new medium for literature. The claim that hypertext has somehow made advances in the mediation of literature will be examined, both in theory and by considering how traditional printed novels might be made available in hypertext. In conclusion, the discussion focuses on whether hypertext can be regarded as a distortion or a fulfilment of the novel's literary aims.

The originator of the term 'hypertext', Theodor H. Nelson, defined it as '[n]on-sequential writing – text that branches and allows choices to the reader, best read at an interactive screen. As popularly conceived, this is a series of text chunks connected by links which offer the reader different pathways'.[2] Nelson named his first hypertext 'Xanadu', prompted by Coleridge's poem, 'Kubla Khan'. Like the poem, which claims to be the vestige of a much more extensive poetic work that preceded it, the hypertext only reveals one fragment of a larger whole, yet implies its existence. As a textual critic, McGann has no doubt that this innovation will have important consequences. Hypertext can demonstrate the properties of texts and their relative status as versions or amendments of versions. It can compromise in its presentation of textual variants in a manner which would be difficult if not impossible in print. In hypertext the various stages in the process of textual production, for example, can be kept in view. If the traditional novel translates experience into a single narrative, hypertext appears to have the potential to translate it into a whole variety of linguistic forms.

Raymond Williams, however, distinguishes between the notion of a medium and that of forms of culture or alternative sign-systems.[3] The same message can be carried by different physical vehicles or different signs with no essential changes, whereas a medium must have some determining effect on the content of the messages it carries. Hypertext can be seen as a new form for delivering the same kinds of texts which have always been written. Long before hypertext was a possibility, novels could be written on separate pages and packaged to be read in any sequence a reader chose. Readers may, in fact, read conventional narratives in any number of random sequences. The difference is not in the medium or the form, but in the reading process. Hypertext makes different ways of reading possible which it would be impractical to organise with a conventional novel.

In literary terms, hypertext is comparable to existing metafiction, where the process of writing is incorporated into the text, and references within the text to the author and to the text itself create a continual reverberation which disappears into an endless *mise en abime*. Hypertext has been seen as nothing more than a continuation of the literary tradition which is exemplified by *Tristram Shandy*.[4] The major distinction between metafiction and hypertext, however, is that in metafiction any reference to what at first sight appears to be the world outside the novel is rapidly assimilated within the fictional world. As Linda Hutcheon has expressed it, '[t]he voice of the narrator is not an exterior authenticating authorial one; it is the voice of a character'.[5] Within the boundaries of the traditional novel, a genuinely metatextual position does not seem to be possible.

As one of the chief proponents of hypertext, George P. Landow argues, however, '[h]ypertext ... blurs the distinction between what is "inside" and what is "outside" the text'.[6] Readers of the hypertext version of T. S. Eliot's *Waste Land* for example, can follow links to different versions, early drafts, sources, and critical works.[7] The very act of choosing such links traverses a hitherto material boundary between the work and its textual versions or commentaries in the act of reading. The primary text may literally disappear in order for us to read about the sources of a quotation. If metafiction is like a vortex which swallows everything up into its own fictional world, hypertext is perhaps like a porous membrane through which the texts of the writer and the world outside intermingle. Metafiction makes every reference part of a fictional world, whereas hypertext makes the distinction between fiction and the external world difficult to identify. Hypertext in principle has more potential than metafiction, demonstrating relations to a textual world outside the text itself which extend the fictional realm rather than draw reality into fiction.

If hypertext literature is not merely metafiction in another form, then it could be argued that it presents an opportunity to deconstruct texts.

Landow has made the case for hypertext as the embodiment of Derrida's theories of language in *Of Grammatology*. When Derrida describes Plato's work as necessarily involved with all contemporary Greek language, Landow seizes the opportunity to assimilate hypertext with this principle: 'Derrida in fact here describes extant hypertext systems in which the active reader in the process of exploring a text, probing it, can call into play dictionaries with morphological analyzers that connect individual words to cognates, derivations, and opposites'.[8]

To achieve this ideal deconstruction, however, the linkages would have to be infinite. To link every word to its etymological sources and to related intertexts would be theoretically possible, but cannot happen in practice. Hypertext at present is also created in what Landow calls 'lexias' or text fragments rather than one word at a time. The internal links are between these fragments and not between words and their origins. Although hypertext appears to present us with an 'open' text, in fact hypertext novels are often no more than a story with an obscure 'discours'. The events in the lexia or chunks of text finally reveal a conventional narrative, with the reader doing the detective work to uncover the elements of the traditional story. Hypertext is not pure unadulterated text in which language speaks by itself. The links which exist are those which the author has created.

Landow also argues that hypertext exemplifies Bakhtin's concept of multivocality, the theory that 'language is peopled with the intentions of others', as Bakhtin puts it. There seems little evidence, however, that hypertext implicitly reveals the way in which the language of a text is composed from the words and phrases of others, any more than it allows language to speak by itself. Nor does it follow automatically that the tyranny of univocality is overcome when the text can represent many competing voices simultaneously. A hierarchy of discourse may still be felt, despite this apparently democratic pluralism.

One element which computer technology does introduce is the ability to manipulate the text to simulate a process. An example of this is Stuart Moulthrop's hypertext novel, *Hegirascope*, which incorporates the term for Mohammed's flight from Mecca, the hegira. The novel begins with a central image which is surrounded by words which have to be selected; if they are not, they change of their own accord in thirty seconds. A word which attracts attention has to be followed quickly. The hypertext clearly has parallels with the notion of a hasty flight and demands that we make similar quick decisions, although the pattern of words which the reader has selected can be displayed retrospectively in a separate window.

In Michael Joyce's *Afternoon*, certain words, if selected, admit us to loops, where the same set of text screens reappear in the same sequence until a way can be found out of the cycle.[9] At various points, the reader encounters the same sequence of screens containing text about the narrator's relationship with his ex-wife as he muses on their sexual life together and recounts their passionate moments. This cycle has to be followed through every time the wife's name is selected. At other times words do not become interactive until the reader has fulfilled certain conditions.

In short, the use of hypertext is not to permit a glimpse of unrestricted textuality, but to compel the reader to follow certain ideas and to pursue certain processes in which we learn both about the text and our response to it. We might therefore say that hypertext is not only an efficient way of delivering the traditional novel with its focus on an individual consciousness, but that it offers a 'directed introspection': our exploration of an individual's psychology and our own curiosity is guided rather than left entirely to the imagination. It is not so much the ability of the computer to open up the text to more numerous ramifications as to offer a more limited range of choices that makes it an attractive medium to some writers.

The nearest analogy for hypertextual configuration of literary texts is the deictic use of the camera in an adaptation of literature for cinema. When a camera is used to point to the signs which the audience should observe and interpret in order to follow the narrative, the potentially open text is, to some extent, made less ambiguous. On such occasions we see the director's vision of a world, and not necessarily the participating characters' perspectives. In a hypertext such as *Afternoon*, we are confined to a certain 'loop' of text at some points and prevented from escaping until we find the correct outlet. This is quite different from the traditional novel where we can switch our attention at will. Technological innovations therefore do have an effect on the content of the novel, since the novel on paper cannot compel us to read in a certain sequence within time, or to see our own choices and what they reveal of our personality as part of the text which we read.

It could be said that certain hypertexts, indeed, far from liberating meaning are actually constraining it. Just as film directs the attention of the viewer to the signs which compose the narrative and identifies what it is important to watch, so too, hypertext can identify the words which should be connected with other words. David Miall's article entitled 'Trivializing or liberating? The limitations of hypertext theorizing' argues that hypertext literature restricts the reader's choice of readings in a way that a printed text such as Derrida's *Glas* does not. Hypertext is like a maze where subjectively the experience is of free movement, but limitations have already been imposed. What is clear when reading a hypertext is that the creator has deliberately led us down certain avenues and the text is not fully 'open'. Michael Joyce's *Afternoon*, for example, eventually reveals that the narrator, who early on states that he believes he has seen his son die, may have been responsible for the death. This revelation makes us doubt the narrator's reliability, and tends to narrow down the variety of possible interpretations. It is difficult to read most hypertext novels without presuming that an overarching plot can be reassembled from the fragments. The literary work remains autotelic because it can only try to draw attention to its own characteristics and shed light on the various textual fragments of which it consists.

Miall has argued of hypertext that '[t]he linking of one text node to another tends to promote superordinate connections and to elicit an analytical response more appropriate to expository prose than to literary texts'.[10] This instinctive rejection of any response which is not entirely 'free', may, however, be unjustified. The assumption underlying the criticisms of Miall is that once a sign has prompted the reader/viewer in the direction of a connection or metaphorical relation, this has eliminated the reader/viewer's task of making sense of the connection and testing its coherence within the text. But the reader of a hypertext, like the viewer of a film, is able to make many connections with the same words and to infer many things from any deliberate juxtaposition.

In 1931 Brecht argued that 'today the bourgeois novel still depicts "a world". It does so in a purely idealistic way from within a given *Weltanschauung*: the more or less private, but in any case personal outlook of its "creator". Inside this world every detail of course fits exactly, though if it were taken out of its context, it would not seem authentic for a minute'.[11] Brecht considered that literature needed film if it was to constitute more than the purely idealistic world of the bourgeois novel. His eagerness to adopt film derived from its suitability for the representation of materialist philosophies where the individual is 'seen from outside'. Social determination and the objectification of individuals could be depicted accurately. Brecht also argued that '[g]reat areas of ideology are destroyed when capitalism concentrates on external action, dissolves everything into processes, abandons the hero as the vehicle for everything and mankind as the measure, and thereby smashes the introspective psychology of the bourgeois novel'.[12]

Theatre and film were complementary for Brecht, as he considered that their combination could show the human being in the round and explain human action in the light of its political and economic determinants. He referred to the possibility that '[s]imultaneous events in different places could be seen together. For example, while a fight was going on between two characters for possession of an Albanian oilfield, one could see in the background warships being launched in preparation for putting the oilfield out of commission entirely'.[13] Brecht anticipated the technical ability to compare divergent perspectives on the same subject, in which the medium does not create meanings which cannot possibly exist elsewhere, but enables the foregrounding of certain features in order to present a particular critical perspective.

The technology of hypertext may become more revolutionary if it can finally achieve what Brecht envisaged, which is the simultaneous presentation of internal and external perspectives on character and the determination of action. If hypertext can combine human action and external information, it can focus a particular mode of attention on the subject. What this juxtaposition does is to create a new relationship between the components which needs to be interpreted afresh. It could be said that hypertext allows the reader to experience the immanence of textuality, the sense that intertexts and references are all simultaneously present, and that the text which is read is not the form which takes ultimate precedence. The self-contained world of Brecht's bourgeois novel can be opened up to external influences wherever textual variants and intertexts exist.

One way of exploring this potential of hypertext is to consider whether it is a modernist or a postmodernist phenomenon. Like much modernist fiction, current hypertext novels are preoccupied with individual consciousness and the processes within the mind. They plunge into the middle of things with no obvious beginning and eschew traditional chronological narrative structures. They are experimental and innovatory in approach and frequently collapse time in order to expand the range of interconnected ideas. But it remains to be proven that hypertext can produce an entirely 'free' postmodernist text, in which readers can construct any reading they please. George Landow regards the readers' freedom to 'author' the text for themselves as the ability to construct multiple plots which integrate the elements of the story. This, however, is no different from many examples of modernism which also reject the closure of realist narratives.

What might be more postmodernist would be to look outside the boundaries of the text, and to examine the ways in which the outside/inside dichotomy can be dissolved. Instead of re-combining the internal elements to construct more narratives within the boundaries of the primary text, hypertext could (in principle) open out the text and place it into dialogue with other texts, including ones written in response to it. Fiction in hypertext may lose its distinct, bounded identity and become imbricated in a mass of information. Rather than formulating a new plot, a postmodern strategy might be to make the novel link outwardly and begin to infuse itself into other narratives. This, however, would involve taking current technology a stage further, perhaps allowing spaces in hypertexts in which notes can be inscribed on particular pages to be linked with other electronic information. Reading the hypertext novel may involve adding to it, and allowing it to grow out from one page of writing, like the imagined poem preceding 'Kubla Khan'.

In the remainder of this chapter, I want to consider what value there might be in transferring a conventional novel into hypertext, through two more or less problematic examples.

Although Thomas Pynchon's *The Crying of Lot 49* was written in 1966, it is a novel which seems to look forward to contemporary hypertext.[14] At the first international Pynchon conference in 1994, at the University of Warwick, Brian Stonehill delivered a paper entitled 'Pynchon's prophecies of cyberspace'.[15] Cybernetics, as Stonehill remarks, is concerned with the sending, carrying, and receiving of information, in much the same way as Pynchon's novels are. The name of the chief character in *The Crying of Lot 49*, Oedipa Maas, refers not only to Freud but to an obscure Afrikaans word which means web or net. Moreover at the very end of the novel Oedipa's state is described as 'like walking among matrices of a great digital computer, the zeroes and ones twinned above, hanging like balanced mobiles right and left, ahead, thick, maybe endless'.[16] Though the references to computers in Pynchon's novel are prescient, however, they exist to demonstrate the pathology of the frame of mind which reduces the world's complexity to binary logic.

Once she is named executor of the estate of her former lover, Pierce Inverarity, Oedipa discovers the mysterious Tristero organisation which seems to be responsible for a vast underground mail delivery system represented by the enigmatic posthorn symbol that recurs wherever she goes. Inverarity's forged stamp collection, the auction lot of the title, seems to contain the evidence that the symbol is used by a secret anarchic organisation. Oedipa states that she 'wants to see if there's a connection' between the various occurrences. One central theme of the novel is the impossibility of establishing whether the coincidences and similarities which Oedipa finds in the course of the narrative signify anything.

The Crying of Lot 49 has been recognised as a novel in which the reader has to produce meanings which are never made explicit.[17] The world can seem to be reduced to a series of mutually exclusive choices – Oedipa is either the victim of a gigantic hoax or not – but the novel suggests that we should not expect such conclusive answers. The process of understanding a phenomenon is not represented here as an either/or choice, but as the selection of a perspective from which a coherent picture emerges. Hypertext, which requires its readers to navigate the text by selecting the links for themselves in order to discover resemblances and themes, is also designed to encourage readers to draw their own conclusions rather than offering a thesis which is either true or false. The choice of whether or not to select a word to see what it might reveal via its hypertext link is analogous to Oedipa's dilemma. In a hypertext version of *The Crying of Lot 49*, therefore, there would be an analogy between the style of reading which is required by the text, and the philosophical underpinning of a postmodern novel such as this. However we negotiate our way through the text, the notion of an underlying *histoire* which explains everything is elusive. The novel's ending is open: the agent of the Tristero does not arrive to buy the lot, and we are left to answer Oedipa's questions for ourselves.

The most straightforward hypertext version of this novel would be an electronic text identical to the published version in which certain words or phrases yielded access to passages elsewhere in the novel. Thus a reader could either read conventionally or decide to pursue certain 'clues' which seem to offer some enlightenment. The events could be related in various ways, since, as Oedipa observes, '[e]very access route to the Tristero could be traced also back to the Inverarity estate'.[18]

On the very first page of the novel, for example, when Oedipa hears of the death of Pierce, '[s]he thought of a hotel room in Mazatlán whose door had just been slammed, it seemed forever, waking up two hundred birds down in the lobby; a sunrise over the library slope at Cornell University that nobody out on it had seen because the slope faces west; a dry, disconsolate tune …'.[19] A hypertext edition could allow the word 'Mazatlán' to give way directly to the next occurrence of the name on p. 82. Here Oedipa wanders into a 'greasy spoon' restaurant and discovers Jesús Arrabal, the anarchist whom she and Pierce met on the beach at Mazatlán when they holidayed there years ago. Arrabal still receives copies of the Anarchosyndicalist paper, *Regeneración*, dated 1904. The year could be a hint that Inverarity is behind the mail delivery, in that the number 49 is concealed in the date.

Another significant date is 1943, when a group of American soldiers were trapped by a lake in Italy and killed by the Germans. The bones were buried at the bottom of the lake, but eventually they were dug up and sold to a company which manufactured cigarette filters on behalf of Inverarity. This desecration of the bones of the dead is echoed in the earlier summary of a supposed Jacobean play, *The Courier's Tragedy*, in which the Lost Guard of Faggio are killed and thrown into a lake, and the name 'Trystero' is once again mysteriously invoked.

Hypertext would enable relationships such as these to be tracked by the reader searching the text independently rather than following the narrative. Either the writer could decide how the interlinking elements should be related in lexias, or the reader could be given the power to assemble all occurrences of certain words. Key words could be traced to show their occurrence throughout the novel and assess their correspondences. References to the same character or to related phenomena might be interlinked, for example, so that they eventually led back to Inverarity and suggested the possibility of a gigantic hoax. This possibility dawns on Oedipa only after some time, and so it would preferably require a concerted effort on the reader's part to echo Oedipa's disillusionment. Some of Oedipa's conclusions might be offered only after certain 'clues' had been visited and explored. In addition to interlinking the related formal aspects of the text, hypertext has the potential to incorporate links with information sources which originate outside the text. Some of Pynchon's references to history, for example, are accurate, and could be consulted on-line or via a CD-ROM.

Hypertext might not seem to represent any more than an opportunity for reading more systematically, but it also has the potential to approach one of *The Crying of Lot 49*'s most important themes: the significance of metaphor. On her visit to the inventor John Nefastis, Oedipa is told of a machine he has built to demonstrate a theoretical possibility in physics known as Maxwell's Demon. The machine is designed to show that the metaphorical use of the term 'entropy' in information theory is 'not only verbally graceful but also objectively true'.[20] The correspondence, if proven, would establish that our use of language reflects the laws of the physical world.

Entropy measures the increasing disorder of the energy in a closed system, which is explained by the laws of thermodynamics. According to the second law, every system tends towards disorder, as the useful energy in it is gradually converted into the form of heat. Maxwell's Demon is a theoretical entity proposed by the nineteenth-century physicist James Clerk Maxwell which would ensure the retention of this useful, ordered energy. Since the second law of thermodynamics states that energy must flow from hotter to cooler areas, the Demon simply sorts hot and cold molecules into two separate compartments. This perpetual segregation of the molecules creates a flow of energy which will continue indefinitely.

The use of the term 'entropy' in information theory is as a measure of the amount of information (that is, in its technical sense, the range of possible messages) contained in a source. Pynchon's John Nefastis has designed a Maxwell's Demon machine into which certain people can telepathically feed back information in order to offset its loss of physical entropy. This is an attempt to make the metaphor of entropy literal and to show that informational entropy can ultimately be assimilated to the principles of thermodynamics.

Oedipa is persuaded to link herself with the machine and to try to make it move by the power of thought. This bizarre experiment fails, of course, but Oedipa reaches a vitally important conclusion. 'What if', she asks, 'the

Demon exists only because the two equations look alike? Because of the metaphor?'[21] What if the similarity were the basis of the machine? In other words, Oedipa raises the question of whether language reflects a pre-existing structure, or whether language itself provides the structure which governs the ways in which the universe is conceptualised.

When the reader of the novel encounters the first reference to Maxwell's Demon, the engineer Stanley Koteks explains that it is a theoretical machine where molecules are continually sorted into hot and cold creating perpetual motion and refuting the second law of thermodynamics. The novel relates Koteks's explanation in free indirect speech so that the reader is not sure whether these statements are spoken by him or with the added authority of the author. There is a certain plausibility about the initial explanation which makes it seem as if there is a genuine connection between information flow and physical entropy. The inclusion of authentic sources of information at this point about Maxwell could add to the attractiveness of the idea. Any non-scientific reader might easily be beguiled by these theories. In its current linear narrative form, the novel suggests that the physical concept of entropy, which is encountered (and was theorised) first, is the fundamental truth, and that other senses stand in a derivative metaphorical relation to it. In hypertext, however, this priority might be reversed, and the view which Oedipa advances might be encountered first.

Oedipa makes her own attempt to establish a metaphorical basis for reality when she encounters a stricken sailor in a doorway and is asked to deliver a Tristero-stamped letter for him. The thought that the man will soon die makes Oedipa feel that '[i]t was as if she had just discovered the irreversible process'.[22] She assimilates information flow entropy with the loss of 'information' when the dead depart and all the experience which they have stored disappears with them. This inspires the thought that the old man's alcoholic delirium tremens, 'DTs', conceals another metaphor, like entropy. The word 'delirium' derives from the Latin for a furrow, and literally means to slip from the straight ridge caused by the ploughshare. Oedipa finds herself recalling the teaching of calculus at university where the letters 'dt' stood for an infinitesimal division of time in calculations. At the theoretical single moment, symbolised by 'dt', '[c]hance had to be confronted for what it was'. There is an elegant verbal connection between the mathematical calculation of the probability of a random moment, disconnected from all previous events, and the state of delirium. To be delirious, perhaps, means to exist in a time which is unrelated to what has gone before or which comes after – a moment when any event may occur. We can easily imagine a theory of delirium based on this linguistic coincidence.

On this occasion, however, any metaphorical connection derives only from the orthographical correspondence. Oedipa's speculations parallel her comparison of information flow with entropy, but outside a known frame of reference there is nothing to sustain them. This is the moment at which Oedipa understands that the law of the excluded middle (either a statement or its contrary must be true) cannot be the full story. She recognises that the validity of figurative language depends on a system of belief: '[t]he act of metaphor then was a thrust at truth and a lie, depending where you were: inside, safe, or outside, lost'.[23]

If Pynchon's novel were presented in hypertext, it would enable readers to approach metaphors in a number of ways, so that an implicit hierarchy of meaning (the distinction of tenor and vehicle, for example), might be overridden. In hypertext, the use of a metaphor can be approached both from within a system of belief by adding all the information which makes it seem plausible, and from outside that system. The circulation can proceed endlessly with no one particular belief system taking precedence. The increasingly paranoid beliefs of Oedipa Maas could also be emulated in the choices presented to the reader of a hypertext version. Although it is not yet a common practice, a ludic novel such as *The Crying of Lot 49* could even invite the reader to 'solve' some of the book's mysteries and require them to play the role of investigator. In a novel where the purpose seems to be to demonstrate the futility of searching for ultimate meaning behind appearances, the act of reading in hypertext could mirror the search which the book describes and parallel its themes.

It remains to be seen, however, whether all novels would derive the same benefits from being transferred into hypertext. In the case of novels which advocate a more positive, writerly philosophy in relation to a serious theme, the value of a hypertext version is questionable, since there is no such obvious productive role for the reader.

Fugitive Pieces is the first novel by the Canadian poet Anne Michaels. In this work, the Jewish poet Jakob Beer tells the story of the death of his parents at the hands of the Nazis and his own subsequent escape.[24] He is rescued by a Greek man, Athos, who smuggles him out of Poland to Greece, where the young Jakob is brought up. Later Athos takes Jakob to Toronto, where he works as a university academic in geology. Jakob attends the university and becomes a poet. Eventually Athos dies and Jakob marries a young woman called Alex, but the memories of those he has lost bedevil Jakob's mind and he cannot forget his sister Bella, whose fate was uncertain. Images of Bella continue to haunt Jakob, until Alex leaves him, unable to tolerate his grief.

Jakob takes Athos's ashes back to Greece and finally learns how to live with the memory of Bella. He then meets another woman, Michaela, and finds happiness with her. In the second section of the novel, Ben, a young writer whose parents were imprisoned in the death camps, discovers Jakob's work and uses it to understand how he should live. When Jakob dies, Ben goes to Greece to find Jakob's notebooks and has an affair, but his passion for Jakob's work ends the affair and enables him to return to his wife, able to love unreservedly and finally overcome the destructive influence of the Holocaust.

Fugitive Pieces is a novel which deals in historical facts and also uses metaphors to establish its themes. The connections between geology and memory, for example, are used to represent the Holocaust as an eternal presence in a way that comes to exceed metaphor: '[i]t's no metaphor to feel the influence of the dead in the world, just as it's no metaphor to hear the radiocarbon chronometer, the Geiger counter amplifying the faint breathing of rock'.[25] Just like the radioactivity of supposedly 'dead' rock, previous generations continue to exercise an influence through memory. If we act on the memories we have then the dead may literally be said to have a continued presence. Ben states, '[t]here's no absence if there remains even the memory of absence. Memory dies unless it's given a use'.[26] The contradiction which is foregrounded here – that the memory of an absence converts that absence into a presence – helps to justify the claim that the past can be kept alive if the memory serves a purpose. This purpose is what is called in the novel, 'the assumption which a person lives by'.

The assumption which Jakob lives by is that 'memory is moral; what we consciously remember is what our conscience remembers'.[27] The task of self-understanding, therefore, is to comprehend the significance of the metaphorical connections which unite the memories that constantly return to us. By understanding why we remember certain events in a certain sequence, we can come to know the moral imperatives that drive us subconsciously, and then we can confront our beliefs. Jakob does this and realises that he has projected his own state on to his images of Bella, and thereby deprived her memory of its glory: 'Bella my brokenness has kept you broken'. It is this realisation which enables him to recognise a different moral imperative, not to join Bella in death but to participate fully in the world. Thus he is able to love his second wife. Ben too realises that the therapeutic visit to Jakob's former home has relieved him of a burden from the past: '[a]t last my unhappiness is my own'.[28]

A novel such as *Fugitive Pieces* would not necessarily be enhanced by hypertext links to factual information, since although it depends upon historical facts it is not simply realist, but the ability to connect metaphorical allusions throughout the text might be a way of allowing the reader to examine its therapeutic principle. If the loss of loved ones is thought of as beyond redemption, then it must always be endured without consolation.

If, on the other hand, memories inhabit a timeless environment, then they can be assuaged; they are always available for contemplation and recuperative action. Hypertext stores all the events of a narrative in a non-linear manner, so that each can be reached as easily as any other. In this sense, it may offer a way of emphasising the novel's fundamental outlook. There is an analogy between hypertext and the novel's 'moral memory', in that hypertext too is selected according to principles of our own making. Memory, like hypertext, is not linear: the recollection of the grave events of the past is dictated in *Fugitive Pieces* by the moral beliefs which prompt those memories to return. One moral theme may recall a number of events which are related by imagery, not time. Hypertext has the potential to offer both the author and the reader new ways of navigating the text which integrate these thematic links or leitmotivs.

Just as a film adaptation does not necessarily begin with the first moment of a novel, so too a hypertext version of *Fugitive Pieces* might be opened at a different point. *Fugitive Pieces* is chronological, but a hypertext could condense the story of Jacob and the story of Ben who later discovers his work. The story of the discovery could 'lie behind' the narrative of Jacob's life, and surface from time to time as a parallel rather than consecutive narrative. Michaels writes 'every moment is two moments': '[h]istory is the Totenbuch, The Book of the Dead, kept by the administrators of the camps. Memory is the Memorbucher, the names of those to be mourned, read aloud in the synagogue'.[29] There are two strands of time in other words: the sequence which is recalled out of moral obligation, and the actual historical sequence. If these two moments coincide, this could be represented in hypertext. The technology could enable either a conscious switching between dimensions or a simultaneous presentation on the screen, once the reader had selected a certain word or phrase to activate a link. The computer screen could in principle represent the absolute time of history and the relative time of memory for us.

It would be vital to ensure that the point of any such adaptation was to emphasise the seriousness of this novel's treatment of historical and moral dilemmas, however, and not merely to find an opportunity to exploit the technical gimmickry. In such a poetic novel, the coincidental relations between verbal images which would appear if a reader were allowed to navigate the text in this way might bring to light or elaborate on certain buried themes. But whether this would result either in a better recognition of the world-view carefully constructed by the author, or in a productive alternative understanding, is a matter for debate. The reader is scarcely likely to be subject to the same mental anguish as the characters, and any parallels between the reader's situation and the content of the novel may not be particularly significant – they may even trivialise that content.

The combining of internal and external perspectives is not so easily envisaged in the case of this novel as in *The Crying of Lot 49*. In the Pynchon, the reader both judges and shares in Oedipa's attempts to unravel the mystery of Tristero, but here the internal perspective of the 'character is paramount, and cannot legitimately be shared. What may become possible, however, is for hypertext to provide an external perspective by adding links to the text at certain points. At present the ability of readers of hypertexts to link to external sources is limited, but if this expands, then the reader might be able to read the text in new intellectual contexts rather than just as the product of a single imagination. Internal and external perspectives on the same phenomena could be presented simultaneously. Like the Xanadu project, the text could theoretically be suspended in virtual space and enmeshed in vast numbers of related links which extend and qualify its meaning.

Fugitive Pieces entertains many contradictions: every moment is two moments, the instant is 'gradual'. In such circumstances the novel proposes a set of simultaneously true alternatives. One proposition is that Jakob has found a unique *modus vivendi* and that his belief in this principle has enabled him to survive. At other times, however, Jakob speaks like a pure pragmatist for whom there is no truth: '[w]hether you live by a lie or live by a truth makes no difference, as long as you get past the wall'.[30] Hypertext could not adjudicate between such beliefs, but it might be able to place them in context.

An external reference which might help here, for example, is Bruno Bettelheim, whose words are echoed in the novel. In *The Uses of Enchantment: the Meaning and Importance of Fairy Tales*, Bettelheim, who has counselled young survivors of the Holocaust, refers to 'separation anxiety' as the most profound fear which a young child might experiences when abandoned by parents.[31] This fear is 'forever transcended when the ideal partner has been found with whom the most satisfying personal relationship is established'. Perhaps this could be related to the 'faith of the body' which sustains Jakob Beer and encourages his optimistic belief that nature will transcend tragedy. Jakob states '[w]hat does the body make us believe? That we're never ourselves until we contain two souls'.[32] In this case, however, any *modus vivendi* would be a mere fantasy, since the body would independently sustain belief and life. There could be no principle to live by, Jakob's convictions become rationalisations of nature, and the novel's metaphorical systems would begin to seem irrelevant.

In *The Name of the Rose*, Umberto Eco suggests that: '[t]he postmodern reply to the modern consists of recognising that the past, since it cannot really be destroyed, because its destruction leads to silence, must be revisited; but with irony, not innocently'.[33] *Fugitive Pieces* also suggests that the past must be relived with a new meaning, if not necessarily an ironic one. A postmodern approach to the novel might be to allow readers to revisit the past through a hyptertext adaptation and relate it to other documents, and events on the World Wide Web. The reader could read the novel's original words and make a detour through historical sources and testimonies as he or she read. It would also be possible to enable coincidences of language or subject-matter to be highlighted by the computer using search tools. Readers could store their own comments alongside the text, and in principle any material at all could be linked to it. Life and art could become much closer. History could be woven into the text. At its most extreme, literature might cease to exist as an autonomous imaginary realm.

The opportunities offered by hypertext fiction at the moment – whether adaptations like those we have considered, or original works – allow the text to be 'open' only to the extent that its elements can be navigated in a number of different ways. Openness is defined by contrast with closure. Theorists such as Landow see the ultimate goal, however, as a novel which can be continually invented afresh by readers who themselves become authors. This involves more than varying strategies of internal navigation. Hypertext theorists are fond of quoting Borges's short story, 'The garden of forking paths': '[i]n all fictional works, each time a man is confronted with several alternatives, he chooses one and eliminates the others; in the fiction of Ts'ui Pen, he chooses – simultaneously – all of them. *He creates*, in this way, diverse futures, diverse times which themselves also proliferate and fork'.[34] This quotation raises the possibility of a truly interactive novel where the reader is free to compose multiple and simultaneous responses to the texts encountered. The reader would become analogous to an author, adding to the ramifications of the novel in the pursuit of an endlessly deferred meaning as each addition generates further questions. In the face of developments like these, to immerse oneself in a traditional print novel might become an act of self-denial, the deliberate yielding of imaginative freedom. Whether hypertext is destined to transform the pleasures and responsibilities of reading or to destroy them, however, remains to be seen.

Notes

1 J. McGann, 'The rationale of hypertext' available on the World Wide Web at http://jefferson.village.virginia.edu/public/jjm2f/rationale.html (unnumbered).

2 G. P. Landow, *Hypertext 2.0: The Convergence of Critical Theory and Technology*, (Baltimore, 1997), p. 3. Nelson's internet site where the Xanadu project is presented can be found at www.xanadu.net/. This claims to be the first hypertext, originated in 1960, and its creator is working towards establishing the hypertext as a 'state' rather than a text with links. Texts in Xanadu are permanently connected with other texts from which they quote.

3 R. Williams, *Keywords* (Glasgow, 1976), p. 170.
4 See J. Cowley, 'Hypertext, electronic writing and its literary tradition', *Moderna Sprak* 87:2 (1994) 129–35.
5 L. Hutcheon, *Narcissistic Narrative: The Metafictional Paradox* (London, 1984), p. 63.
6 Landow, *Hypertext 2.0*, p. 83.
7 Christiane Paul's *Unreal City: A Hypertext Guide to T. S. Eliot's* The Waste Land was published by Eastgate Systems, Massachusetts, in 1996.
8 Landow, *Hypertext 2.0*, p. 33.
9 M. Joyce, *Afternoon: A Story* (Massachusetts, Eastgate Systems, 1992).
10 D. S. Miall, 'Trivialising or liberating? The limitations of hypertext theorising', *Mosaic* 32:3 (June 1999), p. 10.
11 B. Brecht, *Brecht on Theatre*, trans. J. Willett (London, 1964), p. 48.
12 *Ibid.*, p. 50.
13 *Ibid.*, p. 78.
14 T. Pynchon *The Crying of Lot 49* (London, 1979).
15 Available at http://www.pynchon.pomona.edu/gr/bato.html.
16 Pynchon, *Crying of Lot 49*, p. 125.
17 See F. Kermode, 'The use of the codes', in S. Chatman (ed.), *Approaches to Poetics* (New York, 1973).
18 Pynchon, *Crying of Lot 49*, p. 117.
19 *Ibid.*, p. 5.
20 *Ibid.*, p. 73.
21 *Ibid.*
22 *Ibid.*, p. 88.
23 *Ibid.*, p. 89.
24 A. Michaels, *Fugitive Pieces* (London, 1997).
25 *Ibid.*, p. 53.
26 *Ibid.*, p. 193.
27 *Ibid.*, p. 138.
28 *Ibid.*, p. 292.
29 *Ibid.*, pp. 140, 138.
30 Michaels, *Fugitive Pieces*, p. 110.
31 B. Bettelheim, *The Uses of Enchantment: The Meaning and Importance of Fairy Tales* (Harmondsworth, 1978), p. 146.
32 Michaels, *Fugitive Pieces*, p. 189.
33 U. Eco, *The Name of the Rose* (New York, 1980), pp. 530–1.
34 J. L. Borges, *Labyrinths* (Harmondsworth, 1970), p. 71.

bruce robbins

PRETEND WHAT YOU LIKE: LITERATURE UNDER CONSTRUCTION

Literature acquired its modern value as an object of study, in or around the Romantic period, when it was redefined as an alternative and anti-dote to the modern division of labour and the industrial fragmentation of communities, selves, and knowledges. Against the backdrop of industri-alism, disinterested non-instrumental works of creative imagination could acquire a social interest, a paradoxical instrumentality; they could be invested with the value of (in Wordsworth's phrases) 'bind[ing] together by passion and knowledge' a newly threatened 'human society' that felt its need to salvage 'things silently gone out of mind and things violently destroyed'. Whether by the fact that literary texts were written in a pre-industrial era of organic community and were thus thought to look at life in a pre-industrial way, or by virtue of their formal unity and synthetic imagination, which reproduced and sustained that organic vision in otherwise unpropitious times, the post-Romantic concept of lit-erature could be credited with the redeeming public value of affirming endangered species of wholeness and autonomy and evading mechanical division and specialisation – specialisation of just the sort that would go on to produce the modern professions, including the profession of liter-ary criticism.

Though this organic view of literature has long ago gone out of fashion, the paradox it engendered remains familiar. We literary critics wish to see ourselves as professionals in the rigour of our interpretative procedures, the depth and breadth of our specialised knowledge, and (often) the diffi-culty of our theoretical lexicon. Yet we also resist professionalism as a self-description, in large part because we serve an object of knowledge that, though now more associated with indeterminacy than community, contin-ues to be defined by a perpetual rebellion against the necessary one-sidedness of professional perspective and the chastened orderliness of disciplinarity.

When Raymond Williams gave something like the above account of how the concept of literature was historically constructed, he did not underline the ironic state of self-contradiction to which that concept seemed to condemn the professional critic. Though *Culture and Society* furnished his profession with one of its most praised narratives of legitimation, a supremely powerful account of why literary studies was worth professing and, no less important, worth funding, Williams himself continued to use 'professional' as a self-evident and unambiguous term of abuse and thus continued also to lament criticism's putative decline into professionalisation.[1] This inconsistency is probably one reason for his public persuasiveness. As a result of the friction between the anti-professional way in which literature is defined and the professional context in which literature is studied, teachers and students of literature tend, like Williams, to manifest a certain disquiet. And this disquiet, no matter how genuinely it is felt, also performs an unconscious social function. It serves to display both to critics themselves and to others how richly dissonant literature is, how refreshingly incompatible with the society around it, how indispensably critical of the status quo, hence how very valuable and needful. The unease at how literature is studied registers the need for literature to be studied. There can be no better evidence that the malady professional critics are called in to treat is serious than the symptoms of that malady they themselves cannot help but exhibit on their own persons. To be observed squirming with discomfort at one's institutional surroundings is not just to flash a badge of professional membership; it is to offer the profession an unpaid advertisement, a useful if only subliminal rationale for its continued existence.

Like other self-contradictions, this one often takes the diachronic form of decline-and-fall narratives, where one pole of the contradiction represents an impossibly idealised starting point while the other becomes a fallen, unredeemed present which seems to invite uninhibited effusions on a continuum from sarcasm to outrage. This is the case, for example, when the fallen present is represented not by professionalisation per se but rather by, say, 'theory' or 'cultural studies'.[2] In 'The future of cultural studies', a lecture he delivered in 1986, Williams lamented the field's success in passing from a genuine vocation (adult education) to a mere discipline: 'having got into the university, English studies had within twenty years converted itself into a fairly normal academic course, marginalizing those members of itself who were sustaining the original project'. It became 'a professional discipline'.[3] Then, in the 1960s, 'a body of theory came through which rationalized the situation of this formation on its way to becoming bureaucratized and the home of specialist intellectuals … The whole project was then radically diverted'.[4] This is similar to the reservation that George Levine notes in his overview of Victorian studies over the past quarter century: 'literary studies have become cultural studies', Levine says, 'and they have done so on the basis of a body of theory, epitomised in the Foucaultian work of people like Mary Poovey and D. A. Miller, that 'leads invariably to reading against the grain, and almost as invariably to professional advancement'.[5]

Levine is right, I think, that the new Foucaultian-style Victorianism 'needs to be altered to take into account its own professional dominance and the potential incoherence of its own positioning'.[6] And living as we do in what the *Intellectual History Newsletter* has called 'the age of cultural studies', when the term has broken loose from the Birmingham Centre and come to designate a style of inquiry that pervades a wide range of fields and periods, we certainly have good motives for asking how far afield it may have led.[7] Nevertheless, the fact that the word 'professional' pops up in the conclusion of both critiques is a sign that the task of positioning literary criticism more accurately has once again been postponed. As the idealised 'before' term, literature has once again been artificially protected from contamination by its professional 'after'.

Refusing to consider criticism's professional habits as an unpleasant accident that has somehow befallen literature, and choosing instead to recognise the many insistent points of contact between the two, need not entail either accepting Foucault's epistemology of the disciplines wholesale or, worse, offering a degraded sociological reprise of it. As Foucault argued, we cannot assume that disciplines investigate pre-existing objects that offer themselves up ready-made for investigation. We cannot help but consider the extent to which disciplines construct for themselves objects whose manifold mysteries – that is, whose combined invitation and resistance to being known – serve at least some disciplinary purpose. But this perspective is only as vulgar and reductive as one's understanding of those disciplines or professions and the purposes they set for themselves. As I have argued elsewhere, these purposes necessarily include claims to social significance, hence a certain historical openness and even public-spiritedness that does not register either in references to the ideological state apparatus of education (literature as 'what is taught') or in the usual clichés about professionalism's self-enclosed science-imitating specialisation and guild-like conspiracies against the laity.[8] If a book like *Culture and Society* does the work of professional legitimation, then professionalism would seem to be a larger and more generous thing than Williams himself was ready to acknowledge. It should be possible to acknowledge in the same spirit, not as a sneer or a debater's point but as an unembarrassed given of academic discourse, that if literature is a professional construct, then so too (as Levine suggests) is the Foucaultian constructionism that calls it a construct.

To treat literature as a professional object of knowledge is to lower it, in the eyes of many, to an unseemly equality with other, baser sorts of knowledge. But this equality need not be taken as humbling if we can also admit that much of what fascinates us about literature, including its seemingly irreducible mystery, is to be found as well in those other sorts of knowledge. Consider Derek Attridge's eloquent account of the concept of literature in his book *Peculiar Language*. Writers since Wordsworth have always claimed, Attridge says, that literature 'can engage with the language and thoughts of everyone who speaks the same tongue, and that it attains thereby the power to intervene in the ethical and political life of a community or a nation. To push this claim too far, however, is to endanger the existence of literature itself as a distinct entity, for if literature does *not* employ a special language, from what does it derive its appeal and its strength?'[9] Hence there are 'two mutually inconsistent demands – that the language of literature be recognizably different from the language we encounter in other contexts, and that it be recognizably the same'.[10] Attridge's solution to this problem is in effect to define literature as this very impossibility of definition.

In at least one sense, it is a happy impossibility. For this is a paradox that literature can seemingly call its own, and to possess a paradox of your own is to possess a disciplinary distinctness of your own, hence a comfortable professional niche. The problem is that literature *cannot* call this paradox its own. The paradox is shared. As Attridge himself notes, in passing, 'the word *literature*' is 'a term like *writing* or *law*, capable of destabilizing the discourses and institutions within which it has its being'.[11] If even 'law', which is so clearly crucial to the grounding of social and political institutions, does the same subversive work as literature, then how can this subversive or destabilising quantity be *opposed* to the 'discourses and institutions' it inhabits? And how can it be centred in the literary? Those other institutions would themselves have to be intrinsically unstable; literature would have to surrender its claim to a unique power of subversiveness. And this would be all the more true of the objects of knowledge of other academic disciplines. Once we've started with law, why not go on to such disciplinary objects as, say, rhetoric (for composition), or society (for sociology), or culture (for anthropology), or politics (for political science), or space (for geography)? Geographers are often irate at the spatial allusions, fashionable in other disciplines, that treat their object as stable, uncontroversial, self-evident, available for metaphor. Space too, they remind us, is mysterious; it is anything but a firm grounding. Can any object of investigation afford to provide a firm grounding?

This point suggests a general hypothesis. All disciplinary objects seem obliged to stake out and defend a large degree of inscrutability, if only in order to guarantee continuing work for the discipline's practitioners. All disciplines resemble literary criticism in the sense that they too exist in an unstable and precarious relation to a shifty object of knowledge that they can never fully possess or master, an object of knowledge that, like literature, sustains their work only by perpetually threatening to escape from their possession and undermine that work. Though critics like to think that they are blessed or cursed – it hardly matters – by the uniquely recalcitrant nature of what they work with, a wandering, undefinable object of uncertain borders is not a deviation from some supposed disciplinary norm. Yet the wandering and the inscrutability can never be unlimited or uncontrolled. Like literature, the objects of other fields must also satisfy both of Attridge's exigencies – the open mystery of distinctness, but also the impulse toward clarity, closure, and constraint that accompanies the 'power to intervene in the ethical and political life of a community', in other words, that ensures a discipline's social significance.[12]

If Attridge's incisive account of the peculiarity of literature can be taken as a proposal about disciplinary objects in general, then it is this second, 'interventionary' impulse that most clearly requires more discussion. Literature's difference, its seemingly infinite potential to proliferate meanings, its autonomy vis-à-vis the demands of everyday accuracy and instrumentality, is obvious enough – as obvious as a profession's autonomy, its power to control the market for its labour, the number of accredited practitioners, the pace and standards of work. In both cases the *limits* to that autonomy are less obvious, but no less crucial. Taking off from Attridge and the premise that the impulse toward closure and constraint he discerns in literature necessarily accompanies all claims to social significance, we might translate this point into sociological terms: the professionalisation of literature implies a sort of social compact by which society at large acknowledges literature's significance, as it acknowledges the significance of other bodies of expert knowledge. Yet this acknowledgement is never more than provisional, and it depends on a certain closing down of the potential infinity of interpretations in the direction of some criteria of urgency, ethical concern, usefulness, necessity to choose. Hence the professional need for narratives like that of *Culture and Society* which narrow the interpretation of literature in order to explain to society at large why literature matters. Hence too a certain understandable puzzlement as to the status of literature today.

If they would be willing to follow the argument this far, most critics would probably want to ask whether any social compact is still working in the case of literature, whether its significance is still acknowledged, and if not, why not. Looking at concrete matters like enrolments, doctorates, and jobs as well as vaguer issues of relative prestige, many recent observers have offered up titles like Andrew Delbanco's 'The decline and fall of literature'.[13] And the problem, they have suggested, is that the critics themselves have reneged on their part of the compact by no longer concerning themselves with literature at all, but instead drifting off into theory, cultural studies, and so on.

As I've been suggesting, however, it is a mistake to believe that a discipline's health depends exclusively on its firm possession of an object of its own. Like professions, academic disciplines have to demonstrate not the distinctness of their object (it is perfectly possible to share an object with another discipline as long as the approach is different) but the significance or relevance of treating that object as they do, their answers to the question of why it should be studied in that way or studied at all. And these answers are notoriously vulnerable to historical contingency. Not long ago David Damrosch brought up the unsettling example of classics. Aside from some border skirmishes with anthropology and philosophy, classics has not lost its privileged hold over the distinctness of its object.[14] What it has lost, since the days when it claimed pre-eminence among the humanities, is confidence that sufficient others sufficiently appreciate the significance of that object. Anyone who thinks literary criticism can correct its supposed slide by returning to a pure, restricted version of its object, without addressing the more delicate question of literature's contemporary public significance, should therefore contemplate the example. This argument is also pertinent to Richard Rorty's call for literary critics to forget about the interdisciplinary projects of recent years and return to literature itself. Rorty talks about English having succumbed to an attack of 'knowingness', the bane of ordinary disciplines, thereby giving up on its unique, higher, indeed religious task of providing 'inspiration'.[15] This sounds great – who could be against inspiration? But is it really any different from what happens in disciplines like history, philosophy, or religion itself? How did literature come to claim a monopoly on inspiration? Surely it makes more sense to assume that all disciplinary objects are obligatorily 'religious' at least in the sense that like religion, they must preserve an inspiring core of inscrutability. At a minimum, this is true for the simple reason that a core of inscrutability is required in order to ensure the possibility of further interpretation, in other words further work for the discipline's practitioners. And that core must be inspiring for much the same reason; otherwise there will be no work. Indeed, interdisciplinary projects have succeeded in large part because they have been, precisely, inspiring.

Another reason for not leaping headlong into the decline-and-fall story is David Simpson's suggestion that literature has not after all been eclipsed. The problem with literariness, in this view, is its strength, not its weakness – the fact that it refuses to be kept dammed up within proper channels, but has overflowed the boundaries of the literary canon, becoming an aspect of 'discourse' in general and a research programme defining much of what happens in the humanities generally.[16] Like Simpson, other observers have located the real essence of literary studies over the past decades in the urge to see the entire social world, beginning with literature itself, as a set of constructs. For them, in other words, what Ian Hacking calls 'social constructionism' is the imperial strategy by which literary studies has metamorphosed itself into cultural studies.[17] This strategy, if it is one, is at least professionally coherent in that, while it sacrifices some of the distinctiveness of literature, hence also the assumption that literature is 'valuable in itself' (to quote Terry Eagleton), it also preserves and extends the case for literature's significance: to put it crudely, the case that, if literariness is spread about more widely, then the artist's special freedom to create is likewise not so special, but a democratically accessible or at least pervasive freedom to remake the social world.[18]

Constructionism does not of course correspond to literariness in all of that term's many senses. It does not propose, say, aesthetic closure as (in Francis Mulhern's words) an anticipation of 'a healed existence' or 'a recovery of infantile pleasures'.[19] In one of the definitive constructionist moments in one of the most influential constructionist books of the past quarter century, volume one of the *History of Sexuality*, Foucault writes: '[s]exuality must not be thought of as a kind of natural given which power tries to hold in check, or as an obscure domain which knowledge tries gradually to uncover. It is the name that can be given to a historical construct'.[20] The word translated here by 'construct' is the French 'dispositif'. 'Dispositif', which refers to arrangements of parts to form a purposeful whole, emerges from legal, military, and technological contexts, not aesthetic ones. (It shares this of course with the primarily architectural metaphor of construction.) As the editors of a recent symposium on the concept point out, 'dispositif' begins in Foucault as a mediation between the symbolic and the technical, with emphasis arguably already on the latter, and since that time its usage has veered in an ever more technical, more instrumental direction.[21]

Still, it is no coincidence that Kant, who first articulated the concept of the aesthetic on which literary studies has since depended, also figures for Hacking as the 'great pioneer' from whom 'all schools' of constructionism seem to derive.[22] And literature's intimate and paradoxical relations with constructionism are evident in Foucault himself. In an interview published in 1975, Foucault was asked about the status of literature in his work. He admitted that literature was 'not something I analyzed, or reduced, or integrated into the very field of analysis'. Rather, it was 'a badge, a flag'.[23] More than 'literary works or discourses within literature', the texts and authors he cared about served him because he could think of them as 'discourses outside philosophy'.[24] In short, literature had escaped the sort of treatment he was pioneering for other discourses, and escaped it precisely because literature, as a privileged point outside the framework of philosophy, was imaginatively necessary in order for the genealogical enterprise even to be conceived. There was no defensible reason why literature should be thought of as indeed freely transcending the weighty determinations to which all other discourse was subject, and others were quick to bring it back, as one discourse among others, within a Foucaultian perspective. Yet the freedom of literature was and is essential to the constructionist enterprise, which remains literary in the precise sense that its project of de-naturalising involves showing to be products of human imagination, creativity, and discourse, in other words showing to be like literature, concepts in many fields that had been taken to be 'natural givens' and therefore inalterable. At the heart of cultural studies lies, in John Guillory's words, 'a tacit analogy between the constructedness of the literary artifact and the constructedness of the identity categories supporting politically repressive social practices'.[25] Constructionist de-naturalising carries over directly from literature the alienating, strange-making impulses to 'interrogate' and break down collective identities, to problematise the coherence of experience, to render fluid and indeterminate that which has seemed natural and oppressively fixed.

The extensive overlap between literature and constructionism will not come as much of a surprise to anyone who has watched the rise of cultural studies from the sceptical vantage point of some other discipline. That constructionism has been excessively, disablingly literary is for example the point of sociologist Michael Schudson's critique of cultural studies, published in *Lingua Franca* in 1997.[26] But this interdisciplinary debate is one subset of a much broader question: what is the social value of social constructionism? If constructionism is indeed analogous to literature, if what it means to be a construct (open to alternative construction) depends on what it means to be a work of literature (open to alternative imagination), then like the literary programme, the constructionist programme presumably also makes an appeal to society at large, enjoys a professional compact as to the public significance of its intellectual activities, though a compact whose staying power can as yet hardly have been proven. Moreover, its case for its own significance is presumably also continuous with the case for literature. One would expect a rather more complicated relation between the two than simple opposition. Rather than choosing between them, it's perhaps more interesting to ask about their common ground.

Let us suppose that, in Terry Eagleton's words, 'the so-called "literary canon", the unquestioned "great tradition" of the "national literature", has to be recognized as a *construct*, fashioned by particular people for particular reasons at a certain time'.[27] What would follow from this constructionist premise? It would not follow that literature is unreal. As Hacking argues, 'something can be both socially constructed and real'.[28] Nor would it follow that literature 'ought to be done away with'. 'One may realise', Hacking goes on, 'that something, which seems inevitable in the present state of things, was not inevitable, and yet is not thereby a bad thing'.[29] It seems unlikely for example that the classical Greeks applied a post-Romantic notion of literature in their thinking about tragedy and epic. In Aristotle's *Politics*, the word 'catharsis' describes not the disinterested effect of an autonomous artwork but the utility of popular spectacles for keeping the lower orders in check. But doubting that there exists a single continuous concept of literature extending from Aristotle through Kant to the present should not stop us from affirming the historical fact that writers during the last two centuries have been influenced both consciously and unconsciously by the expectations attributed to literature in the post-Romantic sense. Nor need it stop us from exploring what may be gained by applying that set of expectations to the texts of earlier figures who did not even unconsciously write within it. One might well worry over the ideological implications of, say, teaching continuity-with-the-Greeks or disinterestedness-as-depoliticisation or the artist-as-paradigm-of-the-heroically-autonomous-bourgeois-subject, while also insisting on literature's potential usefulness in various historical contexts and circulating as widely as possible its invitation to re-imagine and recreate the social world.

Though 'most people who use the social construction idea enthusiastically want to criticize, change, or destroy some X they dislike in the established order of things', Hacking goes on, there is an important difference between criticising, changing, and destroying.[30] Hacking aligns these three terms with reformist, rebellious, and revolutionary versions of constructionism respectively.[31] As an example of the rebellious version, he takes Judith Butler's attitude toward the construction of gender – to be more precise, her deconstructive refusal of the sex/gender opposition, a refusal which should be understood as criticising but also extending constructionism.[32] Butler does not want merely to unmask the ideological interests behind gender constructions (this would be reformist), but she does not think it possible to abandon gender entirely (the revolutionary option). Compare her with the more absolute refusals of gender expressed in the recent literature of transsexuality, and it's clear how solicitous Butler remains about valuing and preserving the object of her critique.[33]

If Butler's rebellious but not revolutionary take on gender offers one answer to the question of what it might mean to think of literature as a construct, it also turns the tables on this question. That is, it again forces us to consider constructionism as an extension of literature. Butler's concept of 'performativity', the self-consciously theatrical way of playing with identities and revealing their constructedness that Butler finds exemplified by drag, is of course associated with literature's freedom to re-imagine and recreate the social world. To think of gender as performative is 'exhilarating', as Adam Phillips writes, and the deep public appeal of this position clearly has much to do with its insistence that the world is still 'under construction', that biology is not destiny – in other words, that the Romantic programme of creative imagination is still very much alive.[34] Indeed, this generalised, extra-canonical literariness is just what Phillips and other critics react against. Rather than the liberty to perform inventively, Phillips suggests, what Butler describes may be the compulsion to 'act out'. Take away Freud's sense of the heavy constraints on human identity, as revealed for example by the process of mourning, and you get an illusion of untrammelled freedom that does not stand up to scrutiny. 'If the idea of performance frees identity into states of (sometimes willed) possibility', Phillips goes on, 'mourning refers those same identities back to their unconscious histories, with their repetitions and their waste … without the idea of mourning, performance becomes an excessive demand – pretend there's no unconscious, then pretend what you like'.[35]

Pretend what you like: these hard words offer to kick away the foundations of literary study, whether in its narrow canonical or its extended constructionist form. But in doing so, they also teach us something about those foundations. The phrase 'pretend what you like' is very nearly unpronounceable for a literary critic, I would guess, and the reason is that it declares the exercise of imagination too easy, too frictionless, too free from impediment, and thus removes any possible reason why a rational person would want to spend time deciphering and interpreting the products of imagination. If literature were as easy as pretending what you like, then it could hardly be studied in a professional manner. There is something of substance to study only if the freedom to pretend is systematically constrained. And that something is worth studying only if the constraints on the imagination are representative of the constraints on life itself – biological, historical, political, or whatever. The social significance of literature is proportional to the resistance that the (unfree) imagination overcomes or at least recognises and confronts. This is why Hélène Cixous's 'Laugh of the Medusa', to take another influential interdisciplinary example, cannot content itself merely with telling women to write, but must add – whatever the risk of contradiction – that they must write *their own bodies*: must freely create, in other words, precisely that which has been imposed on them by nature.[36] The example underlines the general truth about professional objects of knowledge that I extrapolated above from Derek Attridge: literature, like other disciplinary objects, must somehow combine distinctness and autonomy, on the one hand, and on the other sameness, commonality, translatable significance: the realm of closure and constraint. The same holds for constructionism, whose literariness might be adduced as evidence for, rather than against, this rule.

Butler's intellectual career could serve to illustrate this point, in particular her reaching out toward Freud (and his more determined, burdened, circumscribed model of identity) in self-critical response to objections like Phillips's, but also and even more consistently her ambivalent engagement with Hegel. These engagements have not been factored into the lingering controversy over Butler's literariness, a controversy in which more is at stake than Butler's own work. Consider for example Martha Nussbaum's angry broadside against Butler in *The New Republic*, entitled 'The professor of parody'. 'The idea of gender as performance', Nussbaum writes, 'is Butler's most famous idea'.[37] Indeed, it is ironic in the extreme that critics like Nussbaum should castigate Butler's constructionism as elitist and esoteric, for the idea that gender is constructed is probably the largest public and political success of academic theory in recent memory, one of the few places where theory can be seen to have had unmistakable consequences outside the academy, anchoring itself firmly in the domain of common sense. Nussbaum is surely right to say that this idea has less to do with J. L. Austin's performatives than with the example of the theatre, and I think she is right again, and generous, to admit that the parodic performance of gender as Butler explains it does offer a genuine if limited degree of freedom. But for Nussbaum, as for Phillips, Butler sees too much freedom, too little constraint. Theatricality will be available only to a small number of actors, not to mass movements and practical demands. Freedom does not exist without a 'social agent behind or prior to social forces that produce the self'.[38] The body, for example, is limited by being part of nature; it's 'too simple to write [the body] off as culture'.[39] In short, Butler is again charged with the literary sin of pretending what she likes.

That is certainly not what literature means to Nussbaum herself. In her book *Poetic Justice*, Nussbaum defends the literary imagination 'because it seems to me an essential ingredient of an ethical stance that asks us to concern ourselves with the good of other people whose lives are distant from our own'.[40] Hence 'we can say of the mainstream realist novel what Aristotle said of tragic drama: that the very form constructs compassion in readers, positioning them as people who care intensely about the sufferings and bad luck of others, and who identify with them in ways that show possibilities for themselves'.[41] Literature must be studied because it's a vehicle for preserving and transmitting the experience of those distant from us in space, time, or circumstances.

For better or for worse, Nussbaum's top-down compassion-training may well be the best public case literary critics can currently make for the teaching of literature when challenged, as we recently have been, by the business-oriented counter-programme of composition, which happily dismisses literature from the American high school curriculum in favour of technical 'language skills'. And yet to listen to Nussbaum is to understand once again that for Butler too literariness is not merely free self-creation. It is also – and this is just as representative of how the imagination works – *revulsion* from some of those who are closest to us in space, time, and circumstance, and even a wish that suffering and bad luck may befall them.[42] This revulsion or repulsion, which fellow critics will recognise as a truth of the constrained, actually existing imagination, is something that tends to be forgotten by admirers of literature from outside the profession (here Nussbaum can be allied with Richard Rorty, who argues with unpersuasive idealism that literature need not be politicised because it is always already doing political work). Without repulsion, however, we could never understand why Kant's reason requires his aesthetics. Butler's repulsion is attractive, so to speak, because – like Kant's aesthetics – it makes a space for the recognition of freedom and difference, which we fear may be squeezed out by rational community and which we need to be reassured about before we will voluntarily enter into such a community.

Nussbaum castigates Butler for allowing the imagination both *too much* freedom – from the constraints of the body – and *not enough* freedom – from the constraints of discourse. By oscillating between the charges of voluntarism and determinism, Nussbaum at least recognises, after her fashion, that much of Butler's career has in fact been devoted to complicating the model of 'pretend what you like'. Indeed, that devotion begins with her 1987 book on Hegel. Butler has always been a Hegelian in the sense that her project has been not merely de-naturalising, but rather exploring the dialectic of freedom and constraint and its production of a sort of 'second Nature' (Hegel's phrase). *Subjects of Desire* is the one book of Butler's that Nussbaum omits from her broadside in *The New Republic*. And it is perhaps a symptomatic omission, considering that Nussbaum's own allegiances are so obviously Kantian. Nussbaum's Kant is of course not the Kant who sponsored the romantic imagination and with it contemporary social constructionism. He is the Kant of the categorical imperative (as yet unrescued from abstraction by the aesthetic). It's in the name of Kantian ethics that Nussbaum sums up her objections to Butler's literariness as an objection to Butler's avoidance of norms.

Nussbaum accuses Butler of taking for granted 'an audience of like-minded readers, who agree (sort of) about what the bad things are – discrimination against gays and lesbians, the unequal and hierarchical treatment of women – and who even agree (sort of) about why they are bad … But take that assumption away, and the absence of a normative dimension becomes a severe problem'.[43] 'There is a void, then, at the heart of Butler's notion of politics. This void can look liberating, because the reader fills it implicitly with a normative theory of human equality or dignity. But let there be no mistake … we have to articulate those norms – and this Butler refuses to do'.[44] But why do we have to articulate our norms? If we must be normative, aren't there other, perhaps more effective ways of performing our normative commitments? Lacking a sense of the performative, Nussbaum cannot judge the off-putting effect of her own absolutist articulations of norms, which perversely seem to make those norms more questionable rather than more self-evident. Her case for the compassionate imagination in *Hard Times* sounds a lot like Gradgrind's notion of a circus. Butler, on the other hand, for all the hoopla about her difficult prose style, offers a more compelling aesthetic spectacle. She says she is against norms, and yet she performs the normativity that she denies – and that professional objects of knowledge must possess.[45] The paradox is familiar. The in-group rhetoric about which Nussbaum is so snide works in fact not to exclude but to include. For it makes the reader want to belong, and it sets the price of belonging as tacit, instinctive, 'naturalised' acceptance of just those unacknowledged norms that Butler's desired alternative community would require. Its seemingly unintended literariness aims not at de-naturalising for its own sake, or simply pretending what you like, but at inducing us to embrace a freshly imagined 'second Nature'.

My interpretation of Butler is a recognisably literary one in the sense that it does not allow itself to be put off or shut down by the declared intentions of the author under consideration. But this is not to say that it can avoid the question of authorial authority altogether. Indeed, another way of putting my point would be to say that 'What is an author?' translates as 'What is nature?' A de-naturalising constructionism like Butler's (again I stress that this is not her own self-description) can only be said to postpone this double question, not to transcend it. Like literary studies, constructionism problematises the usual answers, but there is no way it can avoid offering some. It is by now notorious that to exchange 'the creative artist' for more impersonal or collective terms like, say, 'the text' or 'language' or 'discourse' is not necessarily to avoid the difficulties of interpretation to which critics objected in the earlier case. The same is true for constructionism. To say that the world is under construction is merely to switch attention to the agents, brokers, bankers, planners, architects, contractors, government officials, union officials, and many others whose colliding wills will decide when, where, and whether ground is broken, foundations are laid, and beams and girders begin to rise. If X is socially or culturally constructed, what precisely is that 'society' or 'culture' that is supposed to do the constructing? It is these terms that function as a 'second Nature'. Constructionism's freedom – if this was constructed, it can be constructed otherwise – cannot free itself from constructionism's constraint: whatever constructed X also imposed its nature on or invested its meaning in the construction. The regress is potentially infinite; one can always ask what constructs the constructors. The proximity of this regress, which delays the subject- or nature-effect, cannot eradicate it. And yet the delay, which can be described either as the difference between a first and a second nature or, more demagogically, as a (qualified) freedom of self-invention, is nonetheless real and significant.

Literary critics have always been tempted to identify this delay, this defiant floating of all final knowledge, with literature itself. I have been arguing that we must share our claim to virtuous irresolution with constructionism, which generalises it outside the canon, as well as with other more unlikely, more narrowly disciplinary objects and paradigms of knowledge. This is not an argument in favour of constructionism, a gross term for a collective public self-presentation and one that sounds as alien and unpalatable to me as it does, no doubt, to most academics who might be suspected of working within it. Nor is it to say that there are no variations from discipline to discipline or from discipline to interdisciplinarity. My point is merely that the dominant or most successful mode of scholarly knowing today is 'professional' in the specific sense I have extrapolated from Attridge's account of literature: asserting at once its inimitable mystery and its translatability into the language of common concern, obliged at once to put knowledge at a distance and to identify knowledge with the ultimate crossing of that distance. In each case the first term makes a claim to autonomy, the second a claim to social significance. In proposing that even Butler cannot escape this double imperative of the professional compact, and indeed offers a stylistically creative response to it, I have been suggesting that she, like Raymond Williams, does valuable work of self-legitimation for her fellow academics even as she apparently refuses the legitimacy of the collective project, and perhaps collectivity and legitimacy as such. It is because we critics and constructionists have never been free to pretend what we like that we need not feel impelled to narrate our present predicament, for all its dangers and inconveniences, as a fall into unfreedom.

Notes

1 See my discussion of Williams in *Secular Vocations: Intellectuals, Professionalism, Culture* (London, 1993).

2 The following two paragraphs are taken from my 'Presentism, pastism, professionalism', *Victorian Literature and Culture*, 27:2 (Summer, 1999), 457–63.

3 R. Williams, 'The future of cultural studies', in Williams, *The Politics of Modernism: Against the New Conformists* (London, 1989), p. 153.

4 *Ibid.*, p. 157.

5 G. Levine, 'Victorian studies', in S. Greenblatt and G. Gunn (eds), *Redrawing the Boundaries: The Transformation of English and American Literary Studies* (New York, 1992), pp. 144, 150. Levine notes: 'the founding of [the journal] *Victorian Studies*, in 1957, was almost exactly contemporary with the publication of Raymond Williams's *Culture and Society*, one of the most influential books of the last half century' (p. 136). For a brief but insightful discussion of continuities from Arnold to Williams and cultural studies, see C. Gallagher, 'Raymond Williams and cultural studies', *Social Text*, 30 (1992), 79–89.

6 *Ibid.*, p. 150.

7 Symposium on 'Intellectual history in the age of cultural studies', *Intellectual History Newsletter*, 18 (1996), 3–69. To watch another discipline wrestling with cultural studies, see V. R. Dominguez, 'Disciplining anthropology', in C. Nelson and D. Parameshwar Gaonkar (eds), *Disciplinarity and Dissent in Cultural Studies* (New York, 1996).

8 This is the argument of *Secular Vocations*.

9 D. Attridge, *Peculiar Language: Literature as Difference from the Renaissance to James Joyce* (London, 1988), p. 1.

10 *Ibid.*, p. 3.

11 D. Attridge, 'Introduction', in J. Derrida, *Acts of Literature*, ed. D. Attridge, (London, 1992), p. 17.

12 One example is the inimitable, mysterious 'bedside manner' which doctors began to emphasise more heavily when medical 'common sense' first came under attack from scientists wielding new discoveries.

13 A. Delbanco, 'The decline and fall of literature', *New York Review of Books* (4 November 1999).

14 D. Damrosch, 'Can Classics die?', *Lingua Franca* 5:6 (Spring 1995), 61–6.

15 R. Rorty, 'The necessity of inspired reading', *Chronicle* (9 February 1996), A48.

16 D. Simpson, *The Academic Postmodern and the Rule of Literature: A Report on Half-Knowledge* (Chicago, 1995).

17 I. Hacking, *The Social Construction of What?* (Cambridge, Mass., 1999). Philosopher Naomi Scheman, cited by Hacking, takes the opposite position that 'everything that is socially constructed is real … If something has in fact been socially constructed, then it does exist, and so is real!' Hacking disagrees, appealing to the example of satanic ritual abuse, for which none of the charges was substantiated by any evidence whatsoever. Hence Hacking concludes: 'SRA (unlike child abuse) is not real' (pp. 125–6).

18 T. Eagleton, *Literary Theory: An Introduction* (Oxford, 1983), p. 11.

19 F. Mulhern, *Contemporary Marxist Literary Criticism* (London, 1992), p. 21.

20 M. Foucault, *The History of Sexuality*, 1, trans. R. Hurley (New York, 1980), p. 105.

21 See H. Peeters and P. Charlier, 'Introduction: contributions à une théorie du dispositif', in the special number of the journal *Hermès: Cognition, Communication, Politique*, 25 (1999) entitled 'Le dispositif: entre usage et concept'.

22 Hacking, *Social Construction of What?*, p. 41.
23 M. Foucault, 'The functions of literature', interview with R-P. Droit (20 June 1975), trans. A. Sheridan, in L. D. Kritzman (ed.), *Michel Foucault: Politics, Philosophy, Culture, Interviews and Other Writings, 1977–1984* (New York, 1988), p. 307.
24 *Ibid.*, p. 312.
25 J. Guillory, 'The spontaneous philosophy of the critics: science wars and cultural studies', manuscript available from the author. The extent to which literature is felt to define one of those repressive categories, and thus to which a literary constructionism must also aim, however contradictorily, to liberate us from literature itself, remains a matter of lively dispute.
26 M. Schudson, 'Paper tigers', *Lingua Franca* (August 1997), 49–56.
27 Eagleton, *Literary Theory*, p. 11. This is not a difficult thing to suppose. It is no more than Raymond Williams argued in *Keywords*. According to Williams, it was only late in the eighteenth century that the word 'literature' ceased to refer to any writing on any subject that met a certain standard of quality, and acquired something like its more specialised modern meaning of writing that was imaginative, creative, disinterested, non-instrumental (R. Williams, *Keywords: A Vocabulary of Culture and Society* (London, 1988), p. 183 ff).
28 Hacking, *Social Construction of What?*, p. 29.
29 *Ibid.*, pp. 6–7.
30 *Ibid.*, p. 7.
31 *Ibid.*, pp. 8–9.
32 Butler has of course been a critic of constructionism from the beginning of her career. *Gender Trouble* objected that to present gender as constructed was to preserve the notion of sexual body as natural. Butler's critique of 'customary notions of "construction"' (in *Bodies That Matter*, pp. x–xi) describes them as 'not quite adequate to the task at hand' (p. xi). She wishes, she says, to restore the sense of 'constitutive constraint' (p. xi) in construction by insisting on construction as not a 'singular or deliberate "act"' but a 'reiterative and citational practice' (p. 2). This means '"sex" becomes something like a fiction, perhaps a fantasy, retroactively installed at a prelinguistic site to which there is no direct access' (p. 5). See also Pheng Cheah, 'Mattering', *Diacritics* 26:1 (Spring 1996).
33 J. Prosser, *Second Skins: The Body Narratives of Transsexuality* (New York, 1998).
34 A. Phillips, 'Keeping it moving: commentary on Judith Butler', in J. Butler, *The Psychic Life of Power: Theories in Subjection* (Stanford, 1997), p. 153.
35 *Ibid.*, p. 156.
36 H. Cixous, 'Laugh of the Medusa', *Signs*, 1 (1976).
37 M. Nussbaum, 'The Professor of parody', *The New Republic* (22 February 1999) pp. 37–45.
38 *Ibid.*, p. 41.
39 *Ibid.*, p. 42.
40 M. C. Nussbaum, *Poetic Justice: The Literary Imagination and Public Life* (Boston, 1995), p. xvi.
41 *Ibid.*, p. 66.
42 When Nussbaum objects to Butler's assumption that 'there is no agent behind or prior to the social forces that produce the self' (p. 41), her objection to constructionism, or to a literariness-without-the-Author, is really an objection to the absence of norms. For the Author, in her view, is where normativity is necessarily located. No author, no norms. From this perspective, Butler might be seen not as avoiding nor-

205

mativity so much as trying to relocate it outside the author, and thus render it more effective.

43 Nussbaum, 'The professor of parody', p. 42.

44 *Ibid.*, p. 43.

45 To put this another way: the Gramscian struggle for common sense is better fought not by declaring norms, but by performing them.

robert smith

LITERATURE – REPEAT NOTHING

Words, words, words.
(Hamlet)

As I write this essay in the summer of 1998, the latest novel by Ian McEwan, *Enduring Love*, heads the list of best-selling paperback fiction in the United Kingdom. In its title the novel invites images of a romantic relationship surviving adversity with the rich resources of sentimental intensity, only to qualify such images severely as the story gets under way. First, the love portrayed is unrequited; second, it is pathological; third, it is homosexual; fourth, it is a manifestation of Christian fanaticism. The word 'enduring' in the title becomes menacing, suggesting obsession. It also reflects back on the object of the love who must 'endure' the menace such 'love' presents.

The unrequited, pathological, homosexual, Christian-fanatic lover is Jed Parry; his beloved, the novel's protagonist, Joe, through whose first person narrative the novel mainly proceeds. Until Jed comes along Joe, who writes popular science articles for magazines, has an enduring love of his own, of the orthodox, secular, bourgeois kind, with a woman named Clarissa, a lecturer in English literature. Although Joe and Clarissa's relationship gets derailed by Jed's obsessive love for Joe, the couple ultimately reconcile, with Jed by then securely cordoned off in a mental asylum. The structure of the novel provides a fairly obvious defence of such *Gemütlichkeit* as lived by Joe and Clarissa, with the outsider banished from their world after a kind of trial by otherness. Joe and Clarissa's love endures, but so does that of Jed who for years continues undeterred to write Joe impassioned letters from the asylum – letters which the staff do not pass on, in the interests of protecting Joe and, of course, the values he represents.

Issues of class-consciousness aside, *Enduring Love* foregrounds the longevity of love, its tenacity, and its dependence on a notion of perpetuity. Jed embodies it in taking up vigil outside Joe's house: love keeps coming back, indefatigably; love endures. If love is a generally libidinal phenomenon, its libidinality is almost pure energy, ever-burning and inextinguishable, a sustaining fuel which keeps the lover productive and energised, constantly creative and restless in his solicitation of the love object. Indeed, love would have to be libidinal, for only the libido (at least as conceived by Freud) could sustain such unreserved productivity. Jed finds ever-new inspiration for his paeans to Joe, even in despite of Joe's rebuffs; in fact the rebuffs are inconsequential in the face of the sheer prolific engagement of Jed's love.

But therein lies a paradox. Is such libidinal energy creative or destructive? Original or repetitious? Productive or reductive? In his letters Jed can always find fresh material with which to apostrophise Joe and express love for him, but precisely that creativity is obsessive, repetitive and monomaniacal. The letters are always fresh and stale in equal measure: surprisingly new, sometimes absurdly so, so unbounded is their ingenuity; but also crushingly repetitive, with their solipsistically incorrigible insistences and pleas. Is there any fundamental difference between allegedly pathological love and the 'normal' kind? It would only take Joe's acquiescence in the relationship for Jed's love to be normalised. Both kinds of love come under the same stricture to endure, and endurance presents us with a deeply puzzling quality. What kind of resourcefulness is it that the libido harbours? Does it deaden or invent? To the extent that love must endure to prove itself, its libidinal energy channelled towards reaffirmation, cannot its sustainment and repetition over time be seen equally as deathly and reductive as creative and life-affirming? As much as it is energetic, libidinal and resourceful, enduring love is also monotonous, constant, singular, reductive and, in this regard, resource*less*.

This paradox in the notion of libidinal creativity will be my guiding thread, as I transpose it to the creativity involved in literary works (in a sense Jed's tireless, eroticised writing is literary work of its own). I begin with the assumption that whatever else the literary might be, it appertains to 'creative' writing: though not all creative writing is literary, all literary writing is creative. In so far as they are creative, literary works may be grouped with other artefacts and activities that transmute or sublimate libidinal energy into a more or less 'civilised' form. All are expressions, in a sense, of enduring love. What distinguishes literary from other creative works is a question I address at the essay's end. But I begin by filling out the psychoanalytic background condensed in the terminology of the libido and of sublimation that I have already used.

In contrast to the subsequent wealth and sophistication of literary criticism and theory considering itself psychoanalytic, Freud's own writings on the subject of literature as such are few and often surprisingly ingenuous. His most general statement appears in 'Creative writers and day-dreaming (1908 [1907])'. Freud casts creative writing as a form of day-dream or 'phantasy' akin to child's play: '[t]he creative writer [the German word is *Dichter* which carries no necessary implication of creativity, even though it might suggest the same] does the same as the child at play'.[1] This is not to suggest that creative writing is all sweetness and light. The phantasies are displacements of wishes repressed, and never impinge upon a 'happy person': '[w]e may lay it down that a happy person never phantasies, only an unsatisfied one. The motive forces of phantasies are unsatisfied wishes, and every single phantasy is the fulfilment of a wish, a correction of unsatisfying reality'.[2] Being phantasy-driven, creative writing thus labours under the sign of 'unhappiness'. However, the creative writer will transform such subjective misery into objective pleasure, sparing the reader from the indecorousness of the writerly condition, modifying egoistic interests, and proffering aesthetic satisfaction instead. He or she does so through disguises: '[t]he writer softens the character of his egoistic daydreams by altering and disguising it, and he bribes us by the purely formal – that is, aesthetic – yield of pleasure which he offers us in the presentation of his phantasies'.[3] Elsewhere Freud argues for the sexual essence of such aesthetic pleasure, a kind of foreplay or 'fore-pleasure'; here his focus on disguise blends with an argument for the reconstructibility, or rather the aetiological completeness, of the creative or phantasying process. He has already assured us that 'even the most extreme deviations from that model [of the day-dream] could be linked with [creative writing] through an uninterrupted series of transitional cases'; and now he implies again the ideality, so to speak, of the creative psyche which, for all the detours it will have taken, all the masks it will have put on for its phantasy-aesthetic, may nevertheless be tracked back to its motive origin.[4] Though the highways and byways of phantasy be many and wayward, all belong in the same psychic dimension, affirming the latter's unity even as they scramble and warp it.

That motive origin, as throughout Freud's writing, has the libidinal form of a wish, and a wish, because it constitutes the psyche as such, can never be destroyed, only repressed and/or dissimulated. The wish furnishes an impregnable reserve to fund 'creative' activity. The creative, in this case literary, works resulting mark the devious formal or 'aesthetic' accommodations of repressed and refracted wish. In so bursarial a system, the stronger the repression of the wish, the more 'creative' the psyche is likely to be. In an analogous case we shall turn to, Freud proposes that '[t]he greater the resistance, the more extensively will acting out (repetition) replace remembering'.[5] The push-and-pull effect is clear. Creativity increases with repression.

The exchequer of this system is not unproblematic, however. The Freudian psyche, as we suggested, does make for an holistic entity (despite the internal interference it generates), but, importantly, is unable to assume its own integrity. The in this case literary psyche depends for its literary disposition upon a wish, its repression and its subsequent escape from repression, in the camouflage of aesthetic form; it will have duped the censoring mechanism of repression into allowing the now disguised, even beautified, wish into the showplace of representation ('no representation without distortion'). The repressed promises the writer aesthetic treasure, but, being repressed, remains locked to any conscious raiding of it. The writer waits on its whim, powerless to regulate the flow of material which, when it bursts through, he or she will make into literature. The repressed shrinks from intentional appropriations of it; a schism in the psyche has formed, the writer become, to paraphrase Nietzsche, a 'stranger to himself'.

With the repressed now the fount of literary material, what the creative writer has been endopsychically separated from is effectively a muse. Deposed from its deific or transcendent altitude, the muse of classicism has been reallocated by psychoanalytic modernity to the psyche, preserving therein a distance that replicates the effects of such height and authority. What was very high has become very deep. The function remains the same. Where the muse was transcendent, capricious, exterior and yet private, so the literary repressed stands inaccessible, unpredictable, lodging 'within' the psyche as a kind of outside or unbroachable recess. The writer becomes the mere dummy or secretary of an inscrutable force that is at once intimate and foreign, close yet remote. Freud has thus given variation to a long-standing theme in literary tradition. The ablest expositor of this tradition, Timothy Clark, sums it up: '[i]n both the Platonic and the biblical traditions inspiration described the supposed possession of an individual voice by some transcendent authority. The muse speaks, and the poet is only her mouthpiece and servant; or in the medieval Christian tradition the human *scriptor* has authority only as a scribe of divine truth'.[6] The writer merely transcribes his own repressed, his muse.

But evidently, an ambiguity bothers this structure. On the one hand, nothing could be more creative or original than the writer who is 'inspired'. On the other, the inspiration derives from without the writer, or at least outside the precincts of intention, and so circumscribes any creativity claimed. The level of volition and agency defies being specified – a problem traceable perhaps to theological disputation concerning free will (how far are our actions voluntary, how far prescribed?). The muse, the literary repressed: each is the writer's personal other, which dictates imperiously either an already 'known' material latterly veiled through the anamnesis of repression, or an entirely new stock of words. Either way, inspiration comes as a surprise to the conscious mind, and it's not certain that 'the writer', whatever singularity that designates, knows what's going on. At the same time, as much as he or she is possessed *by* this closeted voice of inspiration, the writer is possessed *of* the literary skill which belatedly orders the messages coming through into aesthetic wordings. What, then, is the nature of creativity? For all the aesthetic gain got via this psychic exchange where repressed voices splinter through, its final products – literary works – remain pathogenic objects, even in the aura of their new-found beauty, just as in the Platonic tradition invoked by Clark, inspiration closely resembles mania, and poetry is the cooled fire of frenzy. They result from a process the creativity of which appears spurious, as much a blind irrigation of pulsional urges as the blessed act of free artistry that 'creativity' might suggest.

The ambiguity gets carried over into later psychoanalytic writing. In a Kleinian study titled *Dream, Phantasy and Art*, Hanna Segal avers: '[t]he act of creation at depth has to do with an unconscious memory of a harmonious internal world and the experience of its destruction; that is, the depressive position. The impulse is to recover and recreate this lost world'.[7] Segal's emphasis on reparation, on a paradise regained, construes the creative work as a compensatory epiphenomenon of mental well-being in rather simple opposition to the trauma it supersedes and alleviates, leaving its creativity unclear: note the irresolution in the word 'recreate'. The creator has only redeemed the Atlantis of his inspiration, not made it afresh; and, according to Kleinian teaching, that world would reappear anyway, if not in creative then in destructive and regressive acts of vengeance. The word 'impulse' is equally telling, hedging as it does between conscious and unconscious action. The definite article serves only to mystify it: '*[t]he* impulse'. Whose impulse? Where in the psyche does an impulse spring from? The nearest Segal comes to an answer amounts to a tautology: 'the artistic impulse is specifically related to the depressive position. The artist's need is to recreate what he feels in the depth of his internal world'.[8]

While Segal reproduces the ambiguity there in Freud (not that its resolution is at all obvious), she departs strikingly from the Freudian view of repression. Creativity increases with repression for Freud, whereas Segal points to the 'laxity of repression which is decisive for allowing the expression of phantasy'.[9] The difference opens a deep cleft within psychoanalytic theory, and, as far as I know, little notice has been taken of it. It has to do with a liberalising of Freud, a humanistic eliding of expression with freedom, where repression can be coaxed by means of therapy to step aside and allow the bounty of creation through in all its goodness. The build-up of repressive pressure must be alleviated and creativity will ensue, in a model of aesthetic production that looks innocent next to Freud's recognition of the subterfuge required for artworks to deceive the watchtower of repression. In Freud aesthetic works are only and essentially disguised; in Segal they are the denuded tokens of inner truth.

In the latter view, creativity has become what Clark, glossing Mihaly Csikszentmihalyi, calls 'a vestige of Romantic individualism'.[10] It is moreover 'central' to a 'concept of subjectivity' – a subjectivity which, purportedly bestowed with an inner essence, needs the complementary functions of creativity and expression to bring that essence out and thus confirm it was always there.[11] Creativity supports a doctrine of free, democratic, subjective, essentialist individualism. Other psychoanalytic literature, especially of a therapeutic bent, only endorses the doctrine. A version of it appears in a text by Christopher Bollas, called *Cracking Up: The Work of Unconscious Experience*. Resuming the book's thesis, Bollas writes:

> This process – of collecting condensations which in turn serve as the material of disseminative scattering – is vital to individual unconscious creativity in living. If a person has been fortunate enough to develop this capability, then he will develop in turn a 'separate sense', which evolves from a certain kind of unconscious development and is part of the function of unconscious intuition. However, this kind of inner experiencing may be impossible for an individual whose life is dominated by a trauma, whatever its source.[12]

On the same page Bollas talks of '[u]nconscious freedom, as opposed to unconscious imprisonment', and this dualism sustains the whole book, including the quotation above. What is 'vital' is the freeing-up of an unconscious otherwise in danger of paralytic seizure. Bollas complicates the trope of creative release by giving it the hour-glass shape of 'collecting condensations which in turn serve as the material of disseminative scattering', but the complication leaves the opposition between free and unfree, the quick and the deathly, frozen and thawed, intact. His innovation lies in positing an oxymoronically mature narcissism, whereby the creative individual has evolved an internal 'separate sense', a kind of genius of the psyche, to register creative activity.[13] Bollas has also sublated the difference between aesthetic and non-aesthetic into a general 'creativity in living'. No especial privilege redounds to works commonly considered aesthetic, so that the free, healthy, released practice of absorbed day-dreaming, for example, bears in principle equal 'aesthetic' rank as a work such as *Moby-Dick*, which Bollas discusses. True, Freud also associates aesthetic work with day-dreaming, but he specifically differentiates the aesthetic by its 'formal' quality.

The somewhat facile healthiness in Bollas's portrait of individual creativity has clearly sloughed off the darker, more painfully wrought elements attending Freudian aesthetic work. In both Freud and Segal, in fact, literary products constitute the more or less transparent, more or less displaced, *preservations* of 'trauma' (a term as vague and idealised as 'original sin', and with similar implications), where Bollas regrets that it 'may be impossible' to accede to creativity while under trauma's reign. Within this notion of preservation lie adumbrations of the deathliness of literary production, and one approach to the subject passes through Bollas's own comments on obsession and repetition. Still nursing the binarism of free and unfree, Bollas confides that:

> Psychoanalysts come across many people who lack the unconscious freedom necessary for creative living. Their freedom is restricted, their mind bound in anguished repetitions that terminate the dissemination of the self.
>
> This obstruction to freedom is easily observed in the person who is obsessed.[14]

While the citizens of the demos engaged in creative living fulfil themselves through disburdened expressions of self, the poor, banausic creatures debarred by their own psyches from such liberal favours languish amid immovable terminal repetitions (I put it in these terms because a reading through of *Cracking Up* leads one to suspect Bollas of the naively liberalist agenda also sustaining *Enduring Love*). Bollas's observations return us to our central question: to put it bluntly, does a repetition terminate? Repetition presents a force of continuity, so to charge it with the opposite force of termination, is to beg some questions.

To elaborate them, let us resume our reading of Freud. Several terms are now vibrating together: creativity (especially literary creativity), repetition, termination (death), obsession. We are not sure repetition splits off so readily and so early from creativity, or that the deathliness and vitalism respectively underpinning them can simply be made opposites. Bollas, for instance, appears to hypostatise his terms into ideal values, whereby creativity, life and freedom foster the Good; repetition, termination and unfreedom, the Bad. Freud too appears to keep things apart – or, more precisely, the work done in 'Creative writers and day-dreaming (1908 [1907])' never gets updated in the light of later writings, such as 'Beyond the pleasure principle (1920)', which confound the opposition between life and death. But even in texts roughly contemporary with it, arguments are made which should unsettle or at least revise the creativity sketched out in 'Creative writers'.

Take obsession. Is creativity not obsessive? Of course if we go from Christopher Bollas, obsession is the mortal enemy of creativity: '[p]athological obsession is aimed at maintaining a terminal object that ends all unconscious use of the object: ideational, affective, somatic, or transferential'.[15] That obsession is 'bad' is beyond debate; but in the paradoxical phrase, 'maintaining a terminal object that *ends*', our ambiguity resurfaces. The struggle between maintenance and termination, sustainment and ending, continues unabated, itself interminable. Bollas describes in this context a patient who for years keeps up a moan about her husband, obsessed with his shortcomings: the husband is the 'terminal object' she 'maintains'. Clearly the woman has tapped a source of productive energy, and who is to adjudicate what kind of value it has? Is this not also an enduring love? And why would creative works not be 'terminal objects' that have kept their creator coming back obsessively to address and add to them?

In 'Notes upon a case of obsessional neurosis (1909)', Freud begins by reviving his earlier definition of obsessive actions as 'transformed self-reproaches which have re-emerged from repression and which always relate to some sexual act that was performed with pleasure in childhood'.[16] So much for that: now he wants to make some amendments. In keeping with the theory of disguise and distortion in the slightly earlier 'Creative writers' essay, Freud moves to mix 'ellipsis' into the constitution of obsession, for the 'technique of distortion by ellipsis seems to be typical of obsessional neuroses'.[17] On the next page Freud adds the perhaps surprising qualification that 'in obsessional neuroses the unconscious mental processes occasionally break through into consciousness in their pure and undistorted form', but by and large he wishes now to log ellipsis among obsession's specifications.

The amendment written in, obsession only comes the more to look like creative writing. Where the literary 'impulse' issues in the covert and distorted presentation of a forbidden libidinal pleasure, obsession performs elliptical stagings of repressed infantile sexuality. The difference hardly rings out. They are, moreover, equally 'formal'. Recall, this was already an aspect of literary creation in 'Creative writers'; and Freud, though he does not emphasise this aspect of obsession in 'Notes upon a case of obsessional neurosis (1909)', has already based another whole essay around it. 'Obsessive actions and religious practices (1907)' derived from the insight that the two phenomena discussed share a ceremonious formality; both are disciplines which as such observe certain rules.[18] In fact all three – obsession, religion, and literature – possess such vestimentary traits, the dressed-up, disciplined, artificial and coded tropings of a repressed sexuality. But despite the clear structural sameness that spans from obsessive action and religious practices to creative writing, Freud leaves it unsaid. Is he trying to protect something?

A further, more enigmatic element in the consanguinity of these forms takes the name of repetition, and in this we make another step towards the death instincts. Freud establishes the repetitiousness in religious practices and obsessive actions alike: '[a]ny activities whatever may become obsessive actions in the wider sense of the term if they are elaborated by small additions or given a rhythmic character by means of pauses and repetitions. We shall not expect to find a sharp distinction between "ceremonials" and "obsessive actions"'.[19] One can easily picture the apparatus of the Eucharist, for example, with its prescribed duties and utterances, its rhythmic programme and 'automatic' pattern, and see in it the institutionally approved version of neurotic behaviour obsessed with ritual, with laying things out, with formulaic words, with special clothing, etc. But we should take care in applying this model to literary forms, for a distinction applies, in respect of them, between a writer's activities and the writing produced. Although we can just as readily imagine the writer going through a set procedure before commencing work (washing the hands, unplugging the phone, making coffee, repeating words of private exhortation, etc.), Freud's earlier recognition of the role of aesthetic form directs us, in turn, towards the written. This is not to say the writer might not *also* be an obsessional neurotic who indulges in superstitious preparations; nor that his or her choice of form – the sonnet, say – does not, if repeated, provide a vehicle for personal obsession; but rather that …

I was about to say that when Freud indicates the formal aspect of literary works, matters of genre are claiming his thoughts. But things are more complex. Let's stick with sonnets. Although the sonnet constitutes a 'public' form, a genre, a certifiably 'literary' mode, the writer who employs it thereby makes it his or her own. Conversely, the written sonnet – and it can only ever *be* written – equivocally remains public even in its private appropriation by an author, precisely because it is a form. And because it is a form it does not differ, fundamentally, from any supposedly 'private' ritual or form a writer may develop. Whether stamped as literary or not by prevailing norms, the form a writer selects will endlessly contest this private–public dilemma. Even the most esoteric form becomes, qua form, a repeatable event and, in this regard, potentially public. Likewise, if an obsession, to satisfy its criterion of repeatability, must solicit the 'formal', then it too suffers from the equivocation. Obsessive actions are no doubt personal – they even serve to ratify the alleged particularity of a given psyche – but their repeatability lends them a formal element which simultaneously takes them beyond that psyche's exclusive ownership. The more obsessive one becomes, the more idiosyncratic, but also the more formal, the more theatrical, the more imitable, the more public. Obsession plays host to this intractable ambiguity; and insofar as the formal element of literary works may – and it always may – be abused for personal obsessive ends, those works will shelter the same ambiguity in their very form.

The 'impersonal' side of repetitious and formal obsession emerges in other works of Freud that deal with repetition proper. Earlier we quoted from 'Remembering, repeating and working-through (Further recommendations on the technique of psycho-analysis II) (1914)', in explaining the relation between repression and expression. We heard Freud say that '[t]he greater the resistance, the more extensively will acting out (repetition) replace remembering'.[20] Now, as we have just seen, such repetitions can become elaborate and ritualised, even to the point of obsession. In fact, the greater the resistance or repression, the greater or 'more extensive' will the forms of expression become. To the extent they *ex*press the *re*pressed in complexified or customised form, such repetitions can claim to be 'original' or 'creative' (even though, as we pointed out, that originality also evaporates through their very repetitiousness, which confers a formality that renders them standardised and 'public'). But regardless of how bizarrely or originally a repetition may evolve, regardless of how creative or idiosyncratic a form it develops – and even regardless of, by contrast, how standardised, empty, public and borrowed the very same repetitions might always become – whatever the repetition is, it will always be intrinsically original, creative or deviant, in that it begins in disguise and displacement. Repetition is always already a trope. It tropes a wish which constitutionally it can never imitate, for such blatant presentation of the wish has been forbidden, and repetition stems only from the prohibition. Never could it be orthodox, taking up its task rather as heretical, alternative, heterodox and always different from the repressed wish it tacitly porters along. Coming back to our sonnets, the sheer fact of a writer electing this literary form testifies in principle to a creative, original, eccentric or novel 'impulse', because chances are the form marks or masks the repetition of a wish, and the wish has long been deviated from, following an early obliquity. A repetition has to invent: not only will it have already done so merely by not stating the repressed wish directly; but continues to do so by settling on any literary form whatsoever. It doesn't matter if the form itself is hackneyed or pristine. Both merely accommodate the founding originality of a repetition, and neither affects it, thus making new-fangled literary forms ironically redundant.

None of this yet deals with the aforementioned impersonality of repetition, though it does touch on the grey area circumferenced by modern conceptions of 'the literary'. However else it may be characterised, today's 'literary' must meet the rival requirements to be both creative and 'aesthetic'. It has become a commonplace to note that, in demanding creativity and originality of a literary work, modern expectations reverse ancient, or at least mediaeval, ones which calculate the literariness of a given work from its level of acknowledgement of earlier authorities, thus its imitativeness. Because they seek, in addition to the 'original', to exact the aesthetic from pretenders to literary honour, the expectations can only seem unreasonable at first. At first, the inventively original and the generically formal (aesthetic) appear to be at odds. On closer scrutiny, as we have argued, they merge; and in the light of that scrutiny, we may conjecture that the modern criteria for literariness give voice to an unwitting demand for an object of undecidable status.

As for repetition 'proper', Freud has just given it the alternative name of 'acting out' ('[t]he greater the resistance, the more extensively will acting out (repetition) replace remembering'). The concept of acting out only amplifies the problems we are negotiating. Freud portrays the activity in the following terms: 'the patient does not *remember* anything of what he has forgotten and repressed, but *acts* it out. He reproduces it not as a memory but as an action; he *repeats* it, without, of course, knowing that he is repeating it'.[21] Something mechanical manipulates 'the patient'. A kind of robotic behaviour occurs, whence the 'impersonality' of repetition – but also the opposite. A psychic programming dictates the patient's actions but, *being* psychic, the programming occupies the most private chamber of the personality, its sanctum of authenticity, so to speak, even as it commands these most inauthentic, dispossessed, absurd and puppet-like motions. A highly compromised being appears before us, disporting its unique personality in the contradictory mode of unstoppable autopoetic repetitions which seem to come from some anonymous factory of gestures. The unconscious is at work, in short. In witnessing its dramaturgy we revisit the dialectic of formality and obsession, only in more alienated aspect. Nothing if not repetitious, acting out too achieves formalisation, even to the point of turning its victims into automata; yet, in an agonising paradox, it remains *their* pathology. Repetition obdurately nurtures the internecine twins of private and public, authentic and mechanical, natural and technological, even human and inhuman.

Our affiliated concern was with the possibility or otherwise of *thinking* a form, of bringing anything conscious or original to bear upon the aesthetic form through which creativity demonstrates itself. In the aesthetic form of the sonnet, the creative effort at appropriating it and colouring it with originality triggered a proportionate exappropriation. Subduing a form to conscious, original, thinking, intentional, personal control proved to be possible only to the extent it was also *im*possible. In acting out, the mediating, humanising, thinking moment of remembering gets bypassed, repetition rudely thrusts itself forward, a shell scooped of thought and intention. As with those of the obsessive, the actions played out, no matter how flagrant or contrived, will not be caught, normalised and translated into conscious psychic language, as it were. They press into the world uncouth. Not that in both acting out and obsession, some naked 'trauma' gets pushed on stage: on the contrary, obsession depends, as we have seen, on elliptical and delated figurations, just as the repetition in acting out repeats not a trauma per se but the form of its first reactive, disguised repression (though in the quotation above Freud has relaxed his rigour on this point). It is these convoluted repetitions which their subject fails to think or 'remember' in any cognisant fashion, despite their conspicuous weirdness. The logic of it even suggests that the odder the behaviour, the less noticeable to its subject – which can only be because the form counts more than the content. In other words, the logic supports itself with the truism that 'the patient' – the subject, the obsessive, the priest, the creator, the writer – ceases to apprehend what he or she repeats. Repetition can make a normality of the most aberrant or recondite actions, the form having either numbed all apperception of the content or, more interestingly, commuted each item of content into a moment of itself – a moment of form, that is. In the latter case, the 'form' of the Eucharist would pervade its contents, so that no word ('This is my body … '), nor any item (chalice, wine, wafer, etc.) would represent a content distinguishable from the formal make-up of the ceremony; and in the case of the sonnet not only would the shape of the poem constitute 'form', obviously enough, but so would each line, as if clandestinely saying 'I am the nth line of a sonnet'; and even each word, though varying from sonnet to sonnet and thus creating the impression of content, might be heard to whisper, 'I am the nth word in the nth line of a sonnet' …

But perhaps formal elements cannot be thought. Worse than merely becoming dulled and negligible through repetition, forms, such as aesthetic forms, may be impossible to think *tout court*. Acting out might describe the general as much as the pathological condition of repetition. Perhaps it's not merely *possible* to repeat without understanding, but necessary: repetition kicks in where the understanding falters. We repeat *because* we do not understand. Thus formal elements win their aesthetic quality by overleaping their creator's cognitive mediation of them. After all, such mediation spells their death. Literary form becomes, technically, unthinkable. And when it opts for such a form, the creative act turns into the thoughtless facilitation of a cosmetic object, literariness the effect of suppressing reflection on it.

Though all this makes for a somewhat scandalous theory of creativity, nothing in it disputes the basic proposition that creativity does indeed create. Where there was nothing, now there is something. Even when 'create' really means 're-create', the re-creations fill an erstwhile gap. Even though the creativity falls short of its former freedom and intentionality, nevertheless literary and other aesthetic works *are created*: in the absence of untrammelled 'creativity', creations still arise. I want to come back to the nothingness that precedes a creative act, but for now the sheer 'there-ness' of a so-called creative repetition demands some comment. How did it come to be there? We have exposed the perplexities of its production, the trajectory from wish to repression to deceiving representation, etc., but not substantially interrogated what makes creative repetitions happen.

To enjoy the fruit of Freud's own reflections on this question, we must consult a new source, further on again in the chronology of his essays. In 'The uncanny (1919)' Freud deepens the character of repetition, introduc-ing a phrase, 'compulsion to repeat', which bears a significance well beyond the essay's topic: 'it is possible to recognize the dominance in the unconscious mind of a "compulsion to repeat" proceeding from the instinctual impulses and probably inherent in the very nature of the instincts – a compulsion powerful enough to overrule the pleasure princi-ple, lending to certain aspects of the mind their daemonic character'.[22] A 'compulsion to repeat', then, in the middle of this extraordinarily thought-provoking statement. We are now in the immediate neighbourhood of death. Why are repetitions made? Because of a compulsion. We already knew there was a wish and that it industriously found ways – sometimes very roundabout ways – of gratifying itself in 'repetitions'; and that liter-ary works number among these. Now we also know what drives it, to wit: compulsion.

Painful to say, the notion of compulsion both does and does not further our understanding of the wish as the instrument of the pleasure principle. On the one hand, compulsion takes us further into the psyche, beyond the mere psychology of the wish, into the archaic and, as Freud will later con-tend, *phylogenetic* nest of the instincts. From this point of view the 'com-pulsion to repeat' becomes almost visceral in its functioning, as hard to arrest by conscious will as a heartbeat. On the other hand, since it is a *wish* which pilots repetition, 'compulsion' has already been factored in, for a wish is arguably self-compelling by nature. As *wishful*, the wish knows nothing but motivation, solicitation, identification, and so on, incapable of rest. The wish does nothing but compel itself.

Either way – whether it precedes or accompanies the wish – *there is compulsion*. At this stage in Freud's career (1919), we can say no more; he hasn't yet advanced an explanation for the compulsion at hand. In so far as literary and other aesthetic works provide the formal receptacles for rep-etitions, they too will have been compelled. The wish had to have its way, its compulsive energy relentless in the pursuit of a compromised way round repression. It repeats itself, misunderstood by its agent, in forms which though diverse – aesthetic, obsessive, religious, acting out – enjoy a structural affinity; and it goes on repeating itself, never visiting the consciousness which might find the lever to shut it down. Once again it would be arbitrary to call such energy *either* creative *or* oppressively monotonous. As in the case of Jed Parry in McEwan's novel, it is both. Compulsion offers a more powerful concept than either the creativity or the monotony it may interpretatively be split into.

Freud's explanation of it arrives in a text published the following year, 'Beyond the pleasure principle (1920)'. So far we have conceived repetitions, particularly of the aesthetic variety, as the far-flung, elaborated or 'disseminative' sallies from a repressed wish that has been condensed and displaced: distance inheres in them. The 1920 paper indirectly adjusts this conception. The compulsion to repeat now serves *'a need to restore an earlier state of things'.*[23] This might *prima facie* look like Hanna Segal's 'impulse ... to recover and recreate [a] lost world' (see above), especially given the imprecision of that word 'impulse'. But where Segal identifies a psychological anteriority, Freud's attentions have turned again, as in 'The uncanny (1919)', to the antepsychological realm of the instincts. The *'earlier state'* is much earlier, in short. For all its diversifications and satellites, all the apparent remoteness of its forms, repetition always steers a homeward course towards the instincts. The regionality of its expressions is false. Whatever distance they pretend to have travelled has always already bent back to a prior, nearer location, the innermost of the mind. Indeed the inner-ness is so inwards it has backed through the individual psyche into a phylogenetic past. The intrepid creativity of repetitions could not be more conservative.

In this conservatism lies the kernel of Freud's conception. As it seeks at large the pleasure on which to sate itself (often obliged to light on pathological forms as removed from it as literary works), the wish actually craves *the alleviation of tension* which pleasure affords. Freud's essay opens summarily with:

> In the theory of psycho-analysis we have no hesitation in assuming that the course taken by mental events is automatically regulated by the pleasure principle. We believe, that is to say, that the course of those events is invariably set in motion by an unpleasurable tension, and that it takes a direction such that its final outcome coincides with a lowering of that tension – that is, with an avoidance of unpleasure or a production of pleasure.[24]

Armed thus with his theory, Freud feels emboldened to make the inference that the pleasure principle serves the death instincts, for the state of absolute tranquillity sought from pleasure amounts to the inertia of death. Freud likens it to the extinction of a Buddhist nirvana. And insofar as the death instincts therefore lord it over the pleasure principle, they converge with the compulsion to repeat which, as Freud noted in 'The uncanny

(1919)' (see above), is a 'compulsion powerful enough to overrule the plea-sure principle'. The deathliness of repetition reveals itself at last.

It might be tempting to try to capture Freud's schema in the net of a dialectic, but this would be vain. Repetition tilts between the creative and the monotonous. Impressively creative or flamboyant in its choice of forms, forms which in principle may be as orchidacious and 'aesthetic' as you like, repetition nevertheless drags along the same old wish repressed. Is there a dialectic of identity and difference here? I think not. For a start, any such dialectic could at best be secondary, considering that, as we remarked before, repetitions start off as inventive, coming into existence as improvisatory salvos and, in that, *remaining* inventive, whatever takes place down the line, sameness or variation. But more gravely, the mastery of the death instincts subsumes any dialecticity in the play of repetition into its own overarching, monolithic and irresistible force. Pleasure's sta-tion is not as a partner-in-identity-and-difference for the death instincts, but as its servant. And if that makes us rush to Hegel to help us say that, 'well, if pleasure is the servant of death, and death is pleasure's lord, then the dialectic of power described in *Phenomenology of Spirit* has reap-peared … ', we should pause. For death and pleasure to join together in the *pas-de-deux* of a dialectic, they would have to dance to the same mea-sure. The absolute contemporaneity of the two partners sustains all dialec-tical substitution; there is no time-difference in dialectics. Not only are both partners quite present to each other, but dialectics consists in the effort to comprehend their simultaneity. Death and pleasure, by contrast, inhabit either a dyschronic field, or separate eras which touch. As we noted, the death instincts recede into an archaic past, which Freud now identifies as that of the simple organism. The wish, and the pleasure prin-ciple which governs it, bear an anachronistic relation to the death instincts, as the rebeginning, now in the human species, of an urge for still-ness under the more perspicuous superstructure of the psyche.

A kind of aesthetic double-time develops. No matter the psychical vest-ments worn by aesthetic repetitions, no matter, that is, how expressively they belong to the time of an individual psyche – how far they are the accents of its very modernity – the shadow of an ancient deathliness falls over them. The inaccessible wake of death, both in time and out of time, conditions the aesthetic present while staying ulterior to it. At the very least, the situation restages the problem of the non-individual character of the psyche. It's not just that forms 'creatively' elected by the individual psyche refuse to be subjugated by the private consciousness, but that the death which lays its moon-like light over them ushers them into a past of unassimilable otherness and generality. This older time of the aesthetic object pulls it into at best a phylogenetic ancestry having little to do with psychological continuity, at worst a nameless organicism. But even if we disregard such Freudian arcana, the aesthetic object still snags on a temporal split that prevents its ideal presence-to-self.

Before taking these Freudianisms forward to consider more specifically literary questions, particularly as generated by Leo Bersani and Jacques Derrida from their reading of Freud, let us head off some potential confusion, and do so by drawing again on Timothy Clark.

Eliciting the implications for creativity of Nietzsche's notion of the 'Dionysian', Clark writes that:

> 'Dionysian' creativity, freed from the service of 'higher' values, and become its own end and object, forms a notion of self-creation and re-creation that is, necessarily, also continuously annihilating. Ultimately, it is indistinguishable from a transgressive death-drive: 'The genius – in his works, in his deeds – is necessarily a prodigal: his greatness lies in the fact that *he expends himself* ... The instinct of self-preservation is as it were suspended'.[25]

Two remarks here. First: the 'transgressive death-drive' and '[t]he instinct of self-preservation' are taken to be adversaries. No doubt this agrees with common sense, but in Freud the pair are not only not hostile, they are intrinsically at one. The Freudian death drive aims at just such preservation, by warding off exterior threat, *including* the threat which pleasure, as an experience of agitation, presents; only if it secures its own relief will 'pleasure' be countenanced. 'Death drive' is something of a misnomer for this function. 'Preservation drive' or 'reduction drive' would be more apposite. The Freudian death drive warrants the adjective 'annihilating' only to the limited degree that (a) it carries in its undertow a pleasure principle that smothers or deflects anything disturbing the psychic placidity it protects; (b) it sets its sights on such pared-down placidity, wooing a near-nothing, though strictly this speaks less of a nihilism on its part than a metapsychological minimalism – which sparks a methodological crisis over where to halt the regress of placidity (Freud resorts to recalibrating it at the degree almost-zero of the simple organism). Perversely, the death drive works on behalf of perpetuity, not destruction, and a perpetuity extending both backwards and forwards in time: backwards because a prehistoric past irresistibly beckons it, forwards *because* perpetual. Nothing in Freud really dies: it either lies dormant or – what amounts to the same thing – reintegrates and survives through the hugely powerful processes of memory and memorialisation, processes in which annihilation or pure loss are never allowed to tear holes.

Second: the meaning of death as perpetuity welds it to notions of creation. Both death drive and wish hiddenly buzz with the concentrated energy of continuance, like a sun in eclipse, providing the source of all 'creative' activity. Such energy for creation is a far cry from that trumpeted by Nietzsche, who credits a psychological self-determinism as the ground of creativity that will be denied the Freudian writer. The latter finds him- or herself dwarfed by a metapsychological cosmos, any personal psychology, even where it manages some self-determinism, rendered ineffectual by the chthonic imperatives of death manoeuvring it.

We shall do well to remember the meta- or post-psychological phase of psychoanalysis as we begin our descent towards the literary. But nor ought we so peremptorily to dismiss Nietzsche from the discussion. 'The genius – in his works, in his deeds – is necessarily a prodigal: his greatness lies in the fact that he expends himself ... The instinct of self-preservation is as it were suspended': 'genius' might prove an equally fruitful term with which to configure the literary, but the notion of prodigality or expenditure is what we shall take up. Let us straight away put it into tension with a remark concerning the death drive made by Jacques Derrida: '[a]ccording to a schema that never ceased to guide Freud's thought, the movement of the trace is described as an effort of life to protect itself by *deferring* the dangerous investment, by constituting a reserve (*Vorrat*)'.[26]

It is all a question of how much energy, psychic or otherwise, gets used by creativity, and where it comes from. In Nietzsche, the (creative) genius expends himself, suggesting cavalier self-destruction, but the expenditure is temporary or recoverable, and therefore phoney, each frenzied outpouring only a *petit mort* which can bank on being replenished. Despite its kamikaze recklessness, such psychic orgasm contains itself within what Derrida would call a 'restricted economy', that of the individual mind; we should have to go to Nietzsche's theories of history to see daylight within this otherwise closed system. Derrida specifically lays the charge of 'restricted economy' at Freud's door, and it informs the quotation above. In emphasising the 'reserve' built by the Freudian psyche, Derrida wants to indict the latter for a self-recuperating ideality (along similar lines as his critique of Hegelian dialectics, *inter alia*). In this view, Freudian expenditure would also be phoney. As we were saying, no loss worth the name inheres in the so-called death drive.

And yet the Freudian psyche achieves less continuity with itself than Derrida would have it. Derrida's sureness of the homogeneity of the (Freudian) psychic dimension in which detours are made fails to account for the possible or quasi heterogeneity of its phylogenetic past, which, as we noted, causes a temporal rift and a concomitant loss of psychic presence-to-self. Interestingly, this does not prevent Derrida from envisioning a similar conclusion reached via a different route:

> How are we to think *simultaneously*, on the one hand, *différance* as the economic detour which, in the element of the same, always aims at coming back to the pleasure or the presence that have been deferred by (conscious or unconscious) calculation, and, on the other hand, *différance* as the relation to an impossible presence, as expenditure without reserve, as the irreparable loss of presence, the irreversible usage of energy, that is, as the death instinct, and as the entirely other relationship that apparently interrupts every economy?[27]

As far as Freudian psychology goes, Derrida's construction of the 'economic detour' calls for no objection. But it appears to us that '*différance* as the relation to an impossible presence' already troubled the Freudian psyche in the form of its own phylogenetic – that is, metapsychological – debt. True, the metapsychological '*différance*' (if we can call it that) of the Freudian death instinct does not function – *expressly* does not function – as 'expenditure without reserve … the irreparable loss of presence, the irreversible usage of energy', but then Derrida's courting of so refined an absence looks as idealised as the psychic totality he wishes to disaggregate. On the other hand, metapsychological '*différance*', even if it pertains to an extrapsychic energy (that of phylogenetics) and thereby pollutes the homogeneity of the psychic dimension, pertains to an 'absent' form that *will have been present* and has therefore never been 'impossible'.

It is important to exempt the radical vacuity inscribed in Derridean '*différance*' from any talk of nihilism or annihilation such as we have been party to. If the alleged nihilism in Nietzsche rather fed the creative faculty than killed it, all the more so in Derrida where '*différance*', at first sight so privative, is gifted with an almost transcendental generativity. By stymieing presence, '*différance*' allows it to break from itself and go forward, to defer itself by differing from itself: that is, to become temporalised. Time has to deconstruct itself, lose itself to keep itself. The very possibility of presence – of all that 'is' – depends upon its own cancellation, revealing '*différance*' as the most productive force conceivable. So when Derrida, in the second half of his sentence ('on the other hand, *différance* as the relation to an impossible presence … ') brings in the death drive ('expenditure without reserve … the irreparable loss of presence, the irreversible usage of energy, that is … the death instinct'), an extremely ambivalent phenomenon emerges. If the death drive answers to '*différance*', its economic interfuses with an *an*economic character. Instead of the death drive merely colluding with the pleasure principle (and the reality principle) in a system which postpones pleasure in order to reclaim it later, thereby achieving an overall balance, now that system has a bug in it which impedes its (economic) closure, and thus even the possibility of balance. The bug is '*différance*' which enjoins upon the presence of the present-pleasure-to-be-deferred an absolute loss in principle. The (present) pleasure may indeed be recouped later but only after exiting the system altogether (nor waiting in the sidelines in some virtual system either), and only as incomplete even then. We are beyond all expenditure here. But that same loss will also, through a kind of ultimate risk, create the conditions for all deferral and continuation. '*Différance*' has the peculiar ability to be generative in lieu of any 'reserve' from which to generate: but then having no reserve also means observing no limit. In one respect, '*différance*' is absolute creativity.

In this Derridean view, the death drive succeeds in an affirmative productivity sorely lacking, in the eyes of many commentators, in its Freudian configuration. Witness Leo Bersani:

> What has been repressed from the speculative second half of Freud's text ['Beyond the pleasure principle (1920)'] is sexuality as productive masochism. The possibility of exploiting the shattering effects of sexuality in order to maintain the tensions of an eroticized, de-narrativized, and mobile consciousness has been neglected, or refused, in favor of a view of pleasure as nothing more than the reduction of all tension and the evacuation of all excitement.[28]

Bersani's appeal, powered it seems by a belated Nietzscheanism of its own, for a 'sexuality as productive masochism', raises the good question of why indeed Freud does not permit the death instincts to profit from the energy of the masochism they resemble. I examine that question elsewhere; here we want to board Bersani's relocating of it in the context of the literary (his reading of 'Beyond the pleasure principle (1920)' has been inspired by that of Derrida whose initiative it was to track the strategies of the text's movement).[29] For Bersani something else is going on in Freud's description of the death drive, rather different from our ideas of aesthetic form, that relates profoundly to 'the literary' and concerns precisely its 'productivity'.

For Bersani, a special energy crackles behind the death drive, which Freud is remiss in overlooking. Its character is erotic, and Bersani finds fault with Freud for compacting it into its own antonym, 'the evacuation of all excitement'. Bersani then augments his position: not by extrapolating or refuting Freudian concepts, but by tracing the contours of Freud's rhetoric. He believes the hesitations, solecisms and vaguenesses in Freud's text are the symptoms of this other energy; and he treats them as exemplary, no less, of the general functioning of literary language. He proposes that:

> The linguistic categories of pleasure, reality, sexuality, and death can, at the most, be 'related to', or 'inferred from' or 'correspond to' [Bersani here

mocking Freud's logical and terminological imprecision in 'Beyond the pleasure principle (1920)'] a certain type of insistence in consciousness which it
is the function of linguistic articulation to miss. And we should perhaps
recognise in what, with necessary imprecision, has been called 'literary language' the intrusion of these insistent, silent, productively mistaken replications into a text's line of language. These replications can be verbally
rendered only by such events as the sliding of the word 'pleasure' in Freud's
text, or the indeterminate placing of sexuality in the instinctual conflict
between life and death.[30]

The more vulnerable language becomes to 'the intrusion of these insistent,
silent, productively mistaken replications', the more literary. The intrusion
evidences an eroticised deathliness which knows only such 'mistaken
replications' as a means of propagating itself into the phenomenal and aesthetic world. Ironically, language approaches literariness the more it
divests itself of articulacy, its growing maladroitness the outward sign of a
culture of erotic death parasitically besieging it from within. The literary
comprises telling lacunae created by the absence to articulation of sex and
death which nevertheless indelibly underwrite the literary process. Literature is an effect of the withdrawn presence of the death drive.

Promising though these suggestions are, we should withhold full
approval, for they might just rehabilitate what E. R. Curtius has classified
as literature's 'inexpressibility topoi'.[31] 'Literariness' in Bersani's perspective still trades on the illusion of an inexpressible presence: as he insists,
'*it is the function of linguistic articulation to miss*' these thanatographic
incursions. The ineffable is present to the extent that it cannot be presented. Though Bersani reinvents the literary as its incompetent vessel
rather than its technically skilful or artistic formalisation, the ineffable signified still reigns supreme; and that incompetence under the sway of an
importunate writing force (the death instincts) makes Bersani's design
look like another form of automatic writing.

Despite Bersani's exasperation with, and revision of, Freud, the inaccessible repetitiousness of death in literary form, and the possibility that
literature repeats 'nothing', remain in broad accordance with the master's
views. As with Freud, no room exists in the literary artefact for content. To
be more precise, content has significance only, at bottom, as a form or
mode of the death drive, and in this regard 'the literary' says nothing, it
never posits for itself, it just lets the death drive drive it (where it does say
something, it gives over being literary). Which puts a new spin on an oft-
cited remark of Derrida's concerning literature: '[t]he space of literature is
not only that of an instituted *fiction* but also a *fictive institution* which in
principle allows one to say everything'.[32] From time to time literature
might run up against censorship, but external constraint will not vitiate its

'principle' in the right to 'say everything'. Fictive by birth, literature abounds in an ignorance of all boundaries to the sayable. And by extension, it need never posit anything. Yes, it may do so – a literary work may incorporate positive data, empirical description, factual information, and so on – but it never has to; it is just as literary, even more so, when it dispenses with positive statements.[33] Free of the obligation to posit, literature intrinsically says nothing. In other words, saying nothing and the licence to say everything amount to the same.

So much for productivity when all that gets produced are sweet nothings. Bersani ends up reinstating the emptiness he decried in Freud. Though he salvages the tension of unrelieved eros from the death drive, and exhorts it to destabilise linguistic processes the more to make them literary, what results are deathly gaps in articulation, as aphasic and dumb as they are salutary and vital. In a very general sense this might supply the 'masochism' Bersani petitions for, but is hardly 'productive' in any redoubtable way. Besides, there never was a contradiction in Freud, as we have seen, between creativity and death.

On the subject of masochism, let us remind ourselves that although the death instincts permeate the literary artefact to its superficial core, it feels no pain. Quite the reverse. In our reading of Freud, literary form – and what would a literature without form be? – perpetrates a repetitiousness that defensively keeps all upset at a minimum equivalent to 'pleasure' (or at least its effect). The deportment of the literary, its 'style', is apotropaic by nature: the style protects as much as it adorns, its flamboyant garb also an armour (indeed the word 'ornament' comes from a Latin source meaning 'armour'). This dual aspect of literary style receives its subtlest rendition in a Derridean text 'on' Nietzsche that alludes everywhere to Freud. Elliptical itself, Derrida's essay compresses thus the features of literary style:

> In the question of style there is always the weight or *examen* of some pointed object. At times this object might be only a quill or a stylus. But it could just as easily be a stiletto, or even a rapier. Such objects might be used in a vicious attack against what philosophy appeals to in the name of matter or matrix, an attack whose thrust could not but leave its mark, could not but inscribe there some imprint or form. But they might also be used as protection against the threat of such an attack, in order to keep it at a distance, to repel it – as one bends or recoils before its force, in flight, behind veils and sails (*des voiles*). But let us leave this elytron to float between the masculine and the feminine.[34]

Literary style averts the philosophical 'matter or matrix'. Working complementarily to '*différance*' in its perforation of the present pleasure, the literary 'stiletto' inserts the 'distance' of a *'différance'*-like loss that Derrida will later redescribe in terms of castration. As we were at pains to stress, the loss pertains to no entity; the distance defers no plenary pleasure; no secret essence hides in the background; no transcendental signified or ineffable presence of the ilk rehearsed by Bersani. In its gesture, style attacks as it defends, 'masculine' in its 'femininity' – though the metaphorical value of these terms breaks down in a schema devoid of the essence, truth or literalism in which metaphor might refind its origin. Hence the 'elytron' floats.

As in Freud, literary 'style' consists in the forces of pleasure and pain, principally in the mode of their own deferral, except that Derrida appears to rule out any sensuous, psychological, or metapsychological affect such forces bore in their Freudian format. Lacking any entity or origin to displace, style is nothing but pure deferral or distance, which is as much to say as style is nothing. Crucially, however, that nothing has a 'form' in the literal instrumentality of the style, and its divorced supplementarity to the psyche. It's less that Derrida rules out the sensuous, psychological, or metapsychological affect, and more that he heeds a break in the continuum from psyche to literary artefact, which seems never to have occurred to Freud, despite the latter's awareness of 'form'. Style is not the man, style is the style – a graphic discontinuity in and of the psyche, which curtails the latter's absolute rule over the aesthetic field it thought to have determined. That leaves space for the implements of style – the quills, stilettos, rapiers and bodkins which Derrida inventories – to enact an 'automatism' of their own. Creativity thus discovers a new 'source'. If 'style' brings on the destruction, both offensive and defensive, of the present pleasure it might have otherwise simply deferred, that pleasure and the wish straining after it can no longer support the forays of literary practice, as they did in Freud. Literary style avails itself of a post-psychical independence. But in so doing, style also crashes, for where it was wont to vouch for the singularity of both its author and itself, through the medium of a psychical conduit back to that author, now the psychical reference-point has gone and with it the chance of style staving itself into some singularity. Style, the voice of singularity, has turned plural – and lost its style.

Through Derrida we have encountered a second demand to loosen the literary from its too humanistic or 'post-Romantic' moorings, identify energies of creativity other than those of the individual psyche, and thus tolerate what is separate or alien about the literary. It may be that the literary – indeed any creative work – deserves to be called aesthetic only when it has seceded from psychical ordinance. In the first view, by looking into Freud's notion of aesthetic form, we saw the literary mutate from private to public, and develop separate status. Albeit pathological in origin, the literary adopted a form that necessarily took it away from pathology, according to a logic which Freud, being committed to the universality of psyche, could not entertain. For Freud literary style defers a pleasure and a pain within a psychical dimension that is more or less homogeneous, depending on how far phylogenetics belongs to it; for Derrida literary style defers something more radical, the very condition of possibility of pleasure, namely presence. Such is the destruction that precedes creation that we mentioned above. In both cases (though of the two only Derrida would assent) style breaks free. And although Freud does not address style per se, it falls to the same logic. Aesthetic forms are forms of repetition, as we showed, which led to their 'independence'. The same goes for literary style. Style needs to be repeated to become identifiable as such. A style that 'happens' only once has not yet become a style. In repeating itself style is already becoming a form, and, like a form, becoming susceptible to exappropriation. Long before any Derridean analysis of it, style suffers from the paradox in ownership and singularity. Artefacts of style are again only as creative as they are monotonous.

But we cannot leave it at that. We must not confuse the separateness of the literary artefact with a discrete, bordered, framed unity: it may be independent, but it isn't enclosed. Freud talks about forms, the empiricism of which could easily stop us thinking through the implications of exappropriation. In principle, a literary artefact even of the most integral empirical form (the sonnet again!) will have had to jeopardise its singularity through becoming public, a process which distorts and ruins it; it will have given itself away in the most 'disseminative' fashion in order to win itself back in tidy, consensual shape. In Derrida it gets worse, because no empiricism comes along to validate this or that 'aesthetic' object. With the literary stylus causing rents in the fabric of presence, all 'form' as the collected moments of aesthetic presence becomes impossible. There may be an aesthetic territory for the literary but it no longer coincides with any empirical boundary, especially where that boundary corresponds to an author's psyche, for the literary takes off from the excision of all psychism. The 'space of literature' extends chaotically in all directions, flouting the borders between one psyche and the next, one author and the next, making 'style' the property of the force of writing itself, and preventing us from matching it conclusively to the form of any aesthetic (empirical) object, literary or otherwise (the classification 'literary' has no more distinctness than any other).

Whichever way you look at it, the literary implements deferral. A certain obliquity, and therefore a certain temporality, a certain strategism, a certain rhetoric, carry it ever wayward. In this respect, even Freud and Derrida uphold a tradition. True, Freud adjudges literary artefacts to have risen above the pathologies touching them and saturating other 'formal' practices, but as we have seen, it is arbitrary to do so: the literary is just as perverse as those other practices. And Derrida will elsewhere release the viral energy of the literary into the sanitised space of philosophy, causing philosophy to express a secret delinquency the literary always flaunted – but the literary is still seen as delinquent. Both Freud and Derrida keep the literary in its Platonic place as unorthodox and abnormal, even though they appear to overturn the Platonic evaluation of the literary as 'bad'. What it is is indisputably errant.

The trouble is, its errancy too often incites the desire to chase the literary back to an origin, to counter the authority of a thing which in speaking so much, and ever more copiously, still says nothing – indeed gains its authority from this allusive emptiness. Like death, the literary is all the more powerful for creating the illusion of a substance or content it can never adduce. And indeed such mystificatory authority cannot simply be accepted. The drifting verbosity of the literary has nothing to do with babble, however, or 'stream of consciousness', for its drift, its errancy, its obliquity and ellipses are made up of formal elements, like gaudy jewellery. In the becoming-formal lies the element of the literary's power, but the formalisation does not rectify; it, like an ideological apparatus, institutes an aberration. This aberration is dressed up as everything, but is nothing. Repeat: nothing.

Notes

1 S. Freud, 'Creative writers and day-dreaming (1908 [1907])', in *The Standard Edition of the Complete Psychological Works of Sigmund Freud*, trans. J. Strachey (London, 1959), vol. 9, p. 144.
2 *Ibid.*, p. 146.
3 *Ibid.*, p. 153.
4 *Ibid.*, p. 150.
5 S. Freud, 'Remembering, repeating and working-through (Further recommendations on the technique of psycho-analysis II) (1914)', in *Complete Psychological Works*, vol. 12, p. 151.
6 T. Clark, *The Theory of Inspiration: Composition as a Crisis of Subjectivity in Romantic and Post-Romantic Writing* (Manchester, 1997), p. 2.
7 H. Segal, *Dream, Phantasy and Art* (London, 1991), p. 94. The quotation comes from a chapter which considers Freud's 'Creative writers and day-dreaming'.
8 *Ibid.*, p. 86.
9 *Ibid.*, p. 82.
10 Clark, *Theory of Inspiration*, p. 7.
11 *Ibid.*
12 C. Bollas, *Cracking Up: The Work of Unconscious Experience* (London, 1995), p. 5.
13 Bollas develops the point: '[i]f the ego appreciates the individual's sense, then there is an intrasubjective sensitivity; I think that poets, painters, musicians, and others

engaged in creative work feel pleasure in their ego's contribution to this separate sense ... Creativity in unconscious work responds to any audience delegated by the self' (Bollas, *Cracking up*, p. 155).

14 *Ibid.*, p. 71.
15 *Ibid.*, p. 78.
16 S. Freud, 'Notes upon a case of obsessional neurosis (1909)', in *Complete Psychological Works*, vol. 10, p. 221.
17 *Ibid.*, p. 227.
18 S. Freud, 'Obsessive actions and religious practices (1907)', in *Complete Psychological Works*, vol. 9, pp. 115–27.
19 *Ibid.*, p. 118.
20 See note 5 above.
21 S. Freud, 'Remembering, repeating and working-through', p. 150.
22 S. Freud, 'The uncanny (1919)', in *Complete Psychological Works*, vol. 17, p. 238.
23 S. Freud, 'Beyond the pleasure principle (1920)', in *Complete Psychological Works*, vol. 18, p. 57.
24 *Ibid.*, p. 7.
25 Clark, *Theory of Inspiration*, p. 179. Clark's citation is from Nietzsche.
26 J. Derrida, 'Différance', in *Margins of Philosophy*, trans. A. Bass (Brighton, 1982), p. 18.
27 *Ibid.*, p. 19.
28 L. Bersani, *The Freudian Body: Psychoanalysis and Art* (New York, 1986), pp. 63–4.
29 See my 'A subject is being beaten', *Angelaki* 3:1 (April 1998), 187–96. And for Derrida on 'Beyond the pleasure principle (1920)', see J. Derrida, 'To speculate – on "Freud"', in *The Post Card: From Socrates to Freud and Beyond*, trans. A. Bass (Chicago, 1987), pp. 257–409.
30 Bersani, *The Freudian Body*, p. 66.
31 See E. R. Curtius, *European Literature and the Latin Middle Ages*, trans. W. R. Trask (London, 1953), pp. 159–62.
32 J. Derrida, *Acts of Literature*, ed. D. Attridge, trans. various (New York, 992), p. 36.
33 For elaboration of this point, see my 'Licence', in K. Flint (ed.), *Poetry and Politics* (Woodbridge, 1996), pp. 140–61.
34 J. Derrida, *Spurs: Nietzsche's Styles/Éperons: Les Styles de Nietzsche*, trans. B. Harlow (Chicago, 1979), pp. 37–9.

INDEX